Fashion and Materiality

Fashion and Materiality

Cultural Practices in Global Contexts

Edited by
Heike Jenss and Viola Hofmann

BLOOMSBURY VISUAL ARTS
LONDON • NEW YORK • OXFORD • NEW DELHI • SYDNEY

BLOOMSBURY VISUAL ARTS
Bloomsbury Publishing Plc
50 Bedford Square, London, WC1B 3DP, UK
1385 Broadway, New York, NY 10018, USA
29 Earlsfort Terrace, Dublin 2, Ireland

BLOOMSBURY, BLOOMSBURY VISUAL ARTS and the Diana logo are trademarks of
Bloomsbury Publishing Plc

First published in Great Britain 2020
This paperback edition published in 2021

Cover design by Amelie Varzi
Cover image © Heike Jenss

A catalogue record for this book is available from the British Library.

A catalog record for this book is available from the Library of Congress.

ISBN: HB: 978-1-350-05781-4
PB: 978-1-350-22807-8
ePDF: 978-1-350-05782-1
eBook: 978-1-350-05783-8

Typeset by Deanta Publishing Services, Chennai, India

To find out more about our authors and books visit www.bloomsbury.com and
sign up for our newsletters.

To Gabriele Mentges

Contents

Figures

Acknowledgments

We wish to dedicate this book to Gabriele Mentges, our mentor, a committed scholar and teacher, whose work is deeply concerned with the intricacies of fashion and clothing as material culture. During her twenty-two-year professorship at the *Seminar für Kulturanthropologie des Textilen* at Technical University of Dortmund, she has been a driving force for the development of fashion studies in Germany. Her approach is informed by a rigorous interdisciplinary education across the humanities and social sciences, having pursued a double degree in ethnology, and *Volkskunde/* European ethnology, philosophy, and sociology at the universities of Hamburg, Heidelberg, and Marburg. Her scholarly journey through the fields of clothing and fashion led her from her PhD study on how the sartorial codes and rules of *Tracht* or regional dress acted as disciplinary tools in the socialization, body, and habitus formation of children in nineteenth- and early twentieth-century Germany, to her most recent exploration of the histories and political uses of textiles as national heritage in Central Asia. The way she sees fashion, no doubt, can also be attributed to her ten-year museum career as curator and associate director of the Museum of Everyday Culture in Waldenbuch Castle, a branch of the Landesmuseum Württemberg, Germany. With her background in museum work, and especially being concerned with objects of everyday use and consumption, Gabriele Mentges began to distinctively shape the study programs at the Institute of Arts and Material Culture at TU Dortmund University from 1996 onwards. She challenged her students (including the two editors of this volume) to think critically and holistically about the histories, meanings, effects and affects of clothing and fashion, and she has always been adamant about the need to see fashion in its global interconnectedness, advocating fashion history as "entangled history." Equally, across the historic scope of her work, there is an underlying cultural anthropological interest in the interconnected relationship between humans and things, and their embeddedness in specific social, cultural-historic, and spatial contexts. While promoting a mode of thinking about fashion that is carefully attuned to the various manifestations of fashion—as thing or object, as image, concept, discourse, system—Gabriele Mentges has always highlighted the need to pay attention to the materiality of fashion as an avenue to shed light on how fashion is used and experienced by social actors in time and place. Inspired by these ideas, this edited volume brings together international and interdisciplinary scholars who explore fashion and materiality in various historic and cultural contexts, and as inherently personal and political matters.

Our warm thanks go to all the contributors in this book who together address the materiality of fashion from various points of view and with regard to the dynamics of time and place, movement and transfer. At Bloomsbury Visual Arts, we thank our editors Frances Arnold and Yvonne Thouroude, and, in the early stages of preparation, Hannah Crump and Pari Thomson, for their ongoing encouragement and belief in this book project. Thank you also to the institutions and individuals who provided their various permissions to reproduce images, credited in the list of figures. We also thank our respective home institutions and departments, the School of Art and Design History and Theory and Parsons School of Design, The New School, New York/USA, and the Institute of Arts and Material Culture, Technical University of Dortmund, Germany, for supporting us in our work on this edited volume through funding, enabling translations of selected chapters and image permissions, and especially through the invaluable support of the research assistants, without whom this book would not have met the deadline: Julie Macindoe assisted in the early stages of the book, including literature research, reading draft chapters and translations, and offering, as a student reader, constructive feedback on the book's contents. We are equally indebted to Kalina Yingnan Deng for her thoughtful comments and rigorous proof reading of the manuscript. Thank you also to Neal Bauer, Amelie Varzi and Jasmin Assadsolimani for helping with proof reading, bibliographical, and other queries. Special thanks to Vaishnavi Kambadur for researching literature, working on cover drafts, and organizing image and copyright submissions.

Introduction: Fashion and materiality

Heike Jenss and Viola Hofmann

Fashion plays an intimate material role in the enactment and experience of the body and culture. This includes feeling the imprint of fabrics and garments on the body, from the softness or itchiness of a wool sweater to the shape-lifting effects of body molding sporting gear. The materiality of fashion manifests itself also in feelings of desire and excitement: for example, evoked by the "newness" encountered in physical and virtual shopping spaces that foster ongoing production and consumption; it may also become manifest in experiences of discomfort, self-consciousness, or marginalization, felt through the gaze of others or the perceived misfit of one's clothing according to hegemonic social standards. Fashion and clothing involve all senses and thus can be counted "among the most essential objects of material culture" in closest proximity to the body (Lehnert and Mentges 2013, 8). With a focus on diverse cultural practices in historic and contemporary contexts, presenting case studies from the United States, Europe, Asia, Africa, and Australia, the authors in this book ask how fashion and clothing, as particularly prominent parts of material culture, affect articulations of body and self, experiences of time and place, and the shaping of social and local/global relationships. The chapters in this book take the reader through wide-ranging sites and themes in order to illuminate how the materialities of clothing and fashion shape thinking and acting: from DIY fashion and the concept of "material subjects" to connections between clothing and biography and the early modern collecting of "foreign dress." They further examine local changes and global exchanges that fashion objects materialize in design and production, leading the reader from the popularity of chinoiserie fashion in eighteenth-century Europe to today's "fast-fashion" production in Los Angeles, United States, and Guangzhou, China, to fashion and textiles' role in nation-building in Uzbekistan and Zambia. And they engage with more recent material entanglements between fashion and migration, drawing connections from the distribution of clothing donations for Syrian refugees in Germany to the circulation of "refugee chic" on international fashion runways, to the use of clothing as tools to foster transcultural relationships and integration policies. Together, the chapters in this book scrutinize the dense connections between fashion, clothing, materiality, and humanity, and show the material intricacy and malleability of fashion and clothing in the context of changing cultural processes.

This book is sparked by ongoing debates around the need to address fashion in material terms, including a growing concern about a diminishing "material literacy" resulting from the rapid acceleration of commodity production and the multiplication of and omnipresent exposure to fashion as image. This is not to say that this book is motivated by a nostalgia for the "real," material, and haptic in light of an increasing extension of fashion into the virtual or immaterial realm as we integrate technology into our sense of self (see Turkle 2007, 325). Self-understanding is directly entangled with the flows of images, information, and affects between our bodies and media objects like technological devices. Rather than seeing images and representations in virtual spaces as immaterial, we can understand them as specific forms of materialization. As Sophie Woodward and Tom Fisher have noted, fashion and clothing transmitted through light, sound, and screens "make fashion 'material' in particular ways . . . as part of a multisensory mediation" (2014, 7). In a context of an increasing mediatization of fashion due to digitization and an apparently parallel dematerialization or "flattening of fashion" (see for discussion Rocamora 2017) attributed to the emphasis and distribution of fashion as image on social media, there is, at the same time, a resurging interest in the materiality or "thingness" of fashion, too. Not least because socio-technical practices, such as zooming in and snapping pictures of things in everyday life and their curation and showcasing on platforms such as Instagram, rely on things (such as clothes) to be shown. While the digitization of fashion no doubt spurs an ephemeral consumption of fashion as image, it can at the same time also reinforce and perpetuate the significance of fashion as material things: this is evident in designers showcasing the processes of making online, or in museums and collections (like the Costume Institute at the Metropolitan Museum of Art) providing behind-the-scenes insights into their conservation work on Instagram. The now widely expanded practice and understanding of "curation"—or, in a wider sense, an expanding "care" for—fashion objects beyond the traditional spaces of the museum in everyday contexts further illustrates a resurging interest in fashion as material culture (see Vänskä and Clark 2018; Scatturo 2018).

With this book, we seek to build on and contribute to existing material culture studies of clothing and fashion, which, despite a general acknowledgment of the unique position of clothing as a particularly significant form of material culture, are still proportionally few in number (but for examples see Weiner and Schneider 1989; Mentges ed. 2005b; Kuechler and Miller 2005; Woodward and Fisher 2014; or the journal *Clothing Cultures* edited by Joanne Turney)—especially in considering not only clothing but also fashion as material culture.

Even if the field of fashion studies is increasingly international, it is to a large extent still informed by the legacy of a Eurocentric fashion discourse (Jansen and Craik 2016, 5) that manifests itself, for example, in a terminological and conceptual binary of fashion vs. clothing/dress, whereby the latter has been understood as universal practice and the former as exclusive to the West—or otherwise, if acknowledged to exist in non-Western contexts, seen as a result of globalization or more specifically Westernization of "other" clothing cultures (see for discussion Niessen 2016; Lillethun, Welters, and Eicher 2012; Kaiser 2012; Paulicelli and Clark 2009). In Western thinking, the concept of fashion has been historically allied with the idea of modernity and progress as a unique feature of Western "civilization": a narrative that effectively aided in the construction and self-perception of the West as superior and more advanced than "the rest." This is a way of thinking that has added cultural baggage to the Latin-rooted terms "mode" as well as "fashion," and that, as Sandra Niessen (2003) has argued, makes fashion by definition Western-centric and orientalist. The development of academic sciences, including anthropology, played a substantial role in this conception, by treating non-Western dress as a "non-fashion-foil" (see Niessen 2003, 244) and using "clothing as a way to reinforce cultural and racial types, to distance the colonial subject of the 'primitive'" (Fee 2013, 302).

Similarly, even the realm of Western fashion itself has been riddled with the issues of center-periphery boundaries: for example, the issue of the urban/rural divide that historically marked definitions of fashion, a privileged focus on time over place in studying fashion (Mentges 2005a, 31; Kaiser 2013; and in this book for discussion), or the focus on specific countries or metropolitan capitals within Western fashion/studies, tied to the location of "centers" of the fashion industry as well as of fashion scholarship. However, following various disciplinary paradigm shifts, anthropology, and material culture studies, along with global history and other disciplines, have also been at the forefront in broadening the scholarship of fashion and clothing over recent decades (for select overviews and examples see Hansen 2004; Riello and McNeil 2010; Fee 2013; Welters and Lillethun 2018; Rabine 2002; Maynard 2004; Brand and Teunissen 2005; Paulicelli and Clark 2009; Tarlo 2010; Miller and Woodward 2011; Lehnert and Mentges 2013; Mentges and Shamukhitdinova 2017; special issues in *Fashion*

Theory and *International Fashion Studies*) by providing rich insights into diverse fashion practices and systems across all continents that have helped to address and partly dissolve such binaries, albeit as Niessen (2016) and Jansen and Craik (2016) recently remind us, not entirely.

In order to further help unsettle such binaries, we advocate a need to think of fashion in material terms, and not just as a concept, belief, or value that is temporarily attached to clothing (see for discussion Kawamura 2005, 2–4), but more broadly as material culture that is embedded in time and place in various ways, as a substantial part of human experience and everyday practice (Weiner and Schneider 1989; Mentges 2004 and 2005a). Looking back at the history of the study of clothing and fashion, for example, in anthropological studies or costume history, and in museums, an interest in their materiality has always been at its roots, albeit with shifting foci or interests (see for overviews Taylor 2002 and 2004; Mentges 2004). Where, for example, early material studies were focused on establishing systems of order and categorized objects with an emphasis on technique and formal characteristics, their contexts of use or interaction with the person was considered less significant. Or, otherwise, objects such as clothing were considered as a "reflection" of culture, or read in a textual sense as a sign of underlying social structures. For example, artifacts were understood as "spatial and temporal markers of ethnic identities and primarily reflected ideas in the minds of their makers" (Tilley et al. 2006, 2). The "linguistic turn" in cultural studies brought an emphasis on language and textual or semiotic readings of culture (Barthes 1989), that would inform the development of studies of fashion with a focus on representation and signifying practices, leading the way for the development of today's fashion media discourse analysis, or the unpacking of meaning-making practices and narratives around fashion. The "material turn" in scholarship, and more recently related research introduced under the banner of "new materialism,"[1] marked a renewed interest in "refocusing on matter and materiality" (Rocamora and Smelik 2016, 13). This increased an attentiveness to all forms of materials and material culture, including in the study of clothing and fashion, which in addition to object-based approaches also includes or merges with studies of embodiment, making, production, or consumption, placing an emphasis on the inherently material dimension of these practices. The "material turn" brought a foregrounding of materiality that also provided an angle to "rethink anti-ontologizing dualisms, such as those between the natural and the social, the human and the nonhuman, the material and the immaterial" (Munteán, Plate, and Smelik 2017, 3, referencing Bennett 2010; see also Schneider 2006, 2009). In such a lens, it becomes increasingly difficult to uphold any kind of clear-cut distinction between clothing and fashion along the lines of material and immaterial, since fashion, and not just clothing, is conspicuously material (Rocamora and Smelik 2016, 14): as an object- and image-producing industry and as a symbolic force intimately bound up with embodied experience (see also Paulicelli and Wissinger 2013).

In their study of fashion and everyday life in London and New York, Cheryl Buckley and Hazel Clark state that the various ways in which fashion manifests itself in routine daily lives (e.g., as something that remains with people over time), is handed down, and is recycled or remodeled, show how fashion can also be understood as anti-modern and nonprogressive (Buckley and Clark 2017, 4). Fashion does not define, but it remains a term that demands redefinition, as Clark puts it. Following Judith Attfield (2000), Clark urges to think about "fashion in the lowercase" to accommodate a wider range of practices and ideologies (see the exhibition *fashion after Fashion* at the Museum of Design in New York 2017). This can be aligned with the interests of material culture studies in drawing attention to the rich diversity of the domain of things, or objects and cultural practices, and the "manner in which people think through themselves, and their lives and identities through the medium of different kinds of things" (Tilley et al. 2006, 4).

It is useful here to consider the meanings of fashion as noun and verb. With regard to fashion as a noun, in the sense of fashion as a system and industry that promotes constant newness and change, it can be understood as the "material embodiment of the capitalist system" (Lehmann 2018, 10). It is essentially material, not least as the fashion system produces actual "stuff" yet effectively obscures parts of its materiality, especially by decontextualizing production and labor conditions from consumption and use, and through the production and circulation of fashion as appealing image and spectacle (Woodward and Fisher 2014, 7). Through the rise of mass production, spearheaded by the textile and clothing industry, there occurred a dramatic upheaval in the social relationships between things and people. As a system, it seems as if fashion has withdrawn from the normal everyday object relations in order to virtualize itself in branding strategies and images and narratives with phantasmagorical potential (Mentges 2000, 6). The more fashion is imbricated with capitalism, the more the modes of its use and meaning change. Contemporary fast fashion is an example of this, as it has propelled an unprecedented increase in the consumption of fashion goods, reducing the use time and perceived value of fashion as material object, evidenced by the increasing amount of clothing and textile waste. The ephemerality associated with fast fashion—the quick material turnover in stores and presumably in people's wardrobes—could serve as an example to showcase the idea of the transitoriness of fashion and thus the ephemeral value of fashion as a temporal attribute of clothing. Yet, the material lives of such clothes that are produced as fashion and then designated as waste, because their former user may no longer see them as fashionable, remain. Even if labeled as waste, such fashion matters beyond the initial contexts of use and wear: be it in the form of filling up landfills and causing environmental pollution or in the form of globally recirculating secondhand wares, which can gain or convey a new value for new users as "a resource for self-enhancement" (Schneider 2009, 24).

Like all material things and cultural practices, fashion acts, and is perceived and embedded, within a diversity of cultural interrelations. An example is the dissemination or use of denim across different global locations, where it is treated and interpreted in quite different ways, depending on the specific everyday settings (Miller and Woodward 2011). The use of secondhand clothing, or the global use of denim, show how seemingly fixed or context-specific meanings of clothing and fashion can dissolve entirely, or be carried across into other cultural contexts of use, where, in concrete material interaction, humans incorporate and synchronize them with their own practices of use and patterns of thinking. Even if we have to expect that the meaning of fashion and clothing can never be totally elucidated, in order to grasp and try to make sense of fashion, it is highly productive to consider it in its materiality or as material, not least since the sensuous stimulus of fashion and clothing is such an intrinsic motivation for people to bring them as meaningful materials into their lives. After all, "[m]ateriality is an integral dimension of culture and there are dimensions of social existence that cannot be understood without it" (Tilley et al. 2006, 1).

The Latin roots of the English verb fashion is *facere*, which means to do, to make, to give shape, pointing to an understanding of fashion as a practice and an activity, which by extension points to materiality or the material domain (see also Jenss 2016, 7). While it is acknowledged that the concept of materiality is heterogeneous and ambiguous (see Tilley et al. 2006, 3), per dictionary definition, the term materiality describes the substance and physical properties of things, and "material" is positioned as an opposite of "form" or "formal" (see *Oxford English Dictionary*). If we extend such terminological binary further, we can then think of material in the sense of substance and matter, such as fiber and fabric as opposite to *façon* (Middle French for way, manner, fashion), which also forms a root of the English term fashion. In the vocabulary of tailoring, *façon* is a designated term for "shape," or more specifically the shape of a garment. In that sense, we have to see fashion and material/ity not as separate entities but as interdependent or intimately entangled, since fashion, if understood as form or form-giving (fashioning), shapes material—such as fibers and fabric or bodily matter—and vice versa. Historically the term "material," if understood in the sense of worldly, real, corporeal, or fleshy, has been contrasted to the terms spiritual, mental, or imaginary, thus pointing to the division between mind and body that has long informed Western modes of thinking about the world. Yet fashion and clothing—of all the material goods perhaps in the most immediate way—blur such a separation between the material and spiritual or mental. An example is the potency clothing holds for memory and emotion, which Peter Stallybrass (1999) sees grounded both in the material specificity and in the magic of cloth and clothing as it "receives the human imprint" (1999, 29). The valuing of lasting emotional bonds with clothing are not necessarily in line with capitalism's teaching of the need of the ever-new. However, as the anthropologist Jane Schneider has argued:

> the spiritual and the material are inseparable in the mind of humans everywhere, including those who inhabit capitalist societies. Here too textiles received as gifts are kept and stored. Here too the clothes of the deceased loved ones elicit intense affect, a feeling of connection, while ceremonial robes add substance to the wearer. Here, too, the idea lives on, despite two centuries of modern scientific discourse, that cloth and clothes shore up the person in magical ways, promoting his or her success as vital, loved, admired. (Schneider 2006, 205; see also Schneider 2009, 16)

Fashion is multifaceted and combines material, bodily, sensual, symbolic, and cognitive dimensions. It is a prime example of how human beings simultaneously make—and make meaning with—things, both mentally and physically. Fashion and clothing are, for example, forceful agents in the articulation of historical ideas or social concepts, such as hierarchy, collectivity and individuality, gender, age, race, time, and place and, as such, act upon body and mind in a material and virtual manner. That is, fashion is not only a product of symbolic meaning-making, but in its materiality affects us on a deeper level—it "cuts through emotional and social life" (von Busch 2016, 181). In its various material forms and dimensions, fashion interweaves intimate bodily practices—from the choice of clothing and hairstyles, or the decoration of one's skin—with the formation of cultural identities, social hierarchies, and global economic asymmetries. Equally, fashion forms a complex, globally connected work field and also an attractive belief system, promising individuality, belonging, rejuvenation, or modernity with far-reaching material effects and consequences.

Fashion is not a mere epiphenomenon but constantly and very directly intervenes with our human feelings and social affairs. This occurs not only through adapting to changes in fashion, or following the lead of various influencers, brands, and designers. Although consumers are the focal point for the fashion industry as sign- and image-receiving customers, as everyday users they not only carry a prefabricated symbolic concept of fashion, which Georg Simmel called their own, false fantasies ([1905] 1995, 31), but also cultivate their own poly-sensual relationship to clothing and fashion. By adapting fashion as a physical object to one's own environment, by using, handling, and experiencing it in everyday life, its commodity form can be neutralized. Eventually fashion is made possible through the concrete, material interaction that in everyday practice takes place between humans and their clothing in various contexts and forms—and at various paces.

Thinking, acting, and feeling with the material is a constitutive component of the experience and organization of personal, depersonalized, local, and global relationships. The constellation "fashion and materiality" therefore forms both a thematic focus and a methodological angle for this book. Bringing together an interdisciplinary and international group of authors, the book offers insights into varied material forms and meaning dimensions of fashion in historic and contemporary contexts and also shows diverse approaches and modes of thinking about fashion and/as materiality.

The chapters are organized in four thematic sections: the first section, *Fashion and clothing—materials in time and place*, examines connections between materiality, everyday life, and biography and considers the role of clothing and fashion in experiences of time and place, self and other. It does so theoretically and empirically, by also illuminating how material artifacts, including costume books, dress collections, and archaeological finds, act as historical sources and agents in the formation of knowledge within the field of fashion studies and dress history. The second section, *Materiality in motion—transnational circuits of fashion*, concentrates on the design, production, movement, change, and translation of fashion objects and materials in and across a variety of historic and global contexts. The case studies range from the material circuits of chinoiserie fashion in the eighteenth century to the fashioning of textile materials as forms of national heritage in Uzbekistan and Zambia, to global fast-fashion production in China. The third section, *Materiality and embodiment*, zooms in on bodily experiences of fashion and textile materials. The wearer, fabrics, dress, and clothing items are understood as agents acting together. The reciprocity between body and materials is approached through the material transformation of sports clothes into "athleisure" fashion and the connection between wearer and design/er with the example of Philip Lim's 3.1 line as well as a new materialist approach that examines the "intra-action" of body, dress, and music in heavy metal yoga practice. The fourth section, *Material locations—material exchanges*, expands the book's perspective on fashion and materiality in the light of cultural policies and recent migration and refugee movements to Europe. Reconnecting to the previous sections on the entanglements between fashion, materiality, time, and place, this section highlights how the material intersects forcefully with the personal and political.

Note

1   As Agnes Rocamora and Anneke Smelik suggest in the context of fashion studies, "the claim of novelty of 'new materialism' seems a bit singular" (2016, 14) proposing to speak instead of "renewed materialism," not least as the study of clothing and fashion has always had strands deeply interested in materiality.

References

Attfield, Judy. 2000. *Wild Things: The Material Culture of Everyday Life*. Oxford and New York: Berg.

Barthes, Roland. (1967) 1989. *The Fashion System*. New York: Hill and Wang.

Bennett, Jane. 2010. *Vibrant Matter: A Political Ecology of Things*. Durham: Duke University Press.

Brand, Jan, and Jose Teunissen, eds. 2005. *Global Fashion, Local Tradition: On the Globalisation of Fashion*. Arnhem: Terra.

Buckley, Cheryl, and Hazel Clark. 2017. *Fashion and Everyday Life: London and New York*. London: Bloomsbury.

Fee, Sarah. 2013. "Anthropology and Materiality." In *The Handbook of Fashion Studies*, edited by Sandy Black, Amy de la Haye, Joanne Entwistle, Agnès Rocamora, Regina A. Root, and Helen Thomas, 312–37. London: Bloomsbury.

Hansen, Karen Tranberg. 2004. "The World in Dress: Anthropological Perspectives on Clothing, Fashion, and Culture." *Annual Review of Anthropology* 33: 369–92.

Jansen, M. Angela, and Jennifer Craik, eds. 2016. *Modern Fashion Traditions: Negotiating Tradition and Modernity through Fashion*. London: Bloomsbury.

Jenss, Heike, ed. 2016. *Fashion Studies: Research Methods, Sites, and Practices*. London: Bloomsbury.

Kaiser, Susan B. 2012. *Fashion and Cultural Studies*. Oxford: Berg.

Kawamura, Yuniya. 2005. *Fashion-ology: An Introduction to Fashion Studies*. London: Bloomsbury.

Kuechler, Susanne, and Daniel Miller, eds. 2005. *Clothing as Material Culture*. Oxford: Berg.

Lehmann, Ulrich. 2018. *Fashion and Materialism*. Edinburgh: Edinburgh Press.

Lehnert, Gertrud, and Gabriele Mentges, eds. 2013. *Fusion Fashion: Culture Beyond Orientalism and Occidentalism*. Frankfurt am Main: Peter Lang.

Lillethun, Abby, Linda Welters, and Joanne B. Eicher. 2012. "(Re)Defining Fashion." *Dress* 38: 75–97.

Maynard, Margaret. 2004. *Dress and Globalisation*. Manchester: Manchester University Press.

Mentges, Gabriele. 2000. "Einleitung." In *Geschlecht und materielle Kultur: Frauen-Sachen, Männer Sachen, Sach-Kulturen*, edited by Cornelia Foerster, Gabriele Mentges, and Ruth-E. Mohrmann, 3–19. Münster: Waxmann.

Mentges, Gabriele. 2004. "Überlegungen zu einer Kleidungsforschung aus kulturanthropologischer Perspektive." In *Von Kopf bis Fuß: Ein Handbuch rund um Körper, Kleidung und Schmuck für die interkulturelle Unterrichtspraxis*, edited by Birgitta Huse, 73–82. Münster: Waxmann Verlag.

Mentges, Gabriele. 2005a. "Für eine Kulturanthropologie des Textilen." In *Kulturanthropologie des Textilen: Ein einführendes Handbuch*, edited by Gabriele Mentges, 11–56. Berlin: edition ebersbach.

Mentges, Gabriele, ed. 2005b. *Kulturanthropologie des Textilen*. Berlin: edition ebersbach.

Mentges, Gabriele, and Lola Shamukhitdinova, eds. 2017. *Textiles as National Heritage: Identities, Politics and Material Culture*. Münster: Waxmann.

Miller, Daniel, and Sophie Woodward, eds. 2011. *Global Denim*. Oxford: Berg.

Munteán, László, Liedeke Plate, and Anneke Smelik, eds. 2017. *Materializing Memory in Art and Material Culture*. Abingdon: Routledge.

Niessen, Sandra. 2016. "Afterword: Fashion's Fallacy." In *Modern Fashion Traditions: Negotiating Tradition and Modernity through Fashion*, edited by M. Angela Jansen and Jennifer Craik, 209–18. London: Bloomsbury.

Niessen, Sandra. 2003. "Afterword: Re-Orienting Fashion Theory," In *Re-Orienting Fashion: The Globalization of Asian Dress*, edited by Sandra Niessen, Ann Marie Leshkowich, and Carla Jones. Oxford, New York: Berg.

Paulicelli, Eugenia, and Hazel Clark, eds. 2009. *The Fabric of Cultures: Fashion, Identity, and Globalization*. Abingdon: Routledge.

Paulicelli, Eugenia, and Elizabeth Wissinger. 2013. "Introduction." *WSQ: Women's Studies Quarterly* 41(1+2): 14–27.

Rabine, Leslie W. 2002. *The Global Circulation of African Fashion*. London: Bloomsbury.

Riello, Giorgio, and Peter McNeil, eds. 2010. *The Fashion History Reader: Global Perspectives*. London: Routledge.

Rocamora, Agnès. 2017. "Mediatization and Digital Media in the Field of Fashion," *Fashion Theory* 21(5): 505–22.

Rocamora, Agnès, and Anneke Smelik, eds. 2016. *Thinking through Fashion: A Guide to Key Theorists*. New York: I.B. Tauris.

Scaturro, Sarah. 2018. "Confronting Fashion's Death Drive: Conservation, Ghost Labor, and the Material Turn within Fashion Curation." In *Fashion Curating: Critical Practice in the Museum and Beyond*, edited by Annamari Vänskä and Hazel Clark, 21–39. London: Bloomsbury.

Schneider, Jane. 2006. "Cloth and Clothing." In *Handbook of Material Culture*, edited by Christopher Tilley, Webb Keane, Susan Kuechler-Fogden, Mike Rowlands, and Patricia Spyer, 203–20. Thousand Oaks: Sage Publications.

Schneider, Jane. 2009. "From Potlach to Wal-Mart. Courtly and Capitalist Hierarchies through Dress." In *The Fabric of Cultures: Fashion, Identity, and Globalization*, edited by Eugenia Paulicelli and Hazel Clark, 13–27. Abingdon: Routledge.

Simmel, Georg. (1901) 2004. "Fashion." In *The Rise of Fashion*, edited by Daniel Purdy, 289–309. Minneapolis: University of Minnesota Press.

Simmel, Georg. (1905) 1995. "Philosophie der Mode." In *Georg Simmel Gesamtausgabe*, edited by Otthein Rammstedt, 7–37. Frankfurt am Main: Suhrkamp.

Stallybrass, Peter. 1999. "Worn Worlds: Clothing, Mourning and the Life of Things." In *Cultural Memory and the Construction of Identity*, edited by Dan Ben-Amos and Liliane Weissberg, 27–44. Detroit: Wayne State University Press.

Tarlo, Emma. 2010. *Visibly Muslim: Fashion, Politics, Faith*. London: Bloomsbury.

Taylor, Lou. 2002. *The Study of Dress History*. Manchester: Manchester University Press.

Taylor, Lou. 2004. *Establishing Dress History*. Manchester: Manchester University Press.

Tilley, Christopher, Webb Keane, Susan Kuechler-Fogden, Mike Rowlands, and Patricia Spyer, eds. 2006. *Handbook of Material Culture*. Thousand Oaks: Sage Publications.

Turkle, Sherry. 2007. *Evocative Objects: Things We Think With*. Cambridge: MIT Press.

Vänskä, Annamari, and Hazel Clark, eds. 2018. *Fashion Curating: Critical Practice in the Museum and Beyond*. London: Bloomsbury.

von Busch, Otto. 2016. "Action! Or, Exploring Diffractive Methods for Fashion Research." In *Fashion Studies: Research Methods, Sites, and Practices*, edited by Heike Jenss, 181–97. London: Bloomsbury.

Weiner, Annette B., and Jane Schneider, eds. 1989. *Cloth and Human Experience*. Washington DC: Smithsonian Books.

Welters, Linda, and Abby Lillethun. 2018. *Fashion History: A Global View*. London: Bloomsbury.

Woodward, Sophie, and Tom Fisher. 2014. "Fashioning through Materials: Material Culture, Materiality and Processes of Materialization." *Critical Studies in Fashion and Beauty* 5(1): 3–23.

Section One

Fashion and clothing: Materials in time and place

Introduction

Fashion and clothing can be understood to materialize the otherwise abstract concepts of time and space. For example, changes in the material world, such as fashionable cycles or changing aesthetic preferences throughout one's life, can create impressions of change or continuity and thus affect feelings of time or temporality. As Susan Kaiser discusses in the first chapter of this section, time has been a prominent focus in studies of fashion and dress, which has served ideologies associated with the idea of Western modernity and progress. Early writers on fashion, such as Georg Simmel ([1901] 2004) and Werner Sombart ([1902] 2004) have developed universalizing, time-centered theories that informed the way fashion has become primarily understood as directed by the temporal rhythm of newness and obsolescence. In these theories, fashion and clothing as materials did not matter much beyond establishing the idea that changes in their form and materiality constitute the change of fashion, which, for Sombart, was driven by the capitalist entrepreneur, with minimal involvement from the consumer ([1902] 2004, 313). In order to be competitive, as time is money, fashion entrepreneurs must remain "*at least* up-to-date, to be in possession of the latest collection of patterns, the latest designs" ([1902] 2004, 314). Equally, Simmel's ([1901] 2004) theoretical conception of fashion that focused on the social dynamics between individualization and differentiation, foregrounded time explicitly in aligning fashion with the rhythm of modern (and this meant Western and urban) time. As Susan Kaiser reminds us, however, a shift in "focus from narratives about fashion-time to narratives about materiality enables a more grounded way of dealing with fashion-time," one that also attends to how fashion and clothing practices are situated in place, thereby bringing in view a greater diversity of experiences of fashion in and across time and place. While time, space, and place can be theoretically distinguished, they merge together in the everyday life and "everyday bodies of material subjects." Kaiser's chapter highlights these connections theoretically and empirically by reflecting on the abstract concepts of time and place and examining materiality and fashion as part of bodily articulations, experiences, and productions of place and time. Focusing on a particular moment and movement of people in US history, the Women's March that took place one day after the presidential inauguration of Donald Trump in November 2016, Kaiser uses the concept of "material subjects" to explore how people, time, and place come to converge and diverge through fashion and materiality. One of her material examples is the making and wearing of the pink, knitted "pussy hats" that were intended to be worn as a sartorial sign of solidarity among the protestors, but that also received criticisms tied to discourses around gender and race, as not everyone felt included in the movement or appropriately represented by the sartorial sign of the pink pussy hat. By complicating the concepts of time, space, and place, and linking them with subject positions that include gender, sexuality, race, and nationality, Kaiser furthermore highlights how individuals, and their material and bodily practices, are always bound up with the navigation of larger social worlds, whereby the political context of substantially rising nationalism in various countries around the world has become particularly riddled with anxiety and tension.

As a material object that signifies both a moment of resistance and a moment within history and time, the knitted pussy hat entered the collection of the Victoria & Albert Museum a few months after the 2016 demonstrations. It has thus taken the museum's "historical relevancy hurdle" and might now start to enter new, curated material relationships, where it may be placed, for example, in the company of a "1910 cup and saucer, stamped with the logo of the Women's Social and Political Union, and a striped silk scarf, bearing the words 'Votes for Women'" (Russel 2017). The example points to the wide reach of clothing and fashion as materials in time and place, including the anticipated future-historic value of things beyond their immediate use in time as they transform into historical sources, thus also exemplifying how objects act across or in-between time in the formation of collective memory.

In her conception of "material subjects," Susan Kaiser draws on the work of the American philosopher William James (1842–1910), who highlighted the connectedness between the body, soul, and clothing that co-constitute the human, thus acknowledging the role of clothing in the expression of how one feels and for the maintenance of one's self-image. Even when clothing is a habitual practice, or perceived as a routine act that one might not perhaps think too much about on a daily basis, it involves nonetheless a more or less conscious positioning to the world (Davis 1994). In the following chapter, Christel Köhle-Hezinger shows this through the lives, clothes, and memory of two women in twentieth-century Germany. In her first case study, she draws on the pious life and pious things of Marie Frech, who lived all her long life, from 1895 to 1995, in the small town of Fellbach, near Stuttgart, in the southwestern region of Germany. Her chapter draws attention to the connections between materiality, biography, and spirituality, with Frech growing up in a family and local community that was deeply religious, following the teachings of Johann Michael Hahn (1758–1819). Living through the twentieth century, in which people experienced the trauma of two World Wars, the subsequent separation of East and West Germany, with a rapid expansion of consumer culture in the latter and Germany's reunification, Frech decidedly refused luxury and fashion consumption by decree. The clothing she wore at a younger age during the 1930s looks similar to the clothes she wore later as an older women (Petri 1996, 67), marked by muted colors, indicating that she chose not to draw attention to herself, even if—with time—the maintenance of her early twentieth-century style and devoted religiousness would come to have the opposite effect due to its alterity in the late twentieth century. Her house and all her things, seen as valuable material witnesses of a century and of an apparently anachronistic lifestyle, were exhibited by the town of Fellbach one year after her death. Drawing on oral history and memories of her remaining family members and contemporaries, as well as Frech's written notes and material remains, the exhibition was accompanied by a book that documents and contextualizes the "100 years of Marie Frech" in Fellbach (Beckmann 1996; see also Christel Köhle-Hezinger 1996 and 2011). While Frech's house was demolished thereafter, the Stadtmuseum of Fellbach acquired and now exhibits part of her estate. In her chapter, Christel Köhle-Hezinger draws on the research around this project with a focus on the entanglements of clothing, biography, and memory as well as the order of things in Frech's everyday life, where "everything has its place" and where her clothing provides her with a material and spiritual constant as the world around her changes. Köhle-Hezinger contrasts the case of Marie Frech with her second example Renate K., a women who moved in 1955, six years prior to the building of the Berlin Wall, from East Germany to West Germany, later settling in Stuttgart where she became active in the work of the Free

Democratic Party. While located in geographic proximity, in or near Stuttgart, the lives of both women seem worlds apart, representing different generations, different cultures, and different points of view that Köhle-Hezinger sees at the opposite ends of a "normative traditionality" and "disruptive modernity." We come to learn about Renate K's clothing in the form of a letter in which she memorizes particular sequences of her life through the materiality of her clothes. There is no material constant in place as in the case of Marie Frech's sartorial biography; rather, Renate K's descriptions of different clothing items work like flashes that spotlight various moments of her transforming life. Her autobiographical document points to the role of clothing as agents of change, and as agents of memory.

The chapters in this section make clear that time and also space/place are not absolute, universal, or a natural given, but sophisticated cultural and social constructions that are themselves context-specific and subject to change according to contemporaneous attitudes to time and spatial constellations. As one considers clothing as an evidence of former lives, it is therefore always a challenge not to see time and place only from one's own present-day point of view (Geertz 1973). This is the subject of Daniel Devoucoux's chapter, in which he turns to archaeology and antiquity to discuss the issue of the discrepancy between material sources and representation and its impact on knowledge formation in the history of clothing. The discipline of archaeology, which defined itself "by the very act of unearthing its own source materials not from the depth of dusty archives, but from digs and excavations" (Gaimster 1994, cited in Gerritsen and Riello 2015, 3), has been an important basis for the emergence of material culture studies. The interest in antique objects can be traced back to the fifteenth and sixteenth centuries, when European elites developed an increasing interest in acquiring and collecting objects from distant cultures. Classical Greece and Rome became important as historical points of reference in the context of Renaissance humanism. Archaeological excavations were sponsored by the pope and cardinals in Italy, yet archaeology in a more scientific sense is understood to emerge with the eighteenth-century excavations of the sites of Herculaneum and Pompeii. When Napoleon Bonaparte invaded Egypt later in the eighteenth century, he contributed substantially to the circulation of antique objects by pairing his military campaign with exploratory projects. He brought large numbers of excavated objects from Egypt to France, which were made public through scholarly publications and in the museum of the Louvre (opened in 1793), where the display of the appropriated antique artifacts also came to serve in his political strategy of empire building. To this date, the perhaps most spectacular archaeological find was the discovery of the tomb of Pharaoh Tutankhamun by Howard Carter and Lord Carnarvon in 1922. The discovery sparked a frenzy for Egyptian-style fashion in the 1920s as well as in later decades of the twentieth century when the exhibition of his sarcophagus and mummy, along with other objects from his grave site, went on an international museum tour. To this day, the Tutankhamun show in 1978 was the most visited exhibition at the Metropolitan Museum of Art, which speaks to the popular fascination that material objects from the past arouse in the public imagination.

While substantial scientific advancements have been made in archaeological clothing and textile research, there still remain many gaps. As Devoucoux shows, the terminology and iconography of clothing and archaeological material findings often do not match up. As he discusses in his chapter, there are different conceptions of time at play and also of what constitutes "reality." Based on various examples, his chapter focuses on the relationship between objects and images, clothing and its representation, to demonstrate the complex relationships between knowledge formation and meaning production through material objects.

In the fourth chapter of this section, Jutta Zander-Seidel expands the discussion of connections between material and visual sources in a further direction by examining how clothing objects and descriptions of foreign clothing cultures in early modern costume books and dress collection practices served in the construction of "self" and "other." In her chapter, Zander-Seidel introduces the collector Christoph Kress (1541–1583), who was a member of the Nuremberg elite, stemming from a patrician family that had long-established ties with the world of trade. Kress had a keen interest in the acquisition of clothing and accessories from distant or "foreign" (*fremd*) cultures. While the actual items he had in his collection are mostly extant, the probate inventory from 1584 is kept in the Germanisches Nationalmuseum in Nuremberg, founded in 1852, which holds also a number of rare sixteenth-century garments in its collection. As Zander-Seidel discusses, the collecting and organizing of "strange" or foreign cultural objects emerged among the cities' elites as a way to expand their understanding of the world and also to manifest and showcase in the collection and display of objects their level of education, or what one might liberally call in today's terms "cultural capital" (Bourdieu). In that sense, the examination of Kress's collection can tell us something about how the privileged bourgeois elite saw the world and also themselves through the acquisition of material objects. As Zander-Seidel states, the "list of thirty garments, headgear, weaponry and textiles—all mostly described as 'Indian,' 'Moorish,' and 'Turkish'—represents one the oldest verifiable records of non-European clothing obtained and preserved by bourgeois owners in the German-speaking world." Zander-Seidel draws connections between the collection and categorization of the material clothing items and the rising popularity of European costume books and prints in the sixteenth century that showcased and circulated visual representations of distant peoples. We do not learn much about the "global lives" (Gerritsen and Riello 2016) of the items in Kress's collection, including their "origin" and trajectory before they were acquired. Yet, the manner in which the collected items are described and cataloged, using cultural labels or place names that encompass broad geographic regions, reveals insights into the role such material engagement with foreign clothing cultures—via acquiring and collecting "foreign" things—played in sixteenth-century processes of identity formation within the European context. It is a formation of identity that would evolve in connection to space and an expanding "global imaginary" as well as through "distancing," including the invention of exoticism that also manifests itself in how place names came to be used for exotic goods such as "China" for porcelain (Schmidt 2015, 227–28; see also the chapter by Purdy in the next section of this book), highlighting the important role of language and text in relation to objects. As Benjamin Schmidt notes, this "linguistic phenomenon also demonstrates a broader conceptual approach to the world and to worldly things. It illustrates how the early modern European culture of collecting and consuming had merged with the aesthetic of exotic geography—how exotic places came to be correlated with consumable things" (Schmidt 2015, 228).

Moving from the Women's March in 2016 in the United States to the fifteenth-century collection of foreign clothing in Nuremberg, Germany, this first section of the book not only demonstrates the importance of clothing and fashion in the formation of a sense of self, time, and place, but also points to the constitutive role of materials and materiality in thinking, acting, and knowledge production within and across time and place.

References

Beckmann, Ralf, ed. 1996. *Die 100 Jahre der Marie Frech. Ein Fellbacher Frauenleben zwischen Pietismus und Eigensinn. Eine Ausstellung der Stadt Fellbach vom 12. Mai bis 13. Oktober 1996*. Fellbach: Fellbacher Hefte.

Davis, Fred. 1994. *Fashion, Culture and Identity*. Chicago: Chicago University Press.

Gaimster, David, ed. 1994. *Museum Archaeology in Europe*. Oxford: Oxbow.

Geertz, Clifford. 1973. "Thick Description: Toward an Interpretative Theory of Culture." In *The Interpretation of Cultures*, 3–30. New York: Basic Books.

Gerritsen, Anne, and Giorgio Riello, eds. 2015. *Writing Material Culture History*. London: Routledge.

Gerritsen, Anne, and Giorgio Riello, eds. 2016. *The Global Lives of Things: The Material Culture of Connections in the Early Modern World*. London: Routledge.

Köhle-Hezinger, Christel. 1996. "Ich heisse Frech, aber ich bin nicht frech: Nachdenken über eine schwäbische Biographie." In *Die 100 Jahre der Marie Frech. Ein Fellbacher Frauenleben zwischen Pietismus und Eigensinn. Eine Ausstellung der Stadt Fellbach vom 12. Mai bis 13. Oktober 1996*, edited by Ralf Beckmann, 9–18. Fellbach: Fellbacher Hefte.

Köhle-Hezinger, Christel. 2011. *Alltagskultur: sakral—profan*. Münster and New York: Waxmann.

Petri, Marion. 1996. "Kleidung ohne Luxus." In *Die 100 Jahre der Marie Frech. Ein Fellbacher Frauenleben zwischen Pietismus und Eigensinn. Eine Ausstellung der Stadt Fellbach vom 12. Mai bis 13. Oktober 1996*, edited by Ralf Beckmann, 79–85. Fellbach: Fellbacher Hefte.

Russell, Anna. 2017. "The Victoria and Albert Gains a Pussyhat." *The New Yorker*, April 24, 2017. Accessed April 30, 2017. https://www.newyorker.com/magazine/2017/04/24/the-victoria-and-albert-gains-a-pussyhat

Schmidt, Benjamin. 2015. *Inventing Exoticism: Geography, Globalism, and Europe's Early Modern World*. Philadelphia: University of Pennsylvania Press.

Simmel, Georg. (1901) 2004. "Fashion." In *The Rise of Fashion*, edited by Daniel Purdy, 289–309. Minneapolis: University of Minnesota Press.

Sombart, Werner. (1902) 2004. "Economy and Fashion: A Theoretical Contribution on the Formation of Modern Consumer Demand." In *The Rise of Fashion*, edited by Daniel Purdy, 310–16. Minneapolis: University of Minnesota Press.

1

Material subjects: Making place, making time through fashion

Susan B. Kaiser

Fashion studies scholarship frequently highlights issues of identity: *who* we are, individually and collectively, including critical, intersecting subject positions such as gender, sexuality, ethnicity, class, age/generation, and nationality. In this chapter, I attempt to build on earlier work (e.g., Kaiser 2012) to link such intersectional-identity scholarship with issues of (place) *where* we are and (time) *when* we are through the concept of materiality, or the ways through which processes of fashion (e.g., making, doing) become visible and tangible. I suggest that the intersections between time and place can and should be understood through the concept of *material subjects*: individuals fashioning their bodies as they move through place and time.

Because the place-time interface can be too abstract to comprehend tangibly, I use an overarching case study throughout this chapter, along with other historical and contemporary examples, to illustrate the importance of the body, clothes, and images in making place and making time simultaneously at the women's marches that occurred around the world on January 21, 2017, the day after the inauguration of US president Donald Trump. Figure 1.1 depicts the hundreds of thousands of individuals who occupied space and "made place" in Washington, DC, at a particular, significant time in history. Scattered throughout the crowds in Washington and around the world are homemade hats that have become highly symbolic: pink "pussy hats," each with its own "making" story but connected with a DIY (do-it-yourself) social movement to reassert women's bodily rights. As material subjects, the individuals in Figure 1.1 join millions of protesters around the world, filling (and flowing through) spaces as they make political statements with and through their fashioned bodies and signs. They also make/mark place (Washington, DC) and time (January 21, 2017) simultaneously.

Figure 1.1 Marchers make place (Washington, DC) and time (January 21, 2017) for women's rights. *Photo*: Mario Tama/ Getty Images.

Time and place differ conceptually, but inextricably merge in everyday experience through the styled-fashioned-dressed body (see Tulloch 2010; Kaiser 2012). And what a complicated body it is: itself intersectional—biologically, socially, culturally, and politically constructed through the embodied subject positions of age/generation, class, ethnicity, gender, nationality, "race," sexuality, and so on. These subject positions preexist individuals in the ways that they are mutually constructed by the cross sections among physical characteristics, family background, cultural discourses, and *where* and *when* individuals live and fashion their bodies.

Gertrud Lehnert and Gabriele Mentges (2013) argue for the need to highlight entanglements across places through time. Specifically, they note that the history of European material culture needs to be rewritten to reflect its entanglement with Eastern/Asian material culture. "Fusion fashion" as a concept recognizes that fashion is not just a Euromodern construct or process. Stated somewhat differently, material culture more generally is not static, singular, essentialist, or autonomous. The process of "thinking materially" unleashes fashion from bounded times and places and reflects instead on the flows of bodies and materials through time and place.

Euromodern narratives tend to prioritize time over place: the idea that fashion "started" in Europe sometime in the Renaissance or in the early modern period; that there was little or no change in dress elsewhere in the world prior to the European imagination of progress; and that time in general was on an upwardly linear trajectory in Europe but was basically static elsewhere (Riello and McNeil 2010). For this reason, I have chosen to locate place first in this chapter, to upset this hierarchical dynamic.

Place

We need . . . to think through what might be an adequately progressive sense of place, one which would fit in with the current global-local times and the feelings and relations they give rise to.

Massey 1996, 241

The British cultural geographer Doreen Massey argues for a progressive understanding of place: one that is "not self-enclosing and defensive, but outward looking" (Massey 1996, 237), one that attends to routes through which materials and individuals move through space. From the "silk road" to contemporary migration to fiber/textile/apparel production and distribution patterns, the question needs to be raised about routes: we need to focus on flows and why they matter and how they have shaped global history. In global-local times, there is an intensity of travel and migration of people, transnational networks of the fiber-textile-apparel complex (and hence, complex flows of materials), and digital technologies that make images and narratives widely accessible around the world. During the women's marches on January 21, 2017, for example, many who participated texted family members at other marches, sharing photos and comparing notes. There was a sense of being part of something larger than the places we were making locally. Another aspect of the "pussy hat" DIY movement was that some women who could not afford, or otherwise were not able, to travel to a march but wanted to participate had the opportunity to do so by knitting hats and sending them to distribution centers, often knitting stores. In other words, they did not need to be physically present at a march but could be said to be "materially" present through the items they knitted for other women. Anja Liseth, a Norwegian woman, was quoted in the *Los Angeles Times* as saying, "I feel that my contribution is important, and that since I've knitted these hats, part of me is there at the demonstration" (Mehta 2017). In other words, Liseth was still a material subject who contributed to the making of place and time together.

The issue of who inhabits space (as at a march) or flows across places is a crucial one, however. Not everyone flows freely. At the time of this writing, president Donald Trump has issued his second Executive Order (having modified the first one issued in January 2017; struck down by the courts) to strictly limit travel and immigration from individuals coming from any of the following six predominately Muslim nations: Iran, Libya, Somalia, Sudan, Syria, and Yemen. When the first ban (which included Iraq, eliminated from the second Executive Order) had been implemented immediately in January, protesters around the country flocked to US airports to support stranded and detained individuals from the countries listed (Thrush 2017). Often seen in these protests was a poster that had already circulated widely at the women's marches the day after the president's inauguration: the image of a Muslim American woman wearing the US flag as *hijab*. Figure 1.2 shows an image of a woman similarly dressed and holding the poster at the women's march in Berlin, Germany. I first saw the poster at the march in Sacramento, California; the woman holding it gave it to me to share widely and visibly at the march and beyond. I later learned online about the artist: Shepard Fairey, who had created posters of Muslim American, Chicana, and African American women for a "We the People" campaign, and previously designed the "Hope" poster for president Barack Obama's campaign (Chung 2017). Fairey had based the design on the 2007 photograph taken by Ridwan Adhamis of a Muslim American woman named Ahmed (now thirty-two years old and a freelance interpreter from Queens; Cauterucci 2017). Ahmed was born in the United States, but the travel/immigration bans raised issues regarding the extent to which Muslim individuals were welcomed into the country. The specification of six nations in the travel and immigration restrictions opened

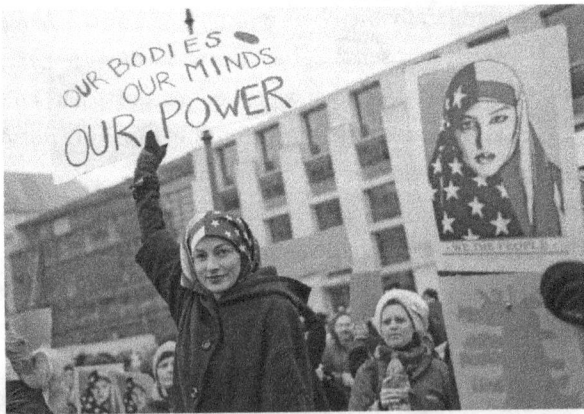

Figure 1.2 A woman at the women's march in Berlin (January 21, 2017) wears an American flag as a headscarf, similar to the poster nearby. With her own sign, she reminds us that material subjects have agency as they move through space and articulate intersectionality (e.g., gender, ethnicity, religion, nation). *Photo*: Steffi Loos/ Getty Images.

up issues of place and space, as they intersected with the subject positions of religion, gender, nation, and ethnicity.

Although the two are highly interrelated, space is a more abstract concept than place. Places are located and have spaces between them. Places are stops along the way for individuals; they are like the embodied pauses in the larger journey of life (Cresswell 2004, 8). The timeframe of these pauses varies from person to person or diaspora to diaspora. Geographer Tim Cresswell (2004, 27) notes that "struggles for place identity" may "appeal to the parochial and exclusive forces of bigotry and nationalism," as well as to us/them distinctions that involve devaluation of "them" and considerations of who is perceived as "in place" versus "out of place." Cresswell also emphasizes that subject positions do not happen "on the head of a pin. They happen in space and place" (Cresswell 2004, 27). This is a helpful reminder for critical fashion studies that place is co-constructed with other subject positions (e.g., gender, class, ethnicity) and becomes a site within space through which fashioned bodies or material subjects flow (Kaiser 2012). Dress histories around the world are replete with case studies of how textiles, clothes, and ways of styling appearance have become identifiable in terms of place (e.g., a village, region), as well as a means for differentiation between places. As a collective process of negotiating "looks" among individuals in everyday settings, fashion is "locatable," albeit subtly at times, even in the context of globalization. The *way* people put their looks together, even if many of the clothes and accessories are very similar, is still part of a localized, social process of style and meaning production (Kaiser, Nagasawa, and Hutton 1991).

In recent years, the field of fashion studies has been critiqued for having an urban or metrocentric bias (e.g., Kaiser 2013; Goodrum and Hunt 2013). Fashion studies' urban focus is shared with many fields of study, according to cultural geographer Doreen Massey, who points to a larger "intellectual infatuation . . . with cities" (2005, 159). She submits that this infatuation has led to the exclusion "not only of other, non-urban places but of wider spatialities of global difference." For example, in fashion discourse there has been a tendency to focus on certain cities (e.g., Paris, Milan, London, and New York) as "world fashion cities" to the exclusion of other, non-Western cities (see Breward and Gilbert 2006).

Time

How, indeed, can we speak of a human life as a story in its nascent state, since we do not have access to the temporal dramas of existence outside of stories

> *told about them by others or by ourselves. . . . I shall not hesitate to speak of a*
> *prenarrative quality of experience.*
>
> Ricoeur 1983, 74

The French philosopher Paul Ricoeur grappled with the paradox of time, summarizing the works of previous philosophers such as Augustine: "How can time exist if the past is no longer, if the future is not yet, and if the present is not always?" (1983, 7). Ricoeur argued that narrative-making or storytelling helps to organize a sense of time and make it humanly possible to articulate it.

There was certainly a movement-making narrative leading up to the women's marches on January 21, 2017, running throughout them, and continuing beyond them. It goes like this: two friends and avid knitters from Los Angeles (screenwriter Krista Suh and architect Jayna Zweiman) launched the Pussyhat Project over Thanksgiving weekend in November 2016, a couple of weeks after the presidential election. They had teamed up with Kat Coyle, the owner of their neighborhood knitting shop to design a simple "pussy power hat" pattern. The project had more than one purpose. First, the Pussyhat Project anticipated the women's march in Washington, DC, and other cities, scheduled the day after the inauguration of Donald Trump on January 20, 2017. The idea was to make a "strong visual statement" at the marches by symbolizing female power through the use of pink, a color connoting "femininity" since at least the 1930s in the United States. Second, it provided simple patterns to foster a DIY movement and enabled knitters who could not attend any of the marches an opportunity to participate by making hats for individuals who were able to attend in person. Third, the pussy hat referenced an earlier videotape, recorded in 2005, in which Donald Trump told Billy Bush, a cousin to former president George W. Bush and *Access Hollywood* host, on board a bus on the way to the set of the soap opera, *Days of Our Lives*, that when you are a famous man, "You can do anything [to women]. . . . Grab them by the pussy. You can do anything." The tape surfaced about one month before the election in November 2016. Shortly after it was aired, Billy Bush was fired from NBC, where he had been a host of the *Today Show* (Yahr 2016). Donald Trump was elected president on November 8, 2016.

Often, fashion stories are hard to tell until after the fact. Ricoeur (1983) argued that narratives in general are preceded by a preliminary period/way of experiencing time that cannot yet easily be expressed in words. He called this the "prenarrative quality of experience" (Ricoeur 1983, 74): a nascent and anticipatory way of knowing, being, and becoming. Somewhat similarly, but with a more direct focus on fashion, the German cultural theorist Walter Benjamin observed that what is so fascinating and compelling about fashion from a philosophical perspective is its "extraordinary anticipations." Like art, fashion often "precedes the perceptible reality by years," and yet Benjamin argues that fashion has "much steadier, much more precise contact with the coming thing" (2004, 63–64). As part of the ambiguity of subjectivity, fashion suggests what is to come, but it does so in an especially compelling way: an embodied way of articulating the present, and anticipation of the future, in ways that cannot yet be verbalized (Kaiser 2012, 44). This process of anticipation operates at both the individual (subjective) and collective (intersubjective) levels of fashion. Street style or runway fashion can strike a chord and feel completely "right" for the present, but at the same time be difficult to describe, much less tell a story. The American sociologist Herbert Blumer attempted to interview audience members at Parisian fashion shows in the 1930s, for example, and was frustrated by the fact that a few styles resonated strongly but could only be described as "chic." He developed a theory of "collective selection" to characterize styles that strike a chord and enable collective adjustment to change: detachment from the past and anticipation of the future (Blumer 1969).

Whether in its prenarrative phase or later, when it becomes organized into an historical narrative or story or period, fashion's way with time does not generally mesh neatly with a linear notion of progress. Indeed, it "complicates notions of time as a linear or cumulative phenomenon" (Riello and McNeil 2010, 3). The story of fashion is a circuitous kind of narrative, with intermittent "tiger's leaps into the past," to use Benjamin's (1968, 261) phrase, for design inspiration. For example, embroidered "peasant" blouses have recurred in popularity in recent years, harkening back to similar styles in the 1970s, when some of them were self-embroidered. A recent advertisement online makes note of this temporal leap into the past: "Give your outfits a bohemian-inspired feel with this chic gauze peasant blouse. The flowy silhouette and long sleeves are finished with pintucked details and paisley embroidery for 70's-inspired flair" (Charming Charlie 2017).

Even stories about fashion periods or cycles become narratives in their own right. China's narratives of fashion change generally revolve around differences across dynastic periods (Hua 2010). Historian James Laver (1937) attempted to compress the history of Western fashion cycles—from the French Revolution until the 1930s—into a linear timeline. Laver's "Law" developed a cyclical continuum of sorts: a given style will look "indecent" 10 years before its time to "daring" 1 year before, to "smart" in its current time, to "dowdy" 1 year after, to "hideous" 10 years after its time, to "amusing" 30 years after, to "romantic" 100 years after, and "beautiful" 150 years after. If Laver's narrative had worked with his historical study and time of writing, it has certainly broken down, with more rapid cycles of recycling since the late 1960s.

There are a number of European-focused "origin stories" of fashion: the fourteenth-century Italian city-state (Steele 1988), the fifteenth-century Burgundian court (Davis 1992), and, more recently, France's emerging fashion system in the twelfth and thirteenth centuries (Heller 2010). Historian Sarah-Grace Heller observes that "there is a noteworthy tendency to discover a birth of fashion in whichever period a scholar studies" (Heller 2010, 26) and that "fashionability is in the eye of the beholder"; she cautions against ignoring periods earlier than a scholar's own temporal and spatial focus (Heller 2010, 34).

Shifting our focus from narratives about fashion-time to narratives about materiality—the life cycle of the body and the materials of fashion—enables a more grounded way of dealing with fashion-time. Individual memories and experiences of time become intertwined with fabric technologies, as well as changing styles and aging bodies. Attempts to become part of a "scene" from a prior period—such as the sixties scene—are limited by available vintage clothes, because the materials themselves are different (Jenss 2015). When we shift our focus to fashioned bodies, Ricoeur's paradox of how time can exist becomes grounded in memories and materials, ambiguities of contemporary style, and anticipation of new styles and narratives in order to make sense of current ambiguities in the future.

Material subjects

The body is the innermost part of the material Self in each of us; and certain parts of the body seem more intimately ours than the rest. The clothes come next. The old saying that the human person is composed of three parts—soul, body and clothes—is more than a joke.

James 1890

The American pragmatist philosopher William James (1890) identified three aspects of the self: the material self, the social self, and the spiritual self, in addition to sheer ego. He did not delve into issues of gender, "race," ethnicity, class, sexuality, and other intersecting subject positions—not surprisingly for his time and place—in relation to these three aspects of self, but here I would like to reflect on the concept of "material self" and revise it for the purposes of this chapter and for the continuing usefulness of the concept in textile and fashion studies to that of "material subjects." It is a plural concept, opening up space for multiple and even conflicting identities, and builds upon intersectional feminist theory and the possibility of partial and overlapping subject positions, which together with subjectivity—the more agential side of subjecthood—comprise what it means to be a subject (see Mama 1995; Kaiser 2012).

The concept of material subjects gets beyond the language of "self" as a unitary, modern agent, who was generally presumed in James' day to be a white, bourgeois, heterosexual male. To illustrate this sense of agency and the only possibility for presumed selfhood or subjecthood imagined in place and time, we can go back in place and time to consider a case study offered by Gabriele Mentges (2002) in her critical analysis of the personal clothing history of Matthäus Schwarz of Augsburg, Germany, between the years of 1496 and 1564. Schwarz's life can be located in a period alternately framed in the period narratives of the Early Modern or Renaissance. Schwarz, an accountant who worked for a wealthy merchant, chronicled—in the form of a visual, diary-like costume book—changes in his own clothing and appearance. The resulting manuscript, in the form of a small, leather-bound book with 137 pages of text and hand-painted, colored illustrations, is a remarkable compendium that "offers present-day readers (and viewers) both a unique insight into the wardrobe of a male individual of the Renaissance period and a seemingly narcissistic glimpse of a masculine Self" (Mentges 2002, 382).

> In his constant wardrobe changes, Matthäus Schwarz also displayed a marked sense of contemporary fashionable taste and extravagance alongside his consistent concern to be on the cutting edge. The slashed fashions he wore from his youth onward permitted a particular flirtation with the fine points of dress and reveal him to have been an elegant man with a highly developed sense of his own body. (Mentges 2002, 386)

Material details abound in Mentges' analysis, as well as in a later book with colorful illustrations both of Matthäus Schwarz's and of his son's self-documentation: *The First Book of Fashion: The Books of Clothes of Matthäus & Veit Konrad Schwarz of Augsburg* (Rublack and Hayward 2015). Mentges points out the lack of female representation in the Schwarz family illustrations. Even upon the occasion of Matthäus Schwarz's wedding, for which his own attire is illustrated, there is no inclusion of his bride's image. The idea of the "Renaissance man"—decidedly European, bourgeois to upper class, and urban—and his importance in forging a new, modern way of being comes to life in Mentges' analysis, which includes "thick description."

Access into the thoughts, priorities, and styles of a material subject's life, including who was missing, such as Schwarz's wife, along with analyses of fabrics and other materials, can be seen as being at the very heart of understanding of what it means to make place, and more generally space, and to make time. The French space theorist Henri Lefebvre emphasized the importance of thinking about time and space together, indicating that "time is known and actualized in space, becoming a social reality by virtue of a spatial practice. Similarly, space is known only in and through time" (Lefebvre 1991, 219). Although space and time can be conceptually distinguished from one another, they cannot be separated in the everyday bodies of material subjects.

Bridging subject positions and subjectivities, *material subjects* include not only bodies as they are gendered, "raced," sexualized and so on, but also bodies as they become dressed, according to overlapping subject positions and subjectivities as well as times and places. During the French Revolution toward the end of the eighteenth century, a radical newspaper in Paris argued that for there to be a real revolution, people had to feel it in their bodies (Sennett 1994, 282). Or, we might say that they had to become material subjects. But whose material subjectivities mattered? One of the primary issues at stake was redefining who counted as citizens of France—who represented the nation. The Revolution needed to invent a "citizen" (Sennett 1994, 285) who somehow looked like "everyman"; the prioritized material subjects were white men who represented a wider spectrum of social classes, including lower- and working-class men. Men of lower classes wore *sans-culottes* (long trousers), which contrasted with and expressed resistance to the more fitted culottes (short breeches) of higher-class men. Other revolutionary symbols included the red Phrygian or "Liberty" cap—a soft, brimless, felt conical cap with the top pulled forward—and the tricolor cockade—a red, white, and blue circular accessory pinned to coats or hats (Wrigley 2002). Worn to Revolutionary festivals in city spaces, these items of dress became part of the material subjects' feelings of resistance, in which "the body is roused to take note of the world in which it lives" (Sennett 1994, 310). But the opportunity for these feelings of resistance to "make" a new place and a new time was not shared equitably across gendered subject positions.

William James (1890) observed that materiality transcends the body and the textiles, technologies, and other materials with which we surround our bodies. These materials, external to our bodies, have their own origins, flows, and lifespans: "cradle to grave," or "cradle to cradle" if they are upcycled (Braungart and McDonough 2002) beyond our own bodies. Popular and scholarly attention to materiality has increased in recent years, perhaps due to trends such as the following:

(a) concerns with sustainability; the lives of materials (including textiles and related substances) do not end with consumers' end-of-use of them (see Hethorn and Ulasiewicz 2015; Kaiser 2015); despite the global counter-trend of fast fashion, there is a movement to think about the lives of materials, including their possibilities for rebirth in new materials;

(b) digital and other televisual technologies challenge consumers and producers alike to wonder about the extent to which representations of fashion on the screen can be materially experienced (e.g., the "touch" of a fabric, the accuracy of the colors);

(c) new "smart" wearable technologies that monitor bodily health and fitness, mood, and various subjectivities;

(d) globalization, along with a discourse on, and increase of, products "made in America" as a reaction to "fast fashion" made in China or elsewhere;

(e) a DIY ethos, including the wide popularity of knitting for aesthetic as well as therapeutic reasons;

(f) renewed media attention to the political significance of dress (not just for politicians, but for lay individuals) (Friedman 2016) and how/why it should be collected and recorded for historical purposes (Jones 2017).

Altogether, the last few trends can be exemplified through an intersectional, material analysis of the pussy hats worn at the women's marches. Through such a lens, we can consider their material production, distribution, and uses beyond, to their "afterlife." The Pussyhat Project is clearly an interesting case study that not only blends the DIY ethos with attention to the political/cultural significance of dress but also helps to focus our attention on issues of intersectional identities, as well as textiles throughout their life cycle. As Sophie Woodward and Tom Fisher have observed, although fashion is "temporary and ephemeral," it is "indexed in material forms" (2014, 3). It is crucial, they argue, that the material and cultural be seen not as separate but rather as co-constitutive (Woodward and Fisher 2014, 12).

In addition to the materially and culturally co-constitutive nature of pussy hats, I would argue that intersectionality among subject positions need to be central to the discussion. Questions such as the following arise: Who made the pussy hats, and how were they made (following the materials themselves)? Whose bodies feel comfortable wearing pink pussy hats? Who feels included, and who might feel excluded? What happens to the pussy hats after the women's marches (January 21, 2017) and International Women's Day (March 8)? To what extent do they become part of documented and collected material culture?

The word spread about pussy hats through the patterns online, social media, and local yarn stores, which in effect became sites of both production and distribution. There was a run on pink yarn, used to knit basic rectangular hats that could be positioned so as to have perky "ears." Other DIYers bought pink sweater-knit fabric or upcycled pink sweaters from thrift stores to fashion their hats with their sewing machines. It was striking at the marches to see so many hats with the same or similar forms, but in various shades of pink and with some unique variations created by the hands of the makers.

Co-constitutively (i.e., materially *and* culturally), pink pussy hats have to be understood in relation to American cultural constructions of the meaning of pinkness. Between the 1930s and the 1950s, pink came to be associated with the color *not* to be worn by infant boys and became hence the color of early childhood femininity (Paoletti 2012). Since the 1950s or so, Susan Kaiser and Angela Flury (2005) have argued, pink represented, albeit ambivalently, modern white femininity in the United States. Feminists in the late 1960s and early 1970s rejected pink due to its linkages with "traditional" femininity, but, by the 1980s, pink had become widely popular again, as represented in the 1986 John Hughes film, *Pretty in Pink* (starring Molly Ringwald). As the American dress historian Jo Paoletti (2012) has documented, there is a certain irony and ambivalence associated with gender-color-coded, baby-boomer parents (born after the Second World War) going through the feminist movement in the late 1960s and early 1970s and resisting pink as the ultimate symbol of hegemonic femininity, yet dressing their infants classified female at birth (or earlier) in pink.

Hence, there is a history of about half-a-century of feminist ambivalence and anxiety surrounding the color pink, which adds to the complexity of interpreting pink pussy hats. These hats became a powerful and empowering visual symbol of the women's marches in resistance to president Trump's earlier 2005 statements dismissing the subjectivities of women themselves—that grabbing women's genitalia was/is a privilege of being a famous (white) man—as well as of the anxieties about potential federal policies that were likely to affect women's bodies, health, and human rights in the future. As though all of this ambivalence and anxiety is not complicated enough, there is then the issue of who felt included in the marches. At the march in Washington, DC, and in various sites around the United States and the world, multiple attempts were made to be inclusive through intersectional feminist perspectives: women of color, men, and queer and transgender women were included in the featured speaking roles and were

Figure 1.3 The Mothers of the Movement (whose sons have died because of gun violence) foster a bridge between Black Lives Matter and women's rights at the march on Washington, DC. Four wear pink pussy hats. *Photo:* Noam Galal/ Getty Images.

represented as participants in many of the marches. Figure 1.3 shows an image of Mothers of the Movement (Black Lives Matter) at the Washington march. Four are wearing pink pussy hats: Sybrina Fulton (mother of the late Trayvon Martin), Gwen Carr (mother of the late Eric Garner), Maria Hamilton (mother of the late Dontre Hamilton), and Lucia McBath (mother of the late Jordan Davis). All of their unarmed sons died from gun violence, two at the hands of police.

Despite some attempts to make the place and time an inclusive space, from an intersectional, feminist point of view, a lot of African American women expressed on social media "the hurt of seeing so many white women coming together for this march, but not showing up when we march" for movements such as Black Lives Matter (Obie 2017). As has been discussed by Laura Beltran-Rubio (2017), the contrast between the seas of pink at the women's marches around the world on January 21, 2017, and the clothing at Black Lives Matter marches (e.g., neutral colors, hoodies) is striking.

In addition to issues of race, there were some critiques of the marches in terms of whether the marches were managed primarily by and for white, straight, cis-gender women. For example, did the color pink capture the subjectivities of nonwhite or transgender women? Did the genital reference in the pussy hats suggest that only individuals classified at birth as female were qualified to participate as "women"? A transgender woman from Modesto, California, said about the march: "The main reason I decided not to go was because of the pussy hats" (Solis 2017).

Symbols, like the material subjects who embody them, matter. And they have afterlives. After the marches around the world, the Italian fashion designer Angela Missoni ended her Fall 2017 fashion show at Milan's fashion week with pussy hats. All of the models, male and female alike, came out on the stage wearing them, and the guests were encouraged to don the free pussy hats left on their seats (Marchal 2017; Miller 2017). Was this high fashion's appropriation of a DIY political movement? Or was this part of the symbol's afterlife, and an attempt to keep the movement going through fashion? Most likely, it was both/ and. The afterlife of the pussy hat was also evident in the London Victoria & Albert Museum's immediate acquisition or "collection" of a pussy hat worn at the women's march in Washington, DC, for its gallery exploring how current global and political events influence design (Jones 2017). Undoubtedly, the hats will also be saved privately and perhaps worn again on relevant occasions. Overall, among the intersectional feminist ambivalences regarding pink pussy hats, it is evident that the hats made by knitters around the world marked and globally connected place(s) at a particular time in history. They symbolized the opening up of place into space.

Material subjects illuminate the need to think about place and time, or space and time, together. The makers and wearers of pussy hats contributed not only to the material manifestation of a movement but also to ongoing and dynamic narratives of resistance, inclusion and exclusion, and cultural anxiety.

References

Beltran-Rubio, Laura. 2017. "The Power of Pink and a Bloodstained Black Lives Matter Movement." *The Fashion Studies Journal*, February 28, 2017. Accessed April 8, 2017. http://www.fashionstudiesjournal.org/commentary/2017/2/28/fashion-and-solid arity-the-power-of-pink-and-a-bloodstained-black-lives-matter-movement

Benjamin, Walter. 1968. "Theses on the Philosophy of History." In *Illuminations*, edited by Hannah Arendt (translated by Harry Zohn), 252–64. New York: Harcourt, Brace Jovanovich, Inc.

Benjamin, Walter. 2004. *The Arcades Project*. Translated by Howard Eiland and Kevin McLaughlin. Cambridge: Harvard University Press.

Blumer, Herbert. 1969. "Fashion: From Class Differentiation to Collective Deletion." *The Sociological Quarterly* 10(3): 275–91.

Braungart, Michael, and William McDonough. 2002. *Cradle to Cradle: Remaking the Way We Make Things*. New York: Durabook.

Breward, Christopher, and David Gilbert, eds. 2006. *Fashion's World Cities*. Oxford: Berg.

Cauterucci, Christina. 2017. "A Q-and-A with the Muslim Woman Whose Face Has Become a Symbol of Trump Resistance." *Slate*, January 25, 2017. Accessed February 8, 2017. http://www.slate.com/blogs/xx_factor/2017/01/25/a_q_a_with_the_mu slim_woman_whose_face_has_become_a_symbol_of_trump_resistance.html

CharmingCharlie.com. "Embroidered Peasant Blouse." Accessed April 28, 2017. http://www.charmingcharlie.com/embroidered-peasant-blouse.html

Chung, Stephy. "'Hope' Artist Shepard Fairey Reveals New Posters to Protest Trump." *CNN*, January 19, 2017. Accessed February 7, 2017. http://www.cnn.com/2017/0 1/19/arts/shepard-fairey-trump-inauguration-posters-trnd/

Cresswell, Tim. 2004. *Place: A Short Introduction*. Malden: Blackwell Publishing.

Davis, Fred. 1992. *Fashion, Culture and Identity*. Chicago: University of Chicago Press.

Friedman, Vanessa. 2016. "When Politics Became a Fashion Statement: The Year in Style 2016." *The New York Times*, December 13, 2016. Accessed May 31, 2017. https://www.nytimes.com/2016/12/13/fashion/the-year-in-style-politics-dressing.html

Goodrum, Alison L., and Kevin J. Hunt. 2013. "The Field as Mall: Redressing the Rural-Urban Divide in Fashion Theory through Equestrian Events." *Critical Studies in Fashion and Beauty* 4(1–2): 17–42.

Heller, Sarah-Grace. 2010. "The Birth of Fashion." In *The Fashion History Reader: Global Perspectives*, edited by Giorgio Riello and Peter McNeil, 25–39. Abingdon: Routledge.

Hethorn, Janet, and Connie Ulasewicz, eds. 2015. *Sustainable Fashion: What's Next?* 2nd edition. New York: Fairchild Books.

Hua, Mei. 2010. *Chinese Clothing*. Cambridge: Cambridge University Press.

James, William. 1890. *The Principles of Psychology*. New York: Henry Holt & Co.

Jenss, Heike. 2015. *Fashioning Memory: Vintage Style and Youth Culture*. London: Bloomsbury Academic.

Jones, Joanna. "'Pussyhat' acquired for Rapid Response Collection." *Victoria & Albert Museum Blog*, March 8, 2017. Accessed April 8, 2017. http://www.vam.ac.uk/blog/ network/pussyhat-acquired-for-rapid-response-collection.

Kaiser, Susan B. 2012. *Fashion and Cultural Studies*. London: Berg.

Kaiser, Susan B. 2013. "Place, Time and Identity: New Directions in Critical Fashion Studies." *Critical Studies in Fashion and Beauty* 4(1–2): 3–16.

Kaiser, Susan B. 2015. "Mixing Metaphors in the Fiber, Textile and Apparel Complex: Moving Forward." In *Sustainable Fashion: What's Next?*, 2nd edition, edited by Janet Hethorn and Connie Ulasewicz, 132–58. New York: Fairchild Books.

Kaiser, Susan B., and Angela Flury. 2005. "Frauen in Rosa: Zur Semiotik der Kleiderfarben (Women in Pink: On the Semiotics of Dress Colors)." *Zeitschrift für Semiotik* 27(3): 223–39.

Kaiser, Susan B., Nagasawa, Richard H., and Sandra S. Hutton. 1991. "Fashion, Postmodernity, and Personal Appearance: A Symbolic Interactionist Formulation." *Symbolic Interaction* 14(2): 165–85.

Laver, James. 1937. *Taste and Fashion: From the French Revolution until Today*. London: George G. Harrap.

Lefebvre, Henri. 1991. *The Production of Space*. Translated by Donald Nicholson-Smith. Oxford: Basil Blackwell Ltd.

Lehnert, Gertrud, and Gabriele Mentges, eds. 2013. *Fusion Fashion: Culture beyond Orientalism and Occidentalism*. Frankfurt am Main: Peter Lang.

Mama, Amina. 1995. *Beyond the Masks: Race, Gender and Subjectivity*. London: Routledge.

Marchal, Nahema. "Women's March 'Pussy Hats' Hit the Runway." *Heat Street*, February 27, 2017. Accessed April 8, 2017. https://heatst.com/life/womens-march-pussy-hats-hit-the-runway/

Massey, Doreen. 1996. "A Global Sense of Place." In *Exploring Human Geography: A Reader*, edited by Stephen Daniels and Roger Lee, 237–45. London: Routledge.

Massey, Doreen. 2005. *For Space*. London: Sage.

Mehta, Seema. "How These Los Angeles-Born Pink Hats Became a Worldwide Symbol of the Anti-Trump Women's March." *Los Angeles Times*, January 15, 2017. Accessed April 28, 2017. http://www.latimes.com/politics/la-pol-ca-pink-hats-womens-march-20170115-story.html

Mentges, Gabriele. 2002. "Fashion, Time and the Consumption of a Renaissance Man in Germany: The Costume Book of Matthäus Schwarz of Augsburg, 1496–1564." *Gender and History* 14(3): 382–402.

Miller, Jenni. "Missoni Grabs Back with Knitted Pink Pussy Hats at Milan Fashion Week." *The Cut*, February 25, 2017. Accessed April 30, 2017. https://www.thecut.com/2017/02/missoni-grabs-back-with-knitted-pink-pussy-hats-in-milan.html

Obie, Brooke. "Woman in Viral Photo from Women's March to White Female Allies: 'Listen to a Black Woman.'" *The Root*, January 23, 2017. Accessed April 8, 2017. https://www.theroot.com/woman-in-viral-photo-from-women-s-march-to-white-female-1791524613

Paoletti, Jo. 2012. *Pink and Blue: Telling the Boys from the Girls in America*. Bloomington: Indiana University Press.

Ricoeur, Paul. 1983. *Time and Narrative*, Vol. 1. Translated by Kathleen McLaughlin and David Pellauer. Chicago: University of Chicago Press.

Riello, Giorgio, and McNeil, Peter. 2010. "Introduction." In *The Fashion History Reader: Global Perspectives*, edited by Giorgio Riello and Peter McNeil, 1–17. Abingdon: Routledge.

Rublack, Ulinka, and Maria Hayward, eds. 2015. *The First Book of Fashion: The Books of Clothes of Matthäus & Veit Konrad Schwarz of Augsburg*. London: Bloomsbury Academic.

Sennett, Richard. 1994. *Flesh and Stone: The Body and the City in Western Civilization*. New York: W.W. Norton & Company.

Solis, Marie. "How the Women's March's 'Genital-Based' Feminism Isolated the Transgender Community." *Mic.com*, January 23, 2017. Accessed April 8, 2017. https://mic.com/articles/ 166273/how-the-women-s-march-s-genital-based-feminism-isolated-the-transgender-community

Steele, Valerie. 1988. *Paris Fashion: A Cultural History*. Oxford: Oxford University Press.

Thrush, Glenn. "Trump's New Travel Ban Blocks Migrants from Six Nations, Sparing Iraq." *New York Times*, March 6, 2017. Accessed April 8, 2017. https://www.nytimes.com/2017/03/06/us/politics/travel-ban-muslim-trump.html

Tulloch, Carol. 2010. "Style-Fashion-Dress: From Black to Post-Black." *Fashion Theory* 14(3): 361–86.

Woodward, Sophie, and Tom Fisher. 2014. "Fashioning through Materials: Material Culture, Materiality, and Processes of Materialization." *Critical Studies in Fashion and Beauty* 5(1): 3–23.

Wrigley, Richard. 2002. *The Politics of Appearances: Representations of Dress in Revolutionary France*. Oxford: Berg.

Yahr, Emily. "Billy Bush is Officially Done at the 'Today' Show after the Donald Trump Rape." *The Washington Post*, October 17, 2016. Accessed April 8, 2017. https://www.washingtonpost.com/news/arts-and-entertainment/wp/2016/10/17/billy-bush-is-officially-done-at-the-today-show-after-donald-trump-tape.

2

Dressed lives: Biography, emotion, and materiality

Christel Köhle-Hezinger

This chapter considers the significance of clothing as a material constant in the lives of two women living in twentieth-century Germany. It foregrounds reflection on the material quality of things as it was considered a central measure of their value in everyday life. Moving beyond a perspective on textiles and clothing as cultural artifacts whose value is primarily defined by fashion and its changes, I seek to approach the materiality of sartorial objects as a window into the biographies of ordinary people, individual wearers, and their historic cultural contexts. Through this, I will show that the apparently "mute" material remains of former lives, once revisited as sources of material culture, can offer unique insights into the biographies and experiences of individual persons, and into their life-world or *Lebenswelt*.

Clothes, or rather significant items of clothing that came to be referred to as the "best dress," have always played a particular role in people's lives, and thus held a particular cultural and social value. Historically, in the private lives of ordinary people such a "best dress" consisted especially of a festive garment, an item of clothing commonly kept and worn on appropriate occasions over a lifetime—one that maintained significant value even beyond the life of its owner. For example, under the system of feudalism, following the death of a peasant, his or her best dress became the property of the landowner, so that the material value of the garment transformed or translated into a kind of final rent payment, functioning as an "alternate currency" (Lemire 1997). In post-feudal times, a deceased person's best dress was handed down to close relatives (Kaschuba and Lipp 1982; Lemire 1997). Due to its long time span of use, a best dress can be understood as a sartorial investment that, in terms of function, form, color, material, and cost, had to fit the wearer for a wide range of social contexts and occasions: it was a garment dressing its wearer appropriately for various festive events, from baptisms and anniversaries to weddings and funerals as well as for the various festivities associated with the liturgical calendar, which meant that the best dress had to be continuously updated and altered according to the situation.

Material and design were traditionally defined and designed for durability; a best dress should not wear out too quickly, or stand out too much, or be too conspicuous. It was meant to be "timeless." Its particular value and appreciation were derived from a set of characteristics that were ultimately perceived to be transcending time itself. That said, the best dress was not rigidly fixed or outside the dynamics of fashion. It was also subject to processes of change and updating, yet these changes usually occurred over the course of the lifetime of a person, and sometimes even over the course of a century. Although material quality and durability remained key elements in these processes of change over time, some details of the best dress were modified according to its own logic. For example, small formal design modifications can be seen as indicators of change within the dynamics of the personal life of the wearer as well as of larger social developments.

In a broader sense, the best dress was clothing defined by secular and religious norms, regulations and laws and their respective sartorial rules. Such secular and religious regulations also governed the formation of traditions, customs, and conventions as a systematic codex that affected both public and more informal private spheres (Mentges 1996). This codex concerned both secular and sacral contexts as well as rituals including *rites de passage* (van Gennep [1909] 1970). Unequivocal, binding, and clearly defined, it was part of the order of everyday life in various historical, regional, and social constellations.

Thus far, my brief definition of the "best dress" has provided a short overview of its material and immaterial entanglements with wider historical and cultural conditions. To better understand its use and place in everyday life, however, it is necessary to consider the wearer themselves, and the social, biographical, and emotional scope of actions the possession and use of the best dress regulated or enabled. How did notions of longevity and continuity that regulated the purchase and use of clothing, affect the wearers and their personal needs, desires, and beliefs? Though everyday objects remain central to the investigation of material culture, such a large question can best be approached in concrete terms by examining individual cases and with a perspective on biography. In the following, I will present insights into the everyday lives and/or sartorial remains, in both material and textual forms, of two women living in twentieth-century

Germany: one a devout Pietist from a small village in southwestern Germany, the other an employee from an urban environment. In very different ways, their wardrobes offer insights into two worlds that, though geographically in proximity to each other, were radically different in outlook. My selection of these two examples is inspired by the silent legacies of these women's wardrobes, which were handed down, given away, or strategically curated in museums. These two collections were to some extent enriched by additional data or methods, including autobiographic narrative and biographical material culture studies. I understand the attention to memories of and narratives around clothing as a mode of retrospection that merges a view on one's life with a view on one's practices of dressing; or, in other words, as a particular material way of meaning-making or sense-making, and also of ordering one's life and biography—for oneself and for others (Weber and Mitchell 2004).

The pivotal question here—how do clothes *make* life and biography?—extends to the metaphorical and the symbolic, and thus inescapably ambiguous levels. Today, speaking in contemporary terms, best dresses are, as favorite clothing, a significant part of one's lifestyle; they are valued due to preferences for specific looks or materials, and feelings of comfort. In my following focus on clothing and lived human experience, I will shed light on the material histories of the two women's lives, which I trace through clothing as items of material culture that have particular "external" material and "internal" emotional qualities. The examples show us how closely material objects and lived practices are interwoven in both religious and secular conceptions of life. The glimpse into the biographical narratives, material remains, and clothing memories of these two women further show us relationships to things that largely precede the shifts in consumer culture that would accelerate, for example, the use and devaluation of clothing that occurred later in the twentieth century.

Marie Frech: pious things, pious dresses?

My first case study asks, in an ethnographic perspective, how "things" integrate with or reflect a world of religious devotion and persistent piety. It follows the life of Marie Frech (1895–1995) (see Figure 2.1), who lived for all the one hundred years of her life in Fellbach, a wine-growing and industrial village just outside the urban center of Stuttgart in southwestern Germany, a region also historically called Swabia. Upon her death in 1995, Frech's house became a curious memorial, an "open air museum for one summer," and, as such, a kind

Figure 2.1 Marie Frech, portrait taken in photo studio *Utz* in Fellbach around 1920. *Photo*: ©StadtMuseum Fellbach.

of focal point for a collective remembering of a German century (Beckmann 1996). A second commemoration took place in 2005 in Halle/Saale, this time as part of the program of a scholarly event, the International Congress of Pietist Studies in the Historical Orphanage of the Franckesche Stiftungen (Kataloge der Franckeschen Stiftungen 2005). In Halle, as well as in her native village of Fellbach, Marie Frech's living quarters represented the material remains of her everyday life, and, in this way, came to represent the memory of ordinary folks, the "quiet people" of the rural countryside (Unseld and Föll 2004, 12). Marie Frech's things were heavily worn items that had been kept in her equally worn-out house for a long time. The pious things in her home open a fascinating window onto the people who inhabited it, and by extension onto the era's pious people, the "religious virtuosi" (Weber [1922] 1968) including men and women, both unmarried ones and also generations of families who developed and lived their own *praxis pietatis*.

Marie Frech's belongings—what she called in her Swabian dialect *das Sach* (or "all her things")—functioned both as things to be used and moved in everyday life and as signs within the order of a religiously devoted life. Though her material things constituted the bulk of Frech's personal estate, this was not just a haphazard collection; rather, it was a whole world, her world, manifesting itself in her goods and property. In Foucauldian terms, the collection embodied her personal "order of things and life" (Foucault [1966] 1970).

This cosmos of things is not only witness to an individual life, but at the same time illustrates the legacy of a specific and very different culture. The image of the pious life we imagine Marie Frech to have led manifests itself in her domestic spaces: in books and wall decorations, in a harmonium, a handbag, a dress, and headwear. For cultural studies, objects like these contain two meanings—as both subjective and objective moments in the varied contexts of tradition, gender, belief, and memory (Köhle-Hezinger 2007). An ethnographic perspective on Pietism necessarily entails the problem of *alterity*, that is, putting the Pietist self in the center of one's analysis. The observer needs to take the categories of space and time—and thus also the interlinking relationship of "having" and "being"—into careful consideration. In this regard, Frech's life is a story about special spaces and locations, about "having things," about a specific habitus (see Figure 2.2). Consequently, it also involves the notion of non-simultaneity. From a cultural studies perspective, comparative and interpretative cultural research is thus needed (see Scharfe et al. 1990; Mohrmann 1997; Bringéus 2000). Material objects are as important as written and oral sources in allowing for the reconstruction of human experience and sense-making. So, the microcosm of a

Figure 2.2 Marie Frech (née Ebinger) and her husband Wilhelm Frech on their wedding day in front of their house in Fellbach, 1933. *Photo*: ©StadtMuseum Fellbach.

pious life—with all its objects and traditions—makes for an indivisible whole in everyday life and belief.

A "system of objects" becomes a "system of meanings," as Jean Baudrillard once put it (1968). It is therefore crucial to take such systems of objects and their affordances for human existence seriously (Wallmann 1990, 7; see also Lächele

2001). This requires researchers in the case of Marie Frech, for example, to pay close attention to the objects and traces of material culture and to recognize and interpret them in a three-dimensional manner, according to particular conceptions of traditionalism, materiality, and spirituality. This trinity is indissolubly connected throughout Marie Frech's pious life, physically inscribed into her everyday experiences, and it manifests itself in the use of her belongings, including her clothing.

In 1991, when Marie Frech was ninety-six years old, she entered a retirement home, wearing her coat and carrying her *Handtäschle*—the Swabian diminutive for handbag—in much the same way that she went to church every Sunday morning or to the afternoon "hour of edification." Four weeks after her one-hundredth birthday, which she had wanted to live to celebrate, she died. What remained was her vintner's cottage, untouched since her departure in 1991, including all the things that had accumulated in it over generations: a collection of 250 books, a harmonium, photographs, prints and pictures with aphorisms, a sewing machine, dresses (the last of which she had sewn at the age of ninety-three), various pieces of linen, twenty-seven black shoes (thirteen pairs and one single left shoe), and an assortment of six indoor and outdoor brooms, some worn down to the shaft (see Beckmann 1996).

In the year 1836, the inventory of Frech's great-grandfather's estate, who was a vintner and also a Pietist, recorded several volumes of the writings of Michael Hahn (1758–1819), edited in 1819/20. Hahn was the founder of the protestant Hahn'sche Gemeinschaft (Hahn Community), which still exists today. He was a farmer's son, a butcher, and a clockmaker, who had experienced a religious awakening at the age of seventeen. At the age of twenty, he had his first central vision (*Zentralschau*) lasting three hours; the second followed at the age of twenty-five and lasted for seven weeks. His followers, the Michelians, pursued his path of internalization and, often, the attendant oath of celibacy, which he himself practiced (see Trautwein 1969 and 1972; Findeisen 1985). At the age of twenty, Marie Frech, who had also been awakened, likewise decided to remain celibate. Around 1900, Fellbach, with its 4,000 inhabitants, counted 600 members among the Hahn's Community; they made up the "large majority of the converted" (Pfarrbericht Pfarrer Bengel 1905). Within one century, the initially rebellious Pietism, an "explosive" culture as Scharfe described it, had become a relatively quiet movement (see Scharfe 2001, 11; see also Scharfe 1980 and 2004). In a very literal way, their separatism had become domesticated: out of a seemingly unfathomable number of conspiratorial networks branching out into many directions, Hahn's teachings had wandered into the living rooms of the pious (Lehmann 1969). The community's great losses brought about by the mass emigration of the famine years of 1816/17 seemed overcome. Once the hopes of an apocalypse, calculated for the year 1836 (Gutekunst 1999), were assuaged, the devout settled in the surviving world.

The framework set by gender positioning and material culture that organized Marie Frech's pious life (see Mentges, Mohrmann, and Foerster 2000) was clearly defined. It was one based on autarky, subsistence agriculture, and cash crops (see Beckmann 1996; Trautwein 1969 and 1972; Findeisen 1985), including viticulture as well as fruit and vegetable farming. It was a culture reliant on trade in proximity to city and local markets and practices of frugality, including make-do and mend, as well as reading, literacy, and self-learning in order to retain tradition and navigate modernity in a rural environment. Of the family's twelve children, only six reached adult age. Like her four sisters, Marie received a dowry. Her sisters married, while she initially remained single. In 1930—five years after her father had died and Marie had been forced to perform his work in the house, fields, and vineyard (livestock breeding was given up)—she asked her mother to issue a dowry certificate. In 1933, she married Wilhelm Frech (see Figure 2.2), a fifty-year-old widower and fellow follower in faith, whom the brothers and sisters selected for Marie according to the conventional belief that a widowed man needed a housewife. He moved into her parental home, adding further things to the devout books, pictures, clothes, and furniture that already occupied Marie Frech's small house. Nothing was thrown away. Their marriage was ultimately a happy one, and the couple reached their silver wedding anniversary. The village made fun of the elderly, pious couple who openly displayed their happiness. In 1968, following Wilhelm's sudden death, a long period of widowhood—and a new departure—followed for Marie. She was seventy-three when she started once again to study her bible and books and write down her findings. She also began to hold prayer meetings, so-called *Schwesternstunden* (sister hours), in her living room. The "brothers" in Stuttgart soon forbade this active spiritual leadership, however, reminding her with sharp, pious words that women were to live in the community in quiet submission (Beckmann 1996, 19–34, Köhle-Hezinger 1996).

Following her death in 1995, "The Pious World of Marie Frech" was publicly exhibited in museum format in 1996 before the house fell victim to urban redevelopment. From an anthropological point of view, the museum is, in the words of Paul Valéry, a disconcerting space because it presents an ensemble of unrelated objects (see Korff 2007, 140). In the context of her life and her traditional culture of piety, Marie Frech's belongings, however, were all combined material witnesses of a period and a faith. Her *Sach*, all her things, were considered authentic relics of a former life and *Lebenswelt* (see Figure 2.3). The exhibition and accompanying book (Beckmann 1996) presented Marie Frech's world of things as one that seemed, in its rustic simplicity and spiritual devotion, strikingly different and alien, especially for the visitors engrained in the lifestyle of the late twentieth century. Visitors to the exhibit frequently asked whether

Figure 2.3 Marie Frech's clothes hanging above books by Michael Hahn in her bedroom. Photo taken for the exhibition of her house in Fellbach (1995). *Photo*: ©StadtMuseum Fellbach.

this overstuffed house was not just simply neglected and run-down. Was Marie Frech not actually a compulsive hoarder, or a *Messie*, to use a German term? Yet, this reading of Marie Frech's home and personality could not be further from the truth. In her world, all things were important; they were "in order" and they had to be kept in this order. And, in accordance with Swabian ideals, no item was to be discarded; they were to be kept, preserved, cared for. All things, according to the teachings of Michel Hahn, are considered to have spirits or souls.

The apocalyptic motif of Christ's return appeared twice in Marie Frech's small house: once in a nineteenth-century print that hung above the marital bed; the other in the version of the *Descent of the King of all Kings from Heaven*, which Beckmann described as "an important part of her domestic world of images" (see Beckmann 1996, 123ff.; see also Föll 2002). There was also a wealth of annual calendars. Behind the last calendar from the year of her departure in 1991 was a whole stack of calendars from the preceding years hanging from the wall. Nothing goes to waste, everything has its meaning. This explains the array of biblical images, images with aphorisms, and photographs adorning Frech's home. In the metaphorical language of Pietism, these are the "final things," that is, the "recovery of all things"—or, in reference to the old question of the adiaphora in Pietism, the "middle things," which from an ethical-religious point of view must be neither condemned nor commanded (see Gestrich 2004, 573–77; Scharfe 1980 and 2004).

The negative catalogue of forbidden things, which seems less ambiguous, defined what is commanded. Forbidden things tended to be of the affluent worlds of the court, the aristocracy, and the bourgeoisie; they were literally objectified in "splendid houses, pleasure gardens, luxurious appliances, jewelry, rides with carriages, sledges and coaches, horseback riding, chic music, dancing, frivolous songs, popular tunes, all kinds of delicious jests, foolish pranks, mockery, resounding laughter" (Kullen 1811 quoted from Scharfe 1968, 26). Up to the end of her life in her house in 1991, there was neither a newspaper nor a radio or television in Marie Frech's life. Her dresses, too, reflected a rigid sense of sobriety. Only at a very advanced age did she buy her first coat, a three-buttoned inter-seasonal made from black poplin.

The black dress and the white dress

For Marie Frech, the black dress and the white dress constituted an order of life. Almost all of her clothing and accessories were black. This included her wedding dress from the year 1933, since only "the robe of Jesus is white" as she noted down (Ms. Frech). In 1919, newly awakened spiritually, she wrote into her notebook in metaphorical language: "If one goes through the daily exercises and enters the way of the cross, one gradually obtains this wedding dress. Blood and justice, this complements man and woman" (Ms. Frech). Such thoughts can be found throughout Marie's notebooks, which she had kept since the end of her school days. Her octavo booklets and loose-leaf sheets start in the year 1908, one year prior to her confirmation. Frech's "written matter"—not all of which is actually dated—was deposited all around her house, revealing the value she invested in objects in an intriguing manner.

Making the connection between material clothing and spiritual belief even more evident, Frech wrote that she "put on a wedding dress, in the spirit of Jesus Christ" (quoted in Petri 1996, 76). In the year 1923, she reported of her difficulties to find the right path:

> Then my vanity became crystal clear to me . . . and I felt a desire to rid myself of it, but in spite of this I believed that it was a dishonor to wear plain dresses. But when my disciplined spirit required me to do it, I followed. This brought inexplicable joy to me, which I am still experiencing today. . . . After all, the savior was forced to hang naked from the cross owing to our vanity. In our eternal life, he will compensate us for everything. For every braid and pleat [in our dress], which we deny to ourselves, he will present us with a beautiful, ornamented wedding dress. (quoted in Petri 1996, 76)

Here, Marie Frech refers to her confirmation motto: "To him that overcometh will I give to eat of the tree of life, which is in the midst of the paradise of God" (Rev. 2:7). Often, she combines this verse with a subsequent one from the Book of Revelation: "He that overcometh, the same shall be clothed in white raiment . . ." (Rev. 3:5).

Throughout her life, Marie Frech retained her fascination with the "white robe" (Ms. Beckmann 1999, see also Hager 1999). She never wore any kind of regional folk dress, but wore clothes resembling the style of her youth, with only small variations and minimal adaptations. In this way, she had consciously, and permanently, opted for the pious dress characteristic of women in the Hahn'sche Gemeinschaft. Nor did she adopt any of the innovations suggested by her biological sisters, not even practical ones such as modern knitwear, which she is said to have called newfangled stuff. In fact, in the course of her life, Marie Frech only wore knee-length open or crotchless underpants made from white cotton, so-called *Schenkel am Bändel* (tied culottes). She never wore a bodice or a brassiere, or any shaping undergarments whatsoever (Petri 1996, 70). Modern knitwear undergarments led to a fierce quarrel with her sister, the youngest of the five daughters, who worked at Bleyle, a knitwear company in Stuttgart. Marie refused to even wash them saying: "I am not going to wash her clothes—that is sinful" (Petri 1996, 70). The new pliant underwear made by the factory was a very real material indicator of the incipient structural and mental changes pervading the rural region (see Köhle-Hezinger and Mentges 1993). In a kind of anachronistic contrast to the developments of fashion, Frech's wardrobe represented a vestimentary defense against the modernizing world. It consisted of an ankle-length black skirt and a tailored top with tucks and a hidden button placket. Between top and bottom, loosely marking the center of the body, was a cloth belt furnished with hooks and eyes. Over all this she wore an apron and a black knitted jacket. It was in this outfit that she left the house—on weekdays to shop in the village, on Sunday mornings to attend church (albeit without the apron), and on Sunday afternoons for her edification "hour," until the year 1995. On her head, she always wore the *Netzle* (hairnet), a fifteen-cm wide scarf made from black wool for the winter months and from black tulle for the summer (Petri 1996, 77). The *Netzle* was meant to adequately cover the head of a female Pietist in everyday and in liturgical contexts (see Mettele 2001).

If traditional clothing is typically thought to signify a "culture of reputable appearance" (*Kultur des Ansehens*), as Hans Medick described it (Medick 1994, 193–212), then we might consider the wardrobe of the pious Marie Frech as participating in the Pietist "culture of sensation" (*Kultur des Aufsehens*). The clothing of the pious people was indeed remarkable—it was different in the sense that they decentered the individual person in an effort to detract from worldly, external matters. Clothing was designed to enable wearers to look up to the heavenly, to final and higher things. Reflecting on Marie Frech's wardrobe, Marion Petri came to the following conclusion in the volume accompanying the Fellbach exhibition:

> The dark silhouette, slightly emphasizing the waistline yet loose, detracts from the body and directs the onlooker's gaze to the face of the wearer. . . . With her renunciation of all elements of fashion, of modern types and norms of clothing as well as of vestimentary luxury, Marie Frech has accomplished something she may not even have noticed: Her clothing created a sensation. (Petri 1996, 77)

Pious clothing is always about the habitus, never the dress itself, as formulated in August Hermann Francke's "rules for living" (*Lebens-Regeln*): the "orderly positioning of the body" is an expression of an externally visible order in a pious world because "the body is the mirror of the soul" (see Gohl-Völker 2002).

In this way, Marie Frech's body, her household, and ultimately her life, each functioned as mirrors (see Köhle-Hezinger 1993 and 2007). The image of the pious housemaid (*Geistliche Hausmagd*) is one of the prominent models (see Bringéus 1985, 121–42; Spamer 1970) that shaped the biblically founded order of the sexes and the accompanying conception of bodies. In Württemberg, this existed all the way into the twentieth century—extending even into the present. When pious men assembled in black suits in the front end of the room at the brethren's table, women were excluded from this space. Like children, they were directed to the side table (*Katzentisch*) where they sat in a modest manner. They wore dark, knitted jackets, aprons, and bonnets or hairnets that restrained their hair. Lard and sugar water were recommended for smoothing the hair, which was parted backward. In this way, pious women sat with bowed heads, listening, praying, and singing along, but otherwise silent.

The life of Marie Frech can be seen as testimony of what was once new and revolutionary, the burgeoning of the early Pietism of the eighteenth and nineteenth centuries. At the same time, her life also reveals something about our own time. The exhibition of Marie Frech's living quarters (both in Halle in 2005 and earlier, upon her death, when her house became a summer-long open-air museum), turned Pietism and its culture into an object of exotic fascination. More specifically, it provoked the insight that parts of one's own culture and tradition, through the distance of time and space, can be perceived as remote, anachronistic, and other.

Renate K.: clothes as memoirs

The life of Renate K. is another example demonstrating the value of sartorial objects. Her written notes, like Marie Frech's, tell revealing stories about the life of textiles, such as her own "best dress" worn for confirmation. Her biography also clearly demonstrates the relationship between materiality and memories, that is, the impact of objects on our inner emotional shapes and designs. In 1984, she started her personal notes with the following words: "the small, inconspicuous placer under my needlework equipment." These notes, which she later turned over to the director of the municipal museum of Gerlingen, a small town outside Stuttgart, are the records of her "life in clothes." Renate K. had felt a kinship with the museum's director because she, too, had "grown up under the dressmaker's table." The placer, a kind of hook used "to button gaiters and bar shoes" (Ms. Renate K.), was a metaphor binding her lived experience with the development of her body through letters and notes—amounting to a vestimentary cultural history.

Renate K. was born in Nordhausen at the edge of the Harz mountains and grew up in nearby Quedlinburg in the former German Democratic Republic (GDR). In her notes, she describes both the household and clothing practices of her childhood as well as her experiences leaving the region and country of her birth. In 1955, Renate K. moved west to the Federal Republic of Germany, settling in Stuttgart. In the GDR, she had been trained as an infant nurse but worked as a train dispatcher; in the West, she first found a job with a freight agency, then in the branch office of the *Schwäbischer Albverein*, a large German mountaineering association. She entered the Free Democratic Party (FDP) and became active in its organization. Her activities and her interest in the arts and cultural matters are all reflected in her notes. All the textiles, which she eventually left to the Gerlingen museum, are directly connected to her larger biography, as was the hook-like buttoner mentioned above. Everything has its relevance, its history: the handkerchiefs, the patches, the shirt (*Tageshemd*) of her mother, the household linen "spun by herself," the christening cloth, and one piece "of which I dispense with deep respect, namely the great-grandmother's shoulder scarf, which had never been completed" (Ms. Renate K.). It became the christening cloth of the grandmother because she was "christened atop the coffin" at the time of her death (Ms. Renate K.) and she was, since she early "surrendered to a young man, one of the last women who still sat in the church on a bench of shame" (Ms. Renate K.).

In 2005, Heidrun Rothe-Wörner's last exhibition, titled "My Favorite Piece" (*Mein liebstes Stück*), was put on display in the municipal museum of Gerlingen. For Renate K., this exhibition would definitely have been another occasion to reminisce, as was an earlier exhibition of ball gowns (titled *Ballgeflüster*—Ball Whispers) in Gerlingen. Following the opening of *Ballgeflüster*, Renate K. wrote a letter to the curator. This letter, whose whereabouts are unknown today (but of which I have a copy), documents the close relationship between clothing, biographical narrative, memory, and emotion in an insightful manner, that deserves to be cited here at some length:

> Your exhibits are always right to the point, but with Ball Whispers you truly hit the mark for me. Especially because I often sew with pearls. It was a trip into the past. I had not been invited to a wedding since 1947—but now I have been to four since last summer. Me, a retired person, what luck! (Ms. Renate K.)

As Renate K. relates in her letter, an "old woman who is moving into a nursing home and unable to take everything with her," gave to Renate K. her self-sewn mother-of-the-bride's dress from the 1960s. "I turned this into a floor-length skirt," she reveals, adding "I like to wear skirt and blouse, because this allows for more variation." After describing her experiences at the different weddings, as well as the various alterations and updating of her skirt, which time and again proved to be a reliable garment for her, Renate K. continued:

> The third wedding was a Eurasian one, I am glad I had the skirt—there were dresses that made me gasp. But I held my own. Just like at the Greek wedding where money didn't play a role. . . . Yes, indeed, skirt and blouse; for a long time, I had my velvet skirt. A bit outmoded, but perfect for concerts in wintertime. That's from the time when I was in the state committee of the Free Democrats. At party conventions, they had dances in the evenings, and, really, I couldn't possibly wear a long dress for that! I was able to adapt it for an event in the countryside (folk-style jacket and blouse). Festive with a black casaque and silver embroidery. Today, I am wearing it with a black quilted gilet and a white blouse. You just have to have something like that. (Ms. Renate K.)

Renate K.'s clothing memoirs show that there was no single "best dress" after the Second World War, just individual pieces combined into an outfit of "best items." She received her very first "best dress" at the age of fourteen for her confirmation. In the letter, recalling that best dress seemed to inspire a lengthy series of further memories interweaving clothing and relationships, and providing insight into the intersections between biography and material culture:

> It was referred to as examination dress. In the church service on the Sunday prior to confirmation we were examined with regard to what we had learned in class, but also with regard to larger matters of faith. During World War II, my Mom managed to grab a beautiful ruby-colored woolen fabric; in 1947, a dove blue military uniform fabric (Air Force!). There was still shirt fabric (white-grey stripes) left from my Dad, that became the blouse. Russian troops were quartered with us for three months. We went to the Soviet military camp and obtained by accident, due to a case of death, a black dress with a jacket—but of course one can change something like that. Impossible for a 14-year-old, unthinkable today. But we got everything together then . . . In the course of a festive church service, a child became an adult. The basics were there. You received your first dress, the basic requirement for a woman at that time was a black dress, . . . it accompanied you in weighty events, in situations of mourning. The so-called examination dress was the afternoon dress; one also needed one of these. On ordinary occasions, you wore whatever you had with emendations. . . . My ball dress was actually supposed to have been the curtain for the bedroom; Mom had bought it just prior to World War II; it was old gold with little red roses, a

light fabric. She saw the windows shot to pieces, destroying the curtains . . . and decided to salvage the fabric for better times! Those times arrived with my dance class ball and with the wedding of my cousin. That dress was left in Quedlinburg and not taken along when we escaped. . . .

When I think back to my confirmation—these were the hard times of the postwar period. 14 days prior to my confirmation, one sole of my only pair of shoes broke. It was mended with a saddlebag, the brand was *Trumpf*. When I kneeled down, the brand name flashed far and wide . . . I had a Mozart braid down to the hips and Mom only had a small black velvet ribbon. There was a very nice old lady, once also a seamstress working from home, a strict Catholic. On the way to her church she sees the narrow velvet ribbon: "What? This for Renate to go to church with? I still have a black velvet ribbon." It was a broad hatband and there I was with this big thing in my neck. Looked as though I was fresh from boarding school. . . . Our minister then added insult to injury, he could not stand perms. There were 56 girls, and those with child-like hairdos were in the first group. Then the ones with old perms, in the end the frilly girls. There were two Renates, they took the lead.

Aunt Lene was also a seamstress working from home—this wasn't just disabled women doing this; a lot of men never came back from World War I. Aunt Lene lived in the Magdeburg Börde, a rich land with large farms. On every evening of the three-day Marksmen's Festival there was a ball, and every year the farmer's wife was given a new long dress. Two existing ones were changed. If they could afford it, they would come with a new dress every evening. They would also go to health spas and every year there had to be something new. If you turned an ordinary dress inside out, you would have a Sunday dress. One third of the year, Aunt Lene worked outside of her home and just before the Marksmen's Festival she hardly ever got any sleep.

All of this I am putting down from memory, as a complement to the opening speech to the Ball Dress Exhibition. (Ms. Renate K.)

This last sentence from Renate K.'s letter to museum director Heidrun Rothe reads like a personal intervention in museum work. An autobiography, remembered and narrated through clothes and inspired by an exhibition, is offered as a "complement" to the museum as a place of collective memory. The texture of her dresses and images preserves her life, spreading out into a series of autobiographical texts: hooks and velvet ribbon; a skirt and a blouse; the Russians and the curtain. These memoirs, written down for a museum show, proved restorative for Renate K., providing an occasion of dialogue and a means to conserve significant vestimentary memories. Unfortunately, Renate K.'s private "Musée sentimental" is now preserved only in fragments. Both, author and addressee, are deceased. The copy of the letter remains with me as a fascinating document reflecting a whole life lived in dresses.

Conclusions

The sartorial memories of Renate K. and the stringent wardrobe practices of Marie Frech show very clearly that clothing, especially significant pieces such as the "best dress," are defined biographically and culturally, embedded in specific constellations of time and space. While Renate K. recorded particular memories that she connected with clothing and textiles, it was the "things" themselves that revealed Marie Frech's lifestyle, and the culture and society in which she lived—mostly without her personal commentary.

The two represent starkly different generations of women in twentieth-century Germany. Renate K. and Marie Frech embody almost polar opposites, standing for a disruptive modernity and a normative tradition, respectively. The interrelated framework of traditionality, materiality, and spirituality that structured Marie Frech's pious life manifests itself in an orderly material cosmos (see Figure 2.4). Even beyond her death, this life can be read in her personal property and furniture. The things of Frech's house are characteristic for a society of subsistence and scarcity, in which sacred and secular objects made up a coherent and permanent whole. Renate K.'s biography, however, stands for modernity—a dynamic and fragmentary departure from tradition, seizing all areas of life—and which can only be grasped materially and emotionally in specific situations. In contrast to Frech, materiality, modernity, and emotionality are indices of a "maddening" transformation. Material objects are no longer grounded culturally, formatted rigidly, and passed on, but are, as the autobiographical notes show, arranged individually, collaged, and interpreted—the kind of self-fashioning that was a constitutive element in Renate K.'s biography.

Above all, both examples demonstrate the significance of biographical case studies, especially with regard to the significance of things and their materiality in the everyday life of private individuals. They demonstrate, too, different levels for the exploration of material culture, whether that be the material legacy of Marie Frech or the autobiographical commemoration in texts like those of Renate K. Both cases are located in very different contexts, times, societies, regions, and even mentalities. They document the non-simultaneity of the processes of modernization to which cultural research must react with methodological sensitivity in both diachronic and synchronic comparisons.

Figure 2.4 Marie Frech shown as an older woman, in front of her harmonium. *Photo*: ©StadtMuseum Fellbach.

The significance of the link between biography and clothing, however, is evident, regardless of whether textiles appear as a material, "objective" legacy or as a written, textual and subjectively remembered one. While clothes are still too often underestimated as bagatelles of everyday culture, they are significant material containers or traces of the everyday practices of former lives, past periods, and cultures, and therefore worthwhile examining.

References

Baudrilliard, Jean. 1968. *The System of Objects*. London: Verso.
Beckmann, Ralf. 1996. "Eine Jugend in Fellbach." In *Die 100 Jahre der Marie Frech: Ein Fellbacher Frauenleben zwischen Pietismus und Eigensinn. Eine Ausstellung der Stadt Fellbach vom 12. Mai bis 13. Oktober 1996*, edited by Ralf Beckmann, 19–34. Fellbach: Fellbacher Hefte.

Beckmann, Ralf. 1996. "Die Bilderwelt der Wohnung." In *Die 100 Jahre der Marie Frech: Ein Fellbacher Frauenleben zwischen Pietismus und Eigensinn. Eine Ausstellung der Stadt Fellbach vom 12. Mai bis 13. Oktober 1996*, edited by Ralf Beckmann, 123–30. Fellbach: Fellbacher Hefte.

Beckmann, Ralf, ed. 1996. *Die 100 Jahre der Marie Frech: Ein Fellbacher Frauenleben zwischen Pietismus und Eigensinn. Eine Ausstellung der Stadt Fellbach vom 12. Mai bis 13. Oktober 1996*. Fellbach: Fellbacher Hefte.

Beckmann, Ralf. 1999. Unpublished manuscript. *Das weiße Kleid—Leben als Konzept. Gedanken zu einem pietistischen Lebensentwurf.*

Bringéus, Nils Arvid. 1985. "Die Geistliche Hausmarkt." In *Jahrbuch für Volkskunde*, edited by Wolfgang Brückner and Nikolaus Grass, Vol. 8. Echter: Würzburg.

Bringéus, Nils-Arvid. 2000. *Volksfrömmigkeit: Schwedische religionsethnologische Studien*. Münster, New York, München, and Berlin: Waxmann.

Findeisen, Hans-Volkmar. 1985. *Pietismus in Fellbach 1750–1820*. Tübingen: Druckerei Joachim Bölk.

Föll, Renate. 2002. *Sehnsucht nach Jerusalem: Zur Ostwanderung schwäbischer Pietisten*. Tübingen: Tübinger Verein für Volkskunde.

Foucault, Michel. (1966) 1970. *The Order of Things: An Archaeology of the Human Sciences*. New York: Pantheon Books.

Frech, Marie. n.d. Notes. Unpag. Stadtarchiv Fellbach.

Gestrich, Andreas. 2004. "Pietistisches Weltverständnis und Handeln in der Welt." In *Geschichte des Pietismus*, edited by Martin Brecht, Johannes van den Berg, Klaus Deppermann, Johannes F. Goeters, Hans Schneider, Ulrich Gäbler, and Hartmut Lehmann, Band 4: Glaubenswelt und Lebenswelten, 557–83. Göttingen: Vandenhoeck & Ruprecht.

Gohl-Völker, Ulla. 2002. *Die Kleidung der Shakerschwestern im 19. Jahrhundert: Die Repräsentanz kategorialer Ordnungsbegriffe*. Münster: Waxmann.

Gutekunst, Eberhard, ed. 1999. *Apokalypse: Endzeiterwartungen im evangelischen Württemberg. Katalog zur Ausstellung im Landeskirchlichen Museum Ludwigsburg vom 10. Juni 1999 bis 16. Juli 2000*. Ludwigsburg: Landeskirchliches Museum.

Hager, Helga. 1999. *Hochzeitskleidung—Biographie, Körper und Geschlecht: Eine kulturwissenschaftliche Studie in drei württembergischen Dörfern*. Tübingen: Tübinger Vereinigung für Volkskunde.

K., Renate. n.d. Notes. Unpag.: Verschollene Briefe an Heidrun Rothe, Leiterin des Stadtmuseum Gerlingen.

Kaschuba, Wolfgang, and Carola Lipp. 1982. *Dörfliches Überleben: Zur Geschichte materieller und sozialer Reproduktion ländlicher Gesellschaft im 19. und frühen 20. Jahrhundert*. Tübingen: Tübinger Vereinigung für Volkskunde.

Kataloge der Franckeschen Stiftungen. 2005. *Hoffnung besserer Zeiten: Philipp Jakob Spener (1635–1705) und die Geschichte des Pietismus*. Band 14. Halle: O. Harrassowitz.

Köhle-Hezinger, Christel. 1993. "Der schwäbische Leib". In *Der neuen Welt ein neuer Rock: Studien zur Kleidung, Körper und Mode an Beispielen aus Württemberg*, edited by Christel Köhle-Hezinger and Gabriele Mentges, 59–80. Stuttgart: Konrad Theiss Verlag.

Köhle-Hezinger, Christel. 1996. "Ich heisse Frech, aber ich bin nicht frech: Nachdenken üeber eine schwäbische Biographie." In *Die 100 Jahre der Marie Frech: Ein Fellbacher Frauenleben zwischen Pietismus und Eigensinn. Eine Ausstellung der Stadt Fellbach vom 12. Mai bis 13. Oktober 1996*, edited by Ralf Beckmann, 9–18. Fellbach: Fellbacher Hefte.

Köhle-Hezinger, Christel. 2007. "Hören, Schreiben, Lesen, Schweigen. Zur Tradition pietistischer Memoria im Spiegel der Geschlechter." In *Gendering Tradition: Erinnerungskultur und Geschlecht im Pietismus (Perspektiven in der neueren und neuesten Geschichte. Kultur, Wissen, Geschlecht, Band 1)*, edited by Ulrike Gleixner and Erika Hebeisen, 281–92. Korb: Didymos Verlag.

Köhle-Hezinger, Christel, and Gabriele Mentges, eds. 1993. *Der neuen Welt ein neuer Rock: Studien zur Kleidung, Körper und Mode an Beispielen aus Württemberg*. Stuttgart: Konrad Theiss Verlag.

Korff, Gottfried. 2007. "Zur Eigenart der Museumsdinge." In *Museumsdinge: deponieren –exponieren*, edited by Gottfried Korff, Martina Eberspächer, Gudrun Marlene König, and Bernhard Tschofen, 140–45. Köln: Böhlau.

Lächele, Rainer, ed. 2001. *Das Echo Halles: Kulturelle Wirkungen des Pietismus*. Tübingen: Bibliotheca Academica.

Lehmann, Hartmut. 1969. *Pietismus und weltliche Ordnung in Württemberg vom 17. bis zum 20. Jahrhundert*. Stuttgart: Kohlhammer.

Lemire, Beverly. 1997. *Dress, Culture and Commerce: The English Clothing Trade before the Factory, 1660–1800*. Basingstoke: Palgrave McMillan.

Medick, Hans. 1994. "Eine Kultur des Ansehens. Kleider und Kleiderfarben in Laichingen 1750–1820." *Historische Anthropologie* 2: 193–212.

Mentges, Gabriele. 1996. "Blicke auf den ländlichen Leib. Zur Geschichte einer Enteignung. Eine Darstellung anhand Kleidungsbeschreibungen aus Württemberg von 1820 bis 1910." In *Körper-Geschichten: Studien zur historischen Kulturforschung*, edited by Richard van Dülmen, 179–99. Frankfurt am Main: Fischer Taschenbuch.

Mentges, Gabriele, Ruth E. Mohrmann, and Cornelia Foerster. 2000. *Geschlecht und materielle Kultur: Frauen-Sachen. Männer-Sachen. Sachkulturen*. Münster: Waxmann.

Mettele, Gisela. 2001. "Der Entwurf des pietistischen Körpers. Die Herrnhuter Brüdergemeine und die Mode." In *Das Echo Halles: Kulturelle Wirkungen des Pietismus*, edited by Rainer Lächele, 291–314. Tübingen: Bibliotheca Academia.

Mohrmann, Ruth-E. 1997. *Individuum und Frömmigkeit: Volkskundliche Studien zum 19. und 20. Jahrhundert*. Münster: Waxmann.

Petri, Marion. 1996. "Kleidung ohne Luxus." In *Die 100 Jahre der Marie Frech: Ein Fellbacher Frauenleben zwischen Pietismus und Eigensinn. Eine Ausstellung der*

Stadt Fellbach vom 12. Mai bis 13. Oktober 1996, edited by Ralf Beckmann, 79–85. Fellbach: Fellbacher Hefte.

Pfarrbericht Pfarrer Bengel. 1905. Stuttgart: Landeskirchliches Archiv Stuttgart. *A 29, Ortsakten Fellbach Büschel 1240.*

Scharfe, Martin. 1968. *Evangelische Andachtsbilder: Studien zu Intention und Funktion des Bildes in der Frömmigkeitsgeschichte vornehmlich des schwäbischen Raumes.* Stuttgart: Müller & Gräff.

Scharfe, Martin. 1980. *Die Religion des Volkes: Kleine Kultur- und Sozialgeschichte des Pietismus.* Gütersloh: Gerd Mohn.

Scharfe, Martin. 2001. "Pietismus und Kultur. Bedenken und Möglichkeiten." In *Das Echo Halles: Kulturelle Wirkungen des Pietismus*, edited by Rainer Lächele, 11–30. Tübingen: Bibliotheca Academica.

Scharfe, Martin. 2004. *Über die Religion: Glaube und Zweifel in der Volkskultur.* Köln: Böhlau.

Scharfe, Martin, and Wolfgang Brückner, eds. 1990. *Referate der Österreichischen Volkskundetagung 1989 in Graz.* Wien: Österreichischer Fachverband für Volkskunde.

Spamer, Adolf. 1970. *Der Bilderbogen von der "Geistlichen Hausmagd": Ein Beitrag zur Geschichte des religiösen Bilderbogens und der Erbauungsliteratur im populären Verlagswesen Mitteleuropas.* Göttingen: Verlag Schwartz.

Trautwein, Joachim. 1969. *Die Theosophie Michael Hahns und ihre Quellen.* Stuttgart: Calwer Verlag.

Trautwein, Joachim. 1972. *Religiosität und Sozialstruktur, untersucht anhand der Entwicklung des württembergischen Pietismus.* Stuttgart: Calwer Verlag.

Unseld, Werner, and Renate Föll, eds. 2004. *Barock und Pietismus: Wege in die Moderne. Katalog zur gleichnamigen Ausstellung des Landeskirchlichen Museums Ludwigsburg.* Ludwigsburg: Kataloge und Schriften des Landeskirchlichen Museums.

van Gennep, Arnold. (1909) 1970. *The Rites of Passage.* Chicago: University of Chicago Press.

Wallmann, Johannes. 1990. *Der Pietismus.* Göttingen: utb.

Weber, Max. (1922) 1968. *Economy and Society.* New York: Bedminster Press.

Weber, Sandra, and Claudia Mitchell, eds. 2004. *Not Just Any Dress: Narratives of Memory, Body, and Identity.* New York: Peter Lang.

3

The discovery of materiality: Archeological clothing finds, representation, and knowledge formation

Daniel Devoucoux

"Sensational discovery in Armenia," reads the headline of the German newspaper *Die Welt* on June 10, 2010: "Archeologists find oldest shoe in the world." Discovered in a cave, well-preserved including shoelaces, the ancient find looks like a contemporary US size 6 moccasin. While it is unknown whether the shoe belonged to a man or a woman, it has been possible to date the find to the period 3500 BCE, making it a few centuries older than the shoes of the oldest mummy Ötzi (approx. 3300 BCE) found in Europe in the Alps. As the many press reports illustrated, a rare archeological find makes for a good media sensation. However, in recent years, archeology has received increased attention not only in popular media but also in academia, including fields such as historical anthropology and dress and textile studies. Archeology shows us that our knowledge about the history of clothing is at best fragmentary. Looking at textile archeology, it becomes evident that there is a need to draw stronger connections between the material discovery and the representation of clothing. Moreover, as I will discuss in the following, there is a need to also draw stronger connections across various fields of research that inform the ongoing knowledge production around textiles and clothing, including textile archeology and the history and anthropology of clothing.

Textile archeology

Since its formation in the fifteenth century, archeology has primarily dealt with discoveries of hard matter such as architectural stone structures, bas-reliefs, or sculptures of varying forms and materials. Because such media carry written and iconographic representations, structures and sculptures have become the body of sources from which we have drawn most of our historical knowledge about ancient textiles and clothing. In the world of archeology, textile discoveries are considered soft sources and even up to the early 1990s they received little consideration in archeology or dress studies. A 1996 investigation of the Neolithic settlement Çatal Hüyük in southern Turkey provides a ranking of the attitudes toward material goods. Though textiles were highly appreciated in its contemporary era, such materials were only cursorily examined in the overall study (Beck and Jakobs 1996). This exemplifies the low status assigned to textiles as historical sources (Maier 2001, 52), which, by extension, also demonstrates the broader academic marginalization of textile and dress history. Extending Pierre Bourdieu's critique of this fundamental hierarchy within the sciences ([1974] 2002), Johanna Banck-Burgess (2012) asserts, in her remarkable archeological study of textiles among the Celts, however, that given the numerous discoveries of fabric and clothing fragments, it requires little imagination to see what a significant role textiles played in everyday life and in tomb furnishings.[1] The importance of textiles should not be underestimated, as they "represent one of the earliest human craft technologies, certainly older than metallurgy, and they have been a fundamental part of subsistence, economy, and exchange. Textiles have an enormous potential in archeological research, and they have been able to tell about social, chronological, and cultural aspects of the past societies" (Andersson Strand 2010, 150). Even if specific methods for finding, excavating, documenting, conserving, and identifying material remains are only slowly developing, they will allow a new, exciting look into archeology (Banck-Burgess 2008, 82).

Yet, nevertheless, compared to those artifacts made of more durable material such as metal, ceramics, wood, or stone, the value of textile artifacts for cultural anthropology and cultural history still remains underexplored, and the bias against textile sources has left many questions around early Egyptian or Medieval clothing unanswered. The marginalization of historic textiles as sources cannot simply be ascribed to the challenges of textile preservation or to the difficulty of reconstructing historic clothing ensembles. Rather, research gaps exist because the current sources for textile archeology are too sparse. Furthermore, there is a specific urge to visualize clothing from ancient history, although the written or visual sources are often not verified, making it difficult to perform a proper reconstruction of historic clothing (Banck-Burgess 2008, 82). It is the paucity of source verification and the need for a nuanced and critical approach to archeological textile finds that I want to focus on by drawing on examples from the clothing history of ancient Egypt.

Confronting sources

Textile discoveries are particularly meaningful when they can be connected to written or iconographic sources. Take, for example, the textiles discovered in the tomb of the chief overseer and his wife—the architect and scribe Kha and his wife Merit—in Deir El-Medina (originally "Set Maat"), a craftsmen's settlement southwest of Thebes (see Schiaparelli [1927] 2008; Janssen 2008). During the mid-eighteenth-century BCE dynasty of ancient Egypt, masons, stonemasons, plasterers, painters, and scribes worked in the "city of the dead," where they lived with their families in near autarky and seclusion, far away from the river, so they could not disclose the locations of the secret burial sites (McDowell 1997, 76–81). Discovered by Ernesto Schiaparelli during an excavation mission in 1906, the grave remains one of the few tombs found intact. In addition to the tomb, the whole craftsmen's settlement yielded a wealth of material culture beyond textiles, including an impressive volume of written documents and drawings on papyri, limestone, and pottery fragments. This rich collection of cultural data provides insight into the everyday life of the settlement, demonstrating the inhabitants' high level of education and prosperous lifestyle (Schiaparelli [1927] 2008). The discoveries in the tomb offer a fascinating window not only into the religion and ritual practices of the settlement but also into various aspects of quotidian life, from village gossip to communal diseases to everyday clothing styles. Today, some clothes from these excavations are exhibited in the Museo Egizio in Turin, Italy.

Not all textile discoveries have been readily linked with written or iconographic materials. One example is Howard Carter's (1874–1939) findings from the excavation of the gravesite of Pharaoh Tutankhamun (c. 1341–1323 BCE) (see Figure 3.1). Regarding the very first chest in the antechamber, Carter noted:

> At the top there were a pair of rush and papyrus sandals, and a royal robe, completely covered with a decoration of beadwork and gold sequins. Beneath them were other decorated ones, which had attached to them upward of three thousand gold rosettes, three pairs of court sandals elaborately worked in gold, a gilt head-rest, and other miscellaneous objects. (Carter [1925] 2007, 67)

Figure 3.1 Floral collar from Tutankhamun's embalming cache (ca. 1336–1327 BCE). *Photo*: Metropolitan Museum of Art.

A few steps further, at the southern wall of the chamber, there was another shrine, which contained "a necklace of enormous beads, gold, carnelian, green feldspar, and blue glass, to which a large gold pendant in the shape of a very rare snake goddess was attached" (Carter [1925] 2007, 73). Moreover, he found "considerable portions of a 'corslet'" (Carter [1925] 2007, 73). In that same chamber, almost next to that shrine, there was "another toilet box" (Carter 2007, 73). It contained "a number of decorated robes, bundled together and thrust in anyhow [sic], and mixed with them were several pairs of sandals. . . . In still another box, jewellery. . . . Others again, were half empty and contained a mere jumble of odds and ends of cloth" (Carter [1925] 2007, 84). In all chambers and the sarcophagus itself, he discovered clothes, pieces of jewelry, and cosmetic instruments (Carter [1925] 2007, 290f.). Although Carter repeatedly insisted on the importance of these textiles, the material sources were not investigated until Rudolf Pfister examined them in 1937, and it took until the 1990s for them to be looked at again by Gillian Vogelsang-Eastwood (1993 and 1999) and Renate Germer (1992). So far, only a very small portion of these textile finds has been analyzed, and much more work remains to be done. One major difficulty in interpreting and reconstructing these historic clothing finds is due to the fact that, according to Egyptologist Elisabeth Staehelin, the material originals and the images of clothing rarely coincide; indeed, they often contradict each other (Staehelin 1992b, 727).

Of the ancient Egyptian clothing that has been excavated, no corresponding images exist, or their graphic representation is very different from any material findings. This is the case for one of the best-known and oldest pieces of clothing produced by human hand, the Tarkhan dress, dating from circa 3482–3102 BCE. Originally mixed within a dirty bundle of cloth and rumpled linen rags discovered by W. M. Flinders Petrie during the 1913 excavations of Tarkhan, the garment was rediscovered by conservationists at the Victoria and Albert Museum in 1977. Other examples are gaiters, such as the ones exhibited at the Egyptian Museum in Cairo or the complex woven fabrics and stockings excavated from the tomb of Tutankhamun (cf. Vogelsang-Eastwood 1993, 77, 83, 85, and 102). Furthermore, there are no existing visual records of the so-called "mss shirts," tunic-like garments with separately sewn and fitted long sleeves, until the Amarna period (18th Dynasty, fourteenth to thirteenth century BCE), although such shirts have been archeologically dated to the Old Kingdom of Egypt (e.g., in the tomb of Mektire, 11th Dynasty, 2137–1994 BCE) (Hall 2008, 27).

Further archeological discoveries from the Old Kingdom include numerous linen fabrics and long, shirt-like garments, some of them pleated and with sleeves. These garments are frequently compared to the modern Egyptian galabiyeh (Riefstahl 1945). Some clothing items, such as the oversized tunic measuring 3.18 meters by 1.70 meters now preserved in a collection at the University of Tübingen, remain enigmatic (Brunner-Traut 1977). The wide range of these discoveries suggests a diverse spectrum of clothing materials. Wool, for example, has only been occasionally dated to prior to the middle of the first millennium BCE, but the material's varied use in wigs, robes, scarfs, and blankets suggests a much wider historical dissemination than previously assumed. Supported by such discoveries, though rarely credited in the literature, wool's increasing popularity throughout the centuries is owed to influences from the Middle East and Mesopotamia. According to Herodotus, wool was used in ancient Egypt's Late Period (fifth century BCE) in everyday clothing (2008, 81). None of these material findings appears prominently in graphic representations or written sources.

On the other hand, the *shenti*, a type of wool skirt (see Figure 3.2) essential to the male wardrobe, while omnipresent in iconographic representations, was rarely found in archives or tombs (Staehelin 1992a, 744). Thus, what needs to be considered in the study of Egyptian textile discoveries is the cultural ambivalence of the found items that were used both in everyday life and in burial rituals. The rediscovery of a concrete material dimension of ancient Egypt's vestimentary world confronts modern research with important questions, including: How

Figure 3.2 Limestone youth (early sixth century BCE) dressed in Egyptian kilt or *shenti*. *Photo*: Metropolitan Museum of Art.

did such a vast discrepancy between visual representation and archeological discoveries of textile and clothing materials come about? And, perhaps more crucially, what answers to such questions are even possible from our modern vantage points?

A brief record of a long series of (mis)interpretations

Textile archeology is not a new discipline. It has a comprehensive research record dating back to the early nineteenth century. Alois Riegel, for example, in an 1889 catalogue for the Imperial Royal Austrian Museum for Art and Industry, had already commented on the textile remains found in the tombs of Saqqara in 1801 (1889, V). Why, then, have the actual material discoveries still played such small role in the study of ancient Egyptian clothing? At first, this seems to be due to an overt reliance on iconographic representations in the study of vestimentary culture, underscoring the centrality of art history, which has long used clothing and textiles as auxiliary instruments in its disciplinary discourse. In the meantime, however, the study of dress has evolved into a rich interdisciplinary field of its own, drawing on approaches from disciplines such as cultural anthropology, history, literary studies, sociology, and media studies. These crosscurrents have, in turn, influenced art history, which has increasingly welcomed questions and methods from cultural anthropology.

A second reason is due to a disregard on the part of researchers in fields such as Egyptology, archeology, or medieval studies, viz. representatives of disciplines seeking and securing traces of material history. As stated above, textile discoveries have until recently been relatively neglected by these fields. Academic self-referentiality still persists in many disciplines, limiting receptiveness to new research and ongoing debates in the evolving fields of dress and fashion studies. Such disregard also manifests itself in a prolonged, uncritical use of early costume history publications, which are often not based on the study of original material sources.

A third reason is closer to home, in the sense that scholars of dress themselves can be remiss in critically questioning and analyzing their sources. Egyptologists have shown a way to overcome the discrepancy between material discoveries and written and iconographic representations of *realia*, recognizing the particular ways the latter are encoded. Submitting to the ancient Egyptian canon, representations should be subject to the key distinctions between the "Absolute" and the idea of the "two realities" in Old Egyptian conceptions of self (Gundlach 1994, 3–6), a process I will address in greater detail below.

Theological principle and the development of the canon

As a basic principle, any analysis of ancient Egyptian sources must take into consideration that representation is based on a theological principle: the reality of action is distinct from its representation. Egyptologists conceptualize this separation as "two realities." Researchers must be careful not to equate or confuse these two levels. The "real," everyday history takes place on the first level, or first reality, which archeology painstakingly works to reconstruct. In the collective consciousness and conviction of ancient Egyptians, however, the representation in texts, murals, sculptures, or monuments establishes a second level, or second reality. This second reality—the official representation—virtually replaces the first level with an adjusted interpretation (Gundlach 1994, 9). Representations of clothing belong almost exclusively to this second reality, one that replaces real time with an immutable ideological time. First, this means that the modern conception of art, and what we have recognized as Egyptian art, was not experienced as "art" in everyday ancient Egypt. Second, and more importantly, these texts and images—"art" items—compose a "monumental" discourse (Altenmüller 1992, 42). Third, and as a direct consequence of this ideological "monumental" thinking, such items' vocabulary follows a religious canon that saturates representation. The canon consists of an ensemble of exclusive, explicit, and normative rules—all religiously motivated and justified—that govern representation and expression in the service of an absolute and eternal truth. In this "style for eternity" (Assmann 1986, 531), all representations, from those of people to those of clothing and ornaments, become syntactical-semantic elements of a higher order, an expression of power and eternity (J. Assmann 2000, 169–74). The represented clothing, as well as its hieroglyphic script, point to the "affirmation of the divine signature of the world" in which secular time is completely abandoned (J. Assmann 1986, 531). In this way, historical analyses of style and clothing, which are normally closely correlated with chronological change, are bound in an ideologically fixed, evergreen time.

Egyptologist Peter Munro describes the representation of ancient Egyptian clothing that is obligated to the canon as follows:

> Clothes are reduced to an utmost minimum. Women are represented in tight strap dresses, men in different forms of aprons. Feet are almost always bare. This same clothing adorns anthropomorphic goddesses and—in exceptional cases—gods. Additional clothing to provide protection from the cold of winter or intensive sun was obviously excluded by the canon as untypical. (1992, 664)

The skimpy clothes featured in these old Egyptian representations "have less to do with prudishness, for example due to an increasingly civilized state," but instead indicated personhood, lineage, and rank "inside the existing order" with a claim toward universality and timelessness (Munro 1992, 664). Such timelessness is evidenced by clothing rendered without folds that would come from movement or external influence. At most, the representational garments only show a single type of pleating as part of the garment style itself. As Munro points out, these criteria are valid for all categories of monuments, but the hieroglyphic conception makes them noticeable with varying emphasis (1992, 665).

In these artifacts, body and clothes are put together as constituents of the monumental writing system, not as autonomous, time-bound representations. The rigidity of the canon, however, should never be understood as a mathematical or mechanical equation or construction but as a living composition with "breath and pulse" (Munro 1992, 665). Thus, the canon does not offer a dynamic representation of time-bound individual scenes but a sort of ideography working together with "pictograms" and syntax (A. Assmann 1994, 135–36).

However, the principle of eternity and the ancient Egyptian theological language is not immune to imperfection. For example, in private tombs where canon rules were less rigidly applied, images, statuettes, miniatures, texts, and textiles provide revealing information about the first reality. Representation of servants as well as images and descriptions of people's faces, hair, and wigs demonstrate a stylistic deviation from the canon of the Middle and New Kingdom. In these deviations, we can recognize change within different phases of ideological development. For instance, oversized ears are characteristic for the Middle Kingdom (2137–1781 BCE) whereas pierced ear lobes signified by ear adornments have been only documented for the New Kingdom (1550–1070 BCE) (Altenmüller 1992, 20). This is also true for the representation of hair and wigs. With its more "realistic" tendency—later considered a heresy—the Amarna period (fourteenth to thirteenth century BCE) provides a richly detailed source of information on clothing practices.

The temporal dimension, which normally remains largely excluded from the canon, assumes a certain significance that can be gathered from clothing. In iconographic representations, archeologists are discovering interesting signs of change. In her examination of more than a hundred skulls from Amarna, Jolanda Bos found that ancient Egyptians used a type of gel to color grayed hair with louder colors, attached hair extensions, and favored braids and short hairstyles. Hair color and texture ranged from curly black hair to medium brown straight hair (Kemp 2014). Several further styles developed during the Greek and Roman eras (332 BCE–395 CE) that provide information about the coexistence of various design forms in ancient Egypt.

Problems of source criticism and the chronotype

The discrepancy between representations and material discoveries of clothing and the problem of reconstructing their historical-material reality cannot be solved without the systematic scrutiny of sources. However, any kind of one-to-one interpretation of clothing mediated through ideography or written sources undermines credible research. The ancient Egyptian representations of "fashion" must be meticulously analyzed, decoded, and adequately reinterpreted. At the core of dress studies research practices, data must be triangulated via time, space, and context or "realities." In the context of researching ancient Egypt, scholars must clarify different chronotypes and, *per* Franck-Burgess, thoroughly scrutinize sources. According to Mikhail Bakhtin, chronotype refers to the connection between space and the passage of time of a narrative that develops its own characteristics with a special graphic intensity (Bakhtin 2008, 7–9). This connection raises a question for scholars of clothing: how do we place these two levels—that of the material everyday world and that of theological narrative—into a coherent relationship?

Clothing phenomena, whether historical or contemporary, encompass the whole cultural discourse of its era. The influence of the space-time configuration on the dynamics of clothing, its chronotypical dimension, is a basic motif in the history of clothing worlds. Materials and forms express the space-time dimension of clothing cultures, including synchronicity, duration, movement, velocity and dynamics, continuity and discontinuity, present and past, and temporal disruptions as well as social or religious spaces, gendered spaces, intercultural contact, among others. The integration of this complex milieu, from the perspective of archeology to one of cultural anthropology, is the true challenge in modern textile and clothing research (Pritchard 2006).

Egyptologist Renate Germer (1992) answered another important question relevant to the discrepancy between material textile discoveries and their representation. In her study of clothing colors, she developed an exemplary mix of chemical and other testing procedures that undermined previous notions about ancient Egyptian clothing dyes, revising the widely held belief that Egyptians used almost exclusively naturally colored linen. Whereas dyed linen was rather rare in the Old Kingdom, extensive textile coloring technologies were developed, starting in the Middle Kingdom (Germer 1992, 135).

The question of the origin or source of this representation leads to a further confrontation, namely with the history of Egypt itself. There has been a standing assumption that these representations use a design vocabulary that creates a narrative about the Old Kingdom as a stable, continuous institution outside of historical change (J. Assmann 1986, 525; Gundlach 1994, 3 and 6). It is the religious tradition, not the changing fashion of clothing, that was emphasized in written texts and visual representations. The Middle and New Kingdoms developed something of a time lag between the "representation" of clothes and their "reality," one that is only slightly diminished by the progressive expansion of the clothes' thematic repertoire.

Monopoly of representability

In contrast to those from ancient Egypt, discoveries of textiles from the Middle Ages are more of a rarity. They do exist, but in the form of thousands upon thousands of small fabric pieces and numerous accessories. Open for interpretation within the larger context of material findings, ornaments span from metal to stone, bone, wood, and glass, and further archeological artifacts such as cosmetic tools and clay or glass containers. The significance of an object starts with its materiality, especially if the materials that compose it are organic. Their significance depends equally on the environment and conditions of preservation (see Figure 3.3):

> Air sealed storage, constant moisture, dryness, or permafrost will stop or significantly slow down the disintegration of textiles. Vegetal and animal fibers

Figure 3.3 Embroidered chasuble back out of Italian velvet (late fourteenth century). *Photo*: Los Angeles County Museum of Art.

differ considerably with regard to their durability in the soil. Animal fibers, with protein as a chief constituent, are sensitive to lye and resistant to acidic environments. With regard to vegetable fibers, where cellulose is the main ingredient, it is the other way around. In this way, discoveries of vegetable and animal fibers exclude each other almost completely in a given excavation. Soils are almost always predominantly acidic so that vegetable fibers are only preserved in special cases. (Kania 2010, 17–18)

These different basic prerequisites Katrin Kania describes for the preservation of vegetable and animal fibers help explain the predominance of wool and silk in archeological findings. During the construction of a parking space in 2002, more than 6,000 textile fragments from the fifteenth century were found inside a city wall in Tours, France, along the Loire River. Given the preserved condition of the materials, it was possible to reconstruct their life cycle from the processing of fibers to textile surfaces, their treatment, coloring, disposal, and reuse (Henri 2015, 48–58).

Compared to ancient Egypt, there are more diverse types of media in the High and Late Middle Ages of Europe. The range of iconographic representation included mural paintings and, later, panel paintings, miniatures (such as books of hours, psalters, and gospels), fabliaux and passionals, sculptures and reliefs, seals, coins, and stained glass (as in churches and cathedrals) (Scott 2009).

Source criticism in this second example also presents us with the problem of what I refer to as the monopoly of presentability, albeit in a different way than in the case of ancient Egypt. This monopoly is upheld by the hegemonic cultures of court and church. Although these cultures came increasingly under attack throughout the Middle Ages, they prescribed modern ideas about medieval clothing and fashion. A good example of the longevity of this perspective is the popular conception of medieval fashion styles in modern reenactments and computer games.

Discoveries by archeologists in Denmark (Herjolfsnes), Norway (Tegle, Bergen, and Finnegarden), Germany (the historical Haithabu, Lübeck, and Kempten), Greenland (Gardar), France (Martres-de-Veyre and Tours), Holland (Amsterdam, Dordrecht, Smeerenburg, and Groningen), Austria (Lengberg), Poland (Gdańsk, Elbing, and Lubin), and England (London, York, Coppergate, and Isle of Wight) have, in the meantime, begun to disrupt this monolithic image. The academy was initially hesitant to accept these new discoveries because these found clothes had no equivalent or complement in the established clothing terminology, iconography, and literature.

This panoply of sources requires certain distinctions to be made regarding their respective interpretative potential. Written sources, for instances, included courtly literature, chronicles, liturgical texts, dress codes, travelogues, legal texts, wills, inventories, archives, accounting books and other lists, and even records of church councils and sermons. In the view of cultural anthropology, normative texts are more significant as such perspectives better reflect everyday practices of clothing. The conventional juxtaposition of image and text creates great problems for the identification of clothing (Vavra 1988, 21–46; Schüppert 1988, 93–141; Blanc 1989, 7–33). The evaluation of archeological discoveries is initially easiest to do from the listing records (Crowfoot, Pritchard, and Staniland 2001).

New media and tools for dress research

The academy as well as the lays have been focused on and fascinated by the use of new archeological technology. In textile research, technology has changed rapidly in recent years. Whereas Renate Germer was still working predominantly with chemical procedures in the 1980s, Egyptologists and medievalists now often deploy the latest procedures and tools from the field of physics. The large-scale use of sonar-scanners to discover traces in the soil is one recent example. Computer tomography now enables researchers to examine mummies from antiquity or the Middle Ages without undressing and thereby destroying them. Reconstructions in 3D then provide clear visualizations of the mummies. CAT scanning has also been used to rediscover covert structures, as in the case of mineralized textiles, in order to digitally reconstruct them in 3D format (Cybulska, Florczak, and Maik 2009, 36–40).

New documentaries, docudramas, and popular science magazines that tend to fetishize technology as the universal means to uncover the secrets of world history have contributed significantly to the new interest in high-tech archeological research. Technological methods such as high-performance liquid chromatography, IR-spectroscopy, X-ray fluorescence analysis, and synchrotron radiation, help to validate the identification and date of materials and heighten the significance of such discoveries. These tools are particularly helpful in the investigation of colors, even when the actual colorants are no longer visible or when the found textiles have disintegrated due to contact with metallic salts from metal objects, jewelry, or tools (Janaway 1989, 21–29). Whereas these tools can be very precise in unveiling material composition and historical dating, they are often limited in providing insights into the historic use or sociocultural context of textiles and clothing.

Traditional microscopy has nowadays been replaced by scanning electron microscopy (SEM) used for the identification of fibers and fluorescence microscopy for the analysis of organic materials. In dealing with bodies or mummies, both DNA analyses and the Centre for Research and Restoration of the Museums of France (C2RMF) method are standard procedures for the identification of any kind of mineralized fiber. These technologies facilitate the investigation of a large volume of archeological textile discoveries, rather than privileging the investigation of particularly impressive or "characteristic" fabrics (Moulhérat 2008, 18–23). These tools also provide information on natural resources and different contexts of use for textile objects. The rapid development of "new genetics" enables the decoding of old fibers, textiles, or even hair, by means of the DNA or RNA analysis. The "[s]tudy of craftsmanship and experimental archeology, archeobotanic and archeozoology" (Andersson Strand et al. 2010, 149) are just further branches of archeology providing necessary background information on textiles, as in, for instance, the systematic investigation of textile production tools (Andersson Strand and Nosch 2015).

Requirements for a paradigm shift

Textile archeology examines textile objects in the typical scientific sequence. This investigation initially includes a precise analysis of material, textile technology, patterns, intended use, possible further use and reuse, dimensions and density, borders, edges, and seams (Biermann 2005, 324). The basic parameters for analysis of textiles include dimensions, construction, colors, textile and yarn structure, threads, ornaments and patterns, irregularities and faults, the conditions of discovery, and the traces of its usage. Subsequent theoretical analyses deal with the object's surroundings—its social, religious, cultural, economic, and political contexts (Biermann 2005, 324). Therefore, archeological research today is more heterogeneous; it no longer concentrates exclusively on fiber identification and the technical description of objects but also integrates qualitative and quantitative investigations and contextual interpretations. After all, "A textile is not simply a binary system of spun, twisted, or spliced fibres, but first and foremost a result of complex interactions between resources, technology, and society" (Andersson Strand et al. 2010, 150).

Despite the many new methods, perspectives, and theories in archeological research, there is still a large-scale disregard for interdisciplinary approaches and methods developed in fields such as material culture and dress studies. These latter fields have explicitly demanded a paradigm shift to open up disciplinary matrixes, incorporating methods from cultural anthropology and textile archeology (Axel 2002, viii). Nevertheless, the extent to which cultural anthropology and archeology can impact new perspectives in textile and clothing research also depends on the particular cultural clothing practices and on the academy's existing perspectives of the same. The study of ancient Egyptian practices—taking into consideration their specific cultural dimensions and experiences of time—require researchers to develop a heightened level of critical self-awareness of our assumptions and socially constructed biases.

Archeological discoveries invite a particular dialogue that could be structured as the consideration of social and cultural practices, including the symbolic forms through which humans come to organize, shape, structure, and regulate their everyday lives. This connects to the investigation of historicity, the space-time continuum of human existence. Moreover, this method should address the discursive and medial changes in the conceptions and descriptions of human experience. However, in any cultural anthropological investigation, perspectives may shift as the sites of cultural-historic experience are not only constituted by human actors but also by the objects, spaces, and discourses that enact or emerge from human action and shape it accordingly. Only such a perspective points beyond the old anthropocentric, and still quite often Eurocentric, perspective. This praxiographic procedure brings the interactions between different artifacts—weapons, tools, means of transportation, and clothing—into focus, turning them into both media and actors. Following such a direction, textile archeological research could reposition itself and assume a different relevance.

Pursuing textile archeology or dress studies informed by cultural anthropology also means abandoning the old master narratives of art and costume history and the modes of perception and interpretation it perpetuated, including unsubstantiated ideas around *longue durées* of style and form. Instead, following current developments in dress history studies, scholars should embrace smaller time-space contexts with thematic foci. The example of archeology shows that where we had formerly assumed homogeneity, there actually coexisted a diversity of clothing worlds (Hägg 1983, 316–67). To return once more to Bakhtin, research must come to appreciate the plurality of clothing discourses (heteroglossia) and the complexity of clothing narratives (plurivocality) (Bakhtin 1981, 4–6). The idea of border regimes and intercultural points of contact and exchange gain special significance here, since the history of ancient Egypt cannot be viewed as a unified whole but rather in the context of historic development (Merimde culture, Naqada and Badari periods) as well as geographic development (Ancient Nubia, Kingdom of Kush, Meroë, Hittites, Assyria, Persia, and Greek and Roman dominion). This is especially true with regard to textile cultures.

Following Michel Foucault, even the notion of archeology can be extended. Thus, I propose that critics begin to speak of fashion archeology or dress archeology rather than costume history, with the aim of creating a new dynamic and ambitious horizon for the study of clothing. As *The Oxford Handbook of Archaeology* asserts, archeology is interested in human actors and their material remains (Graves-Brown and Harrison 2013, 9–12). Such an approach enables and requires shared approaches in the search, discovery, and understanding of textile and clothing traces.

Note

1 Several institutions in the area of archeology have helped to advance the study of textiles. For example, Gillian Vogelsang-Eastwood, the director of the Stichting (Foundation) Textile Research Centre, Leiden, Netherlands designed a pioneering exhibition on ancient Egyptian clothing in Leiden and Hanover in 1995. In addition, the Center for Textile Research (CTR) of the University of Copenhagen in Denmark has edited the flagship *Archaeological Textiles Review* since 2008. In Athens, Greece, the Hellenic Centre for Research and Conservation for Archaeological Textiles (ARTEX) closely cooperates with museums around the world, including the Quai Branly Museum in Paris and the Victoria and Albert Museum in London. The Institute of Archaeology and Ethnology at Łódź, Poland, also examines archeological textile discoveries using modern methods of analysis.

References

Altenmüller, Hartwig. 1992. "Stilkriterien." In *Lexikon der Ägyptologie*, Vol. 6, edited by Wolfgang Helck, Eberhard Otto, and Wolfhart Westendorf, 18–22. Wiesbaden: O. Harrassowitz.

Andersson Strand, Eva, and Marie-Louise Nosch. 2015. *Tools, Textiles and Contexts: Investigating Textile Production in the Aegean and Eastern Mediterranean Bronze Age.* Oxford: Oxbow Press.

Andersson Strand, Eva, Karin Margarita Frei, Margaita Gleba, Ulla Mannering, Marie-Louise Nosch, and Irene Skals. 2010. "Old Textiles—New Possibilities." *European Journal of Archaeology* 13: 149–73.

Assmann, Aleida. 1994. "Ent-Ikonisierung und Re-Ikonisierung der Schrift." *Kunstforum* 127: 135–41.

Assmann, Jan. 1986. "Viele Stile am Nil?" In *Stil: Geschichten und Funktionen eines kulturwissenschaftlichen Diskurselements*, edited by Hans-Ulrich Gumbrecht, Karl Ludwig Pfeiffer, and Armin Biermann, 519–37. Frankfurt am Main: Suhrkamp.

Assmann, Jan. 2000. *Das kulturelle Gedächtnis*. München: Beck.

Axel, Keith Brian, ed. 2002. *From the Margin*. London: Durham.

Bakhtin, Mikhail M. 1981. *The Dialogic Imagination*. Austin and London: University of Texas Press.

Bakhtin, Michail M. 2008. *Chronotopos*. Frankfurt am Main: Suhrkamp.

Banck-Burgess, Johanna. 2008. "Ein lange vernachlässigter Fachbereich." *Denkmalpflege in Baden-Württemberg* 37(2): 82–87.

Banck-Burgess, Johanna. 2012. *Mittel der Macht. Textilien der Kelten: Instrument of Power. Celtic Textiles*. Darmstadt: Theiss.

Becks, Ralf, and Tina Jakobs. 1996. "Çatal Hüyük. Zur Rekonstruktion von Prestige innerhalb räumlicher Strukturen." In *Prestige—Prestigegüter—Sozialstrukturen. Beispiele aus dem europäischen und vorderasiatischen Neolithikum*, edited by Johannes Müller, Reinhard Bernbeck, and Dana Ottenbreit, 57–79. Bonn: Holos.

Biermann, Daniela. 2005. "Archäologische Textilien aus Peru." In *Kulturanthropologie des Textilen*, edited by Gabriele Mentges, 323–39. Berlin: Ebersbach.

Blanc, Odile. 1989. "Historiographie du vêtement: un bilan." *Le vêtement, histoire, archéologie, symbolique vestimentaire au Moyen-Age. Cahiers du Léopard d'or* (Paris) 1: 7–33.

Bourdieu, Pierre. (1974) 2012. "Haute Couture et Haute Culture." *Questions de sociologie*. Paris: Editions de Minuit.

Brunner-Traut, Emma. 1977. *Die Grabkammer Seschemnofers III*. Tübingen: MUT.

Carter, Howard. (1925) 2007. *The Tomb of Tutankhamun*. London: Little Books.

Crowfoot, Elisabeth, Frances Pritchard, and Kay Staniland. 2001. *Textiles and Clothing: c. 1150–1450*. London: The Boydell Press.

Cybulska, Maria, Tomasz Florczak, and Jerzy Maik. 2009. "Virtual Reconstruction of Archaeological Textiles." In *North European Symposium for Archaeological Textiles X*, edited by Eva Andersson Strand, Margarita Gleba, Ulla Mannering, and Cherine Munkholt, 36–40. Havertown: Oxbow Books.

Germer, Renate. 1992. *Die Textilfärberei und die Verwendung gefärbter Textilien im alten Ägypten*. Wiesbaden: O. Harrassowitz.

Graves-Brown, Paul, and Rodney Harrison. 2013. *The Oxford Handbook of the Archaeology of the Contemporary World*. Oxford: Oxford University Press.

Gundlach, Rolf. 1994. *Die Zwangsumsiedlung auswärtiger Bevölkerung als Mittel ägyptischer Politik bis zum Ende des mittleren Reiches*. Stuttgart: Franz Steiner.

Hägg, Inga. 1983. "Viking Women's Dress at Birka: A Reconstruction by Archaeological Methods." In *Cloth and Clothing in Medieval Europe: Essays in Memory of Professor E.M. Carus-Wilson*, edited by Neidhart B. Harte and Kenneth G. Ponting, 316–67. London: Heinemann.

Hall, Rosalind. 2008. *Egyptian Textiles*. London: Bloomsbury.

Henri, Delphine. 2015. "Production et consommation textiles à Tours aux Xvè et XVIè siècles: Approche archéologique." PhD dissertation, Université de Tours.

Herodotus. 2008. *The Histories*, Vol. 2. Translated by Robin Waterfield. Oxford: Oxford University Press.

Janaway, Robert. 1989. "Evidence Preserved in Corrosion Products: New Fields in Artifact Studies." Proceedings of a Joint Conference between UKIC Archaeology Section and the Council for British Archaeology Science Committee, Leeds, United Kingdom 1983. London: [s.n.].

Janssen, Jac. J. 2008. *Daily Dress at Deir el-Medîna: Words for Clothing*. London: Golden House Publications.

Kania, Katrin. 2010. *Kleidung im Mittelalter: Materialien—Konstruktion—Nähtechnik*. Köln: Böhlau.

Kemp, Barry. 2014. "Tell-El-Amarna." *The Journal of Egyptian Archeology* 100: 1–34.

Maier, Marion. 2001. "Çatal Hüyük und seine Bedeutung für die Textilkultur." In *Kultische Textilien: Dortmunder Reihe zur kulturanthropologischen Studien des Textilen*, edited by Gabriele Mentges and Heide Nixdorf, 19–78. Dortmund: Ebersbach.

McDowell, Andrea G. 1997. "Die Schriftkultur einer altägyptischen Siedlung." *Spektrum der Wissenschaft* 2: 76–81.

Moulhérat, Christophe. 2008. "Archéologie des textiles. Nouvelle méthodologie appliquée à l´étude des tissus minéralisés." *Archéologie des Textiles et Teintures Végétales* 114: 18–23.

Munro, Peter. 1992. "Gewand und Körper." In *Lexikon der Ägyptologie*, Vol. 6, edited by Wolfgang Helck, Eberhard Otto, and Wolfhart Westendorf, 664–68. Wiesbaden: O. Harrassowitz.

Pritchard, Frances. 2006. *Clothing Culture: Dress in Egypt in the First Millennium AD*. Manchester: Whitworth Art Gallery.

Riefstahl, Elizabeth. 1945. *Patterned Textiles in Pharaonic Egypt*. New York: Brooklyn Museum, Brooklyn Institute of Arts and Sciences.

Riegel, Alois. 1889. *Die ägyptischen Textilfunde im K.K. Österreichischen. Museum: Allgemeine Charakteristik und Katalog*. Wien: Waldheim.

Schiaparelli, Ernesto. (1927) 2008. *La tomba intatta dell'architetto Kha, nella necropoli di Tebe / The Intact Tomb of the Architect Kha in the Necropolis of Thebes*. Turin: AdArte.

Schüppert, Helga. 1988. "Bezeichnung, Bild und Sache." In *Terminologie und Typologie mittelalterlicher Sachgüter: Das Beispiel der Kleidung*, edited by Heinrich Appelt, 93–141. Wien: Österreichische Akademie der Wissenschaften.

Scott, Margaret. 2009. *Medieval Dress and Fashion.* London: British Library.

Staehelin, Elisabeth. 1992a. "Tracht." In *Lexikon der Ägyptologie*, Vol. 6, edited by Wolfgang Helck, Eberhard Otto, and Wolfhart Westendorf, 743–45. Wiesbaden: O. Harrassowitz.

Staehelin, Elisabeth. 1992b. "Schurz." In *Lexikon der Ägyptologie*, Vol. 6, edited by Wolfgang Helck, Eberhard Otto, and Wolfhart Westendorf, 726–37. Wiesbaden: O. Harrassowitz.

Vavra, Elisabeth. 1988. "Kritische Bemerkungen zur Kostümliteratur." In *Terminologie und Typologie mittelalterlicher Sachgüter: Das Beispiel der Kleidung—internationales Round-Table-Gespräch Krems an der Donau*, edited by Heinrich Appelt, 21–46. Wien: Österreichische Akademie der Wissenschaften.

Vogelsang-Eastwood, Gillian M. 1993. *Pharaonic Egyptian Clothing.* Leiden, New York, and Köln: E.J. Brill.

Vogelsang-Eastwood, Gillian M. 1999. *Tutankhamun's Wardrobe: Garments from the Tomb of Tutankhamun.* Rotterdam: Barjesteh van Waalwijk van Door.

4

Appropriating the world through clothing: Christoph Kress's foreign dress collection

Jutta Zander-Seidel

Clothing has always played an important role in the way the West has imagined and mediated foreign cultures. At medieval court festivities, Europeans dressed up as "Tartars," "Saracens," and "Orientals." In 1331, the English king Edward III and his entourage participated in a tournament donning *panni tartarici* (Wardwell 1988/89) and a Tartar mask. The "Turkish Masquerades" held at the court of Holy Roman emperor Maximilian I in 1494 featured men attired in "oriental" women's gowns and with their faces hidden behind grids (Franke and Welzel 2013, 37–38). When distant nations were brought into contact following Europe's "discovery" of America and other regions around the world, economic and cultural practices of colonialism and new bourgeois elites shaped the construction and perception of the "Foreign," including the idea of "the clothed Other" (Paresys 2006; Rublack 2010, 177–209; Mentges 2013, 33–34). The fundamental significance of vestimentary culture in the modern European world made clothing an ideal vehicle for cross-cultural comparisons. How outward appearances, materials, and techniques as well as habitus, consumption, and social categories of clothing were perceived underscored the complex role fashion and materiality played in cultural exchange.

To explore a concrete example of such material engagement with the "foreign world" through the medium of clothing, this chapter focuses on the collection of Nuremberg patrician Christoph Kress (1541–1583) (see Figure 4.1). In the probate inventory of 1584, Kress's collection was recorded under the title "All Kinds of Foreign Nations' Clothing and the Like" (*Allerley Frembter Nationen klaidung und dergleichen*) (Kress 1584). The list of thirty garments, headwear, weaponry, and textiles—all mostly described as "Indian," "Moorish," and "Turkish"—represents one of the oldest verifiable records of non-European

CHRISTOPHORUS KRESS.
Reipublicæ Noribergensis
Senator. Natus Año 1541.
Denatus A° 1583.

Figure 4.1 Posthumous portrait of Christoph Kress (copper engraving, around 1700). *Photo*: Germanisches Nationalmuseum.

clothing obtained and preserved by bourgeois owners in the German-speaking world. Additional objects in this collection included oriental jewelry, Arabic coins, Turkish textiles, geographic maps, and costume books. Given its breadth, the collection can be considered a systematic attempt to acquire ethnographic knowledge, a goal Kress defined for himself early on. As a seventeen-year-old student in Leipzig, he wrote to his father that "it might now be time that I would understand another language beyond Latin . . . so I could get to know also the customs and behavior of foreign people" (von Kress 1895, 133). Over the course of his life, this interest led to a vast collection in which clothing, both in its material dimension and as visual-verbal representation, became the principal medium for his acquisition of knowledge about the world of his time.

Kress not only collected foreign clothing but also stockpiled costume books, many from the genre of instructional fashion literature that emerged in the second half of the sixteenth century (see Mentges 2007 and 2015; Rublack 2010; Taylor 2004; Paulicelli 2014). Therefore, this chapter also contributes to the study of costume books as visual, textual, and artistic resources, including their reception by contemporaneous audiences. There is still limited historical understanding of the intentions of the buyers of costume books, and even less regarding the relationship between printed costume collections and the actual clothes amassed from around the world and stored in aristocrats' and patricians' cabinets of art and curiosities (*Kunstkammern*). Similar to research on collectors of the critical fashion commentary that circulated on broadsheets (Schilling 1990; Zander-Seidel 2015, 135–36), such investigations of costume book readership help to position these less studied publications in the context of the media of its time. Akin to the scholarly reconstruction of the collections and libraries themselves, costume books provide information on the life patterns and educational ideals of the early modern elites.

In the catalogue of a recent exhibition on fashion from the Renaissance and Early Baroque in Nuremberg, Gabriele Mentges emphasized the need to critically investigate costume books (Mentges 2015, 150). Indeed, the effects of this genre were wide-ranging, from appropriated design motifs transferred to family registers and *Alba Amicorum* (friendship albums) to extracts from costume books collated by publishers to produce travel souvenirs for towns and regions (Kuhl 2008). One prominent example of a transfer of motifs from costume books is a large embroidered tablecloth with twenty-four female costumes dated from the first half of the seventeenth century (Petrasch 1991, 397–99; Rublack 2010, 146–47; Zander-Seidel 2015, 174–76). Costume books can help to reconstruct not only a previous world of clothing and masquerades but also former modes of textile production. Understood as imaginary collections in themselves, costume books function as a form of parallel *Kunstkammern* (Mentges 2015, 150–51). Kress's collection with its juxtaposition of foreign or "exotic" garments with costume books exemplifies this.

The collector

Christoph Kress III was born in Nuremberg on November 10, 1541. This southern German imperial city and trading center was located at the intersection of important European commercial routes. It was a destination for emperors and kings, and a center of early modern craftsmanship, science, and humanism (Smith 1983). As the oldest son of Christoph Kress II (1515–1560) and his wife Dorothea, née Haller (d. 1554), Kress belonged to an old, established patrician family. The Nuremberg patricians owed their wealth and influence largely to the wholesale and long-distance trade that many of its families had been engaged in since the Middle Ages. For centuries, these families had also maintained oligarchical rule over the city government. The biography of Christoph Kress III was thus characteristic of his rank (von Frank 1936, 352–57; Fleischmann 2008, vol. 2, 655). His broad training reflected the great significance the city's elites placed on education and literacy (Endres 1983). Following elementary education in writing and arithmetic, Kress attended Latin schools in Nuremberg and Leipzig. As with most members of his social group, he pursued further studies in Bologna, in northern Italy, where he spent more than two years, from 1559 until 1562 (Knod 1899, 276). Once back in Nuremberg, he held important city offices, including that of city councillor, mayor, and member of the jury.

During his time in Bologna, Kress corresponded regularly with his father. Letters dating from 1559 and 1560 document how the eighteen-year-old developed an astute interest in his new cultural surroundings and attempted to acquire knowledge of the Italian culture. From the very beginning, Kress had an Italian instructor, who read "every day one hour of Italian with me so that I would get to know the language as soon as possible along with all of my other studies" (von Kress 1895, 142). On the third day of his arrival in Bologna, he sold his fatigued horse and used the proceeds to attire himself "according to local customs" (von Kress 1895, 143). His casual remark indicates how Kress adapted his own clothing to that of his host country, a habit that was documented for travelers and people living abroad from medieval times into the modern era. The reasons for such explicit, material embrace of the other culture are varied, ranging from the wish to adapt to social and religious vestimentary norms to simply acclimatizing to weather conditions. Visitors desired to "pass," viz. not to be immediately identified as strangers; sometimes this was a safety measure, at other times it was born from the desire to communicate social status in the sartorial vocabulary of the host country. Especially in the Middle East, religiously motivated rules forced Westerners to adopt local clothing trends (Rodenbeck 2001; Trauth 2009, 206–08). One example of a practical consideration was documented in the eighteenth-century encyclopedia *Zedlers Universallexikon*, which recommended donning dark travel clothing because it soils less easily.

Examples of stylistic clothing changes between early modern Italy and Germany are also documented in the "book of clothes" by Matthäus Schwarz, a citizen of Augsburg and bookkeeper of the Fugger family, who recorded his outfits in precise drawings and descriptions. In 1516, Schwarz presented himself in Venice "ala zentilhomo" with a long jacket and, upon his return to Augsburg, reverted into the German mode, with a short vest and slit trousers (Fink 1963, 114–15; Rublack 2015, 80–81 and 248–50). Another example of the norms of aristocratic clothing exchange is the Spanish coat that Stephan Praun, who, like Kress, was a member of the Nuremberg patriciate, acquired on his pilgrimage to Santiago de Compostela in 1571. The coat survived as part of the art collection of his brother Paulus Praun. Today it is on loan from the Praun Family Foundation to the Germanisches Nationalmuseum at Nuremberg. *Per* Abraham de Bruyn's contemporaneous costume book *Diversarum gentium armatura equestris*, this coat can be unequivocally identified both by nationality and social rank, and we can safely assume that Stephan Praun acquired this coat to match the clothing characteristic for the Spanish elite (Zander-Seidel 2015, 117–19).

Christoph Kress's letters from Bologna also communicated the collector's interest in preserving his goods. For example, in a July 1560 letter, he asked his father to check on the books he had left in Nuremberg and to place herbs into the book chest to guard them against worms. By adding "they mean a lot to me and are also rather expensive," Kress expressed the upper-class educational ethos and bourgeois sense of economy that pervaded the father-son correspondence (von Kress 1895, 170). Unfortunately, we do not know how Kress preserved his foreign clothing collections into later years, though airing and brushing out were the most common procedures (Zander-Seidel 2015, 220–31). Records regarding the care of the vast wardrobe of English Queen Elizabeth I, for instance, describe a range of advice, including the use of clothing bags made from leather and cotton to protect from dust and vermin, the burning of wood and coal in order to keep rooms dry, as well as placing silk or cotton pouches filled with rose-perfumed powder between clothes and shoes (Arnold 1988, 232–34).

In 1562, Kress returned to Nuremberg. Between 1562 and 1563, he apprenticed under Dr. Abraham Löscher (1520–1575), a lawyer, humanist, poet, and member of the Imperial High Court at Speyer. As of April 1563, the twenty-two-year-old Kress returned to live in Nuremberg, where he married Ursula Tetzel (1539–1574), the daughter of a patrician family, one year later. Following Tetzel's death, he would marry once more, in 1579. On June 23, 1583, Christoph Kress III died at the young age of forty-two.

The collection

We can assume that Kress created his collection of foreign clothing in the last two decades of his life, the period when most Renaissance costume books were published. At the same time that the authors of costume books surveyed the world through the medium of clothing, aristocratic and bourgeois collectors were enticed to incorporate and exhibit material gowns in their *Kunstkammern*, as if they were rare, miraculous artifacts unearthed from nature. As representations of a new, global, or cosmopolitan vision of the world, these clothing collections overtly displayed the knowledge and education of their collectors.

The documentation of the collection in Kress's probate inventory requires further explanation of the source's significance. Probate inventories were official documents required by law, and their compilation after a person's death primarily served inheritance arrangements. In principle, probate inventories were generated for all classes of the population, but their significance and impact increased with the scope of the recorded property. The upper classes not only bequeathed larger and more abundant holdings but they were also able to employ competent writers for the documentation. These appraisers registered what they found in the houses arranged by subject groups and/or rooms, so that itemization included nearly all sectors of material culture.

When nineteenth-century cultural historians discovered the corpus of the probate inventory as a historical source, they first published the inventories based on their limited understanding of the records. Starting in the 1970s, an international inventory research movement emerged and evaluation of these sources began (van der Woude and Schuurman 1980; Mohrmann 2003; Simon-Muscheid 2004, 27–33). Studies by Janet Arnold (1988), Jutta Zander-Seidel (1990), Maria Hayward (2007), and Karen Stolleis (e.g., 1977) deal especially with the inventories of early modern clothing. One fundamental difficulty in the evaluation of inventories is that historical terminology tends to have strong regional inflections, complicating the connection between signifier and signified. While the inventories themselves, with their large volumes of data, are often the subject of digital quantitative analysis, based on selected classes of objects, they become a useful source for material culture studies only when used alongside additional, comparative sources.

In Kress's probate inventory, only the collection "All Kinds of Foreign Nations' Clothing and the Like" (*Allerley Frembter Nationen klaidung und dergleichen*) forms a self-contained record. Other non-European items are recorded according to the specific genre or type of object. Thus, the jewelry of the deceased includes "an Oriental pomegranate with three pearls in gold setting" and "an Oriental jasper in a gold setting with a pearl pendant" (Kress 1584, 13v). He owned "Arabic coins" and "Heathen pennies" (10v, 11v), as well as a "Moorish neck ring made from gilded copper, and an Indian Nut and a small piece of nacre" (18r). The costume books and prints were in the writing room together with maps of "Germania," Jerusalem, and Europe, with an emphasis on the Nuremberg region (34v), underscoring the fact that the comparison between the domestic and the foreign was a motivation for early modern collectors (Rublack 2010, 177–209; Mentges 2013 and 2015, 148).

The foreign clothing collection included the following objects, with the accompanying valuation based on the sixteenth-century three-stage Nuremburg coinage consisting of guilder fl. (*Gulden*), pound (*Pfund*), and pennies (*Pfennig*) (see Scholler 1912):

Item one Indian gown and one pair of shoes, together fl. 4.-.-.
Item one silken striped Moorish coat and one white shirt, fl. 4.-.-.
Item two Moorish shirts, fl. 6.-.-.
Item one white Moorish shirt with red braids, fl. 3.-.-.
Another one all white Moorish shirt, fl. 1.-.-.
Item one Moorish bonnet, fl. 1.-.-.
Another small golden Moorish bonnet at one half guilder, together fl. -.4.6.
Item one red Hungarian small bonnet at 10 kreutzer, fl. -.1.12.
Item three pairs Turkish boots, another pair of shoes and one pair of mules together fl. 3.-.-.
Item two Turkish turbans with woven golden braids, one at 2 guilders, together fl. 4.-.
Another good Turkish turban, fl. 2 .-.-.
Item two white Turkish turbans, one with striped braids, fl. 3.-.-.
Item three poor Turkish turbans, one at one guilder, together fl. 3.-.-.

Another Turkish turban at one-half guilder, together fl. -.4.6.

Item one Turkish colorful napkin fl. 1.-.-.

Another poor Turkish napkin at three ort, together fl. -.6.9.

Item one Turkish napkin and a like handkerchief, together fl. 1.-.-.

Item two Turkish bows including quivers and arrows, also two Turkish shoes, together fl. 2.4.6.

Item one English bow and twenty-four arrows in sheath together fl. 2.-.-.

Item two Turkish scourges together fl. -.-.18.

Item four poor Turkish bows, together fl. 1.-.-.

Item one pair pointed mules, brass shod at ten Kreutzer, together fl. -.1.12.[1]

The description of the foreign clothing items employs the owner's well-versed vestimentary terminology. That is, like the typology of the costume books, the known provides the framework for the unknown. Distance between cultures of origin was expressed through the description of unusual materials such as gold decoration or "red braids." Irrespective of its specific design, a "Moorish shirt," given the generic term shirt, looks like the European version: wide, long-sleeved, and made from linen- or silk-like fabric.

Clothing and textiles

A close analysis of the inventory items requires a critical approach to the sources, initially differentiating between the different types of clothing and accessories. In addition to seven outer garments, the collection boasts three bonnets, six pairs of shoes (including three pairs of boots and two pairs of mules), nine turbans, four handkerchiefs and napkins, plus a host of weapons. The objects' origins are predominantly "Indian," "Moorish," and "Turkish." The only pieces of European origin are "Hungarian" and "English."

In early modern Europe, the term "Moorish" flagged a variety of perceived or imagined vestimentary styles, typically construed as foreign or exotic. In Albrecht Altdorfer's "Triumph of Maximilian I," painted in the years 1512 to 1515, and showing one of the earliest presentations of foreign peoples in European art, the emperor himself determined the visual display of the "people of Calicut" as "naked with a loincloth," "naked the Indian way," or clothed "Moorish" (Madersbacher 1992, 325–26; Michel 2015, 384). In Hans Weigel's costume book, printed in Nuremberg in 1577, the terms "Moor" and "Moorish" are ambiguous, too. In the two illustrations "Female Moor in the Empire of Grenada" and "Female Moor from Grenada," the women are represented as Moriscos, former Muslims who had converted or were forced to convert to Christianity. Additionally, there is the "Moor from Arabia" and the "Arab or Moor from Lybia," the "Female Moor at Constantinople," and "Female Moors in Turkey" (Weigel and Amman 1577, Taf. CLXIII, CLXIIII, CLXXVI, CLXXXIIII, CCX, CCXIII). The collection's other references to cultural origin are also imprecise. In the sixteenth century, "Indian" could refer to all overseas countries and territories (Heikamp 1970, 205), "Turkish" stood for the Ottoman Empire, and "Hungarian" and "English" referred to European collection items.

Even though the "Moorish shirts" of the *Kunstkammern* do not indicate a specific type of clothing, we may assume that they refer to the tunic- or kaftan-like vestimentary format of the Arabic-African region. The style may be likened to the mid-length silk gown, with a pattern of woven stripes and a long vertical opening at the front, that was given to the Nuremberg Public Library as a "Turkish Priest Robe" in 1683 (see Figure 4.2) (Zander-Seidel 2015, 171–72). The object is said to have been obtained from the victorious battles against the Turkish siege of Vienna in 1683 and had been given to its previous owner, a German physician, by Ludwig Wilhelm von Baden (1655–1707). Margrave Ludwig's

Figure 4.2 Turkish garment collected in the *Kunstkammern*, donated to the Nuremberg Public Library (around 1683). *Photo*: Germanisches Nationalmuseum.

portion of the Viennese "Turkish Booty" preserved in Karlsruhe, contains not only further "Turkish shirts," but also a "book depicting Muslims," that can likely be understood to be a costume book (Petrasch 1991, 463).

The increasing proportion of Ottoman clothing in costume books toward the end of the sixteenth century is strongly embodied in Venetian painter Cesare Vecellio's costume book, which was published in several editions starting in 1590 (see Figure 4.3) (Vecellio 1590). Gabriele Mentges explains the intensity in these representations not only through "the close relationship between Venice and the Ottoman Empire, but also with the interest in and the attention given by Europeans to the manifold ranks within Ottoman society, which seems comparable to that of Europe in this respect" (Mentges 2015, 147; see also Paulicelli 2008, 2014). Vecellio's representations of Ottoman dignitaries in turbans, a very exotic object in the eyes of Europeans, may have been a counterpart to the eight "Turkish turbans" in the Kress collection. Thus, Kress may well have sought a material equivalent to the "painted" diversity and hierarchy he found among Turkish headwear in the costume books. The Kunsthistorisches Museum in Vienna preserves a turban from the *Kunstkammern* of Archduke Ferdinand from the second half of the sixteenth century, which, though reassembled in 1980, provides an illuminating window into the equivalent record in the archducal

Figure 4.3 "Turco di grado in casa," illustration in Cesare Vecellio's costume book, 1598. *Photo*: Germanisches Nationalmuseum.

inventory: "a turban as worn by the Turkish emperor with a red silken kulah" (Wien KHM 2017).

In Kress's inventory, the listed turbans are followed by entries of four "Turkish" decorative cloths referred to as *Fatscheinlein* or *Fatzinetlein*, the terms used in early modern Nuremberg for napkins and handkerchiefs (Zander-Seidel 1990, 310–15). The records state that one of these was "colorful" while another was "poor," viz. damaged. As in the records on domestic clothing, the state of these foreign garments was carefully registered, something that was critical for their financial appraisal. The high appreciation or high value for textiles and clothing in the early modern context manifests itself not only in the multiple uses and repairs that were so common, even among the upper classes, but also in their inventories. Nevertheless, information regarding material and design is frequently missing so that a more precise identification of clothes is hardly possible.

Costume books and prints

In the Kress inventory, textile household goods, which also included Turkish cloths and rugs (Kress 1584, 30v–31r; Zander-Seidel 1990, 355–75), are followed by the voluminous section titled "Paintings and all kinds of beautiful engraved books and prints." It includes numerous paintings with religious and secular themes, as well as portraits on both wood and canvas and various maps and prints. Moreover, there are illustrated books and prints, of which three costume books and an unidentified number of costume prints are of interest with respect to Christoph Kress's foreign clothing collection (Kress 1584, 33v–37v, bes. 34v, 35r, 36v).

> Item one illustrated book with various foreign garb in folio and kopert binding, fl. 6.-.-. (34v)
> Item another illustrated book with various foreign costumes in folio and kopert binding, fl. 3.-.-. (35r)
> Item one costume book of various German and foreign nations, fl. 2.-.-. (35r)
> Item several paintings of Turkish costume, in quarto and white kopert binding, one half guilder, together fl. -.4. 6. (35v)[2]

As is the case for the other objects, the book and print entries cannot be unequivocally identified. The first two books may have been in a foreign language due to their general reference as illustrated costume books. The volume titled "Trachtbuch von allerley Teutscher unnd frembter Nation," may have been Hans

Weigel's *Trachtenbuch: Darin fast allerley und der fürnembsten Nationen die heutigs tags bekandt sein Kleidungen*, published in Nuremberg in 1577 (Weigel and Amman 1577). This section of the Kress inventory, also records costume books, maps, travelogues, and portraits, images of Roman emperors as well as a *Schembart-Buch* with carnival processions of masked people in Nuremberg and a "Bachelor Tournament on Paper" (*Gesellenstechen auf Paper*). All of these items show the collector's interest in larger vestimentary contexts, where clothing indicates social distinction. The *Gesellenstechen* of young Nuremberg nobles, equivalent to aristocratic tournaments, was a distinguishing feature of patrician identity. One is tempted to think of the large-sized color painting on paper by Jost Amman showing the last Nuremberg *Gesellenstechen* on March 3, 1561. The splendid armor of the combatants renders the event as one of the urban elite, but there is no indication that this painting, which is currently located at the Bavarian National Museum in Munich, is the same as in the painting in Kress's inventory record (Pilz 1932; Smith 1983, 275). Adolescent patricians participating in the *Schembartlauf* (carnival parades) wore fanciful costumes, and so, in the same way, the Roman imperial portraits were distinguished by their clothes and regalia.

The reconstruction of Paulus Praun's book collection also demonstrates the existence of costume books in the libraries of Nuremburg citizens (Isphording 1994, 95–99, Nr. 1787–1790). Among the 197 titles contained in the 1719 inventory, Ferdinando Bertelli's *Omnivm fere gentium nostrae aetatis habitvs* (1573) and Cesare Vecellio's *Habiti antichi & moderni di tutto il mondo* (2nd edition, 1598) are classical costume books. Jost Amman's ecclesiastical book of trades *Ständ und orden der heiligen Romischen Catholischen kirchen* (Estates and Orders of the Holy Roman Catholic Church), published in 1585, and Nicholas Nicolai's *Vier bücher von der raiß und schiffarth in die Türckey . . .* (Four books on the Trip and Sea Voyage to Turkey), published in 1576 in Antwerp, round off this collection. The latter book contained sixty-one male and female figures, "drawn from life, according to the different countries, and their use, with a description of the manner and life of each, both in peace and in war time" (Löcher 1994, 382–85, Kat. 216, 217).

Unfortunately, we cannot know what the costume book collection actually meant to Kress, or how he used it. Did he appreciate his costume books because, as Gabriele Mentges (2015, 149) stated, the genre communicated circumstances in fashion as well as ethnology in a graphic and entertaining way to the early modern reader? Did he view the "Moorish" shirts, "Indian" coats, and "Turkish" turbans more as costumes and masquerades or did he have a genuine ethnological interest in foreign clothing? In any case, we may assume that the Nuremberg patrician, who had left Germany only for those two years of study abroad in Bologna, used the clothing of distant countries to gain knowledge about known and unknown regions of the world.

Agents and provenances

While compiling his collection, Kress utilized agents to procure objects. From the extant correspondence, we also know that he especially asked his brothers residing abroad to look out for suitable exotic objects for purchase. Kress then absorbed the expenses, at times through barter transactions, or by fulfilling requests for goods from his homeland.

The clothing collection possibly profited from his brother Hieronymus Kress (1546–1596), who participated in a Spanish military campaign in Tunis. His war journal from the year 1571 until 1576 tells of the events that culminated in the capture of Tunis. Hieronymus Kress reported of many shot or stabbed "Moors" in the alleys and streets, and of the looting mercenaries: "Foremost, we have partially captured large volumes of Moorish dresses, made from beautiful silk, damask and gold delicately and beautifully, and also found much beautiful, soft pieces of linen and many silver rings which they wore, according to their custom, around the arms" (Loose 1881, 65). It is likely that Hieronymus Kress also helped himself here and sent his brother some coveted items. In any case, the inventory of the Kress collection includes both "Moorish clothes" and gilded silver bangles. At the same time, his brothers Karl (1550–1578) and Hans (1553–1576) sent him Roman medals and coins (Kress 1575). In February 1574, Hans Kress asked his brother Christoph for fur skins for boots, for which he promised "a Spanish dagger" or an "old Moorish cloth" "because there are many curious things in this country" (Kress 1572–1574).

As with Christoph Kress's entire estate, the collection "All Kinds of Foreign Nations' Clothing and the Like" (*Allerley Frembter Nationen klaidung und dergleichen*) was appraised according to its material value. Perhaps remarkably, the listed monetary amounts for the various pieces in the collection are not fundamentally different from those of the personal Western clothes of the deceased. Obviously, neither their complicated ways of acquisition nor the perceived exoticism of the objects influenced the appraisal values. A "Moorish shirt" at three guilders was appraised at the same amount as the "fine male shirt" some pages earlier. The "Indian dress" together with a pair of shoes was appraised at four guilders, the same amount the appraisers assessed the marten lining of a robe. A turban was appraised at a maximum of two guilders, the same apportioned for a velvet beret. Altogether, the appraisals were in the range of high-quality dresses of the period, but the peak value of fifty guilders for Kress's "best black coat with marten lining and a fur collar" (Kress 1584, 19r) was not matched by any other object, foreign or not.

Patrician Christoph Kress's collection demonstrates the ethnographic interests of early modern elites, spotlighting, in particular, yet another previously unpublished example of the Nuremberg context of social distinction and way of life (Rublack 2010, 194–206). Travel, books, and (art) collections constituted a significant part of elite education. This social performance was intertwined with personal interests and histories, as many of the leading Nuremberg families owed their reputation and prosperity to long-distance trade. Even though the collection no longer exists materially, the careful documentation of the objects in the inventory of the deceased demonstrates the social prominence that existed beyond the death of the collector, as well as the collector's cultural knowledge and symbolic pride in social rank and as part of the patrician family legacy.

Research perspectives connected to the evaluation of inventories and similar sources require the broadest possible data set to contextualize early modern clothing in the area of material culture. In the best possible case, the data will also include family and household books as well as diaries and letters that comment on the collection from the perspective of its users. The quantitative and qualitative analysis of these sources complements today's naturally external perspective on the historical dress code with contemporary insider views. To reflect the multifaceted realities of cultural life, historical vestimentary research must reach and analyze all its aspects and contexts.

Notes

1   Item Ein inndianisch Klaidt und Ein par schuch, zusammen umb fl. 4.-.-.
Item Ein seiden gestraimbten Mörischen Rock, sambt einem weißen hembt, umb fl. 4.-.-.
Item Zwey Mörische Hembter, umb fl. 6.-.-.
Item Ein weiß Mörisch Hembt mit roten Strichen umb fl. 3.-.-.
Mer ein ganntz weiß Mörisch Hembt umb fl. 1.-.-.
Item Ein Mörische Hauben umb fl. 1.-.-.
Mer Ein Mörisch guldes Heublein umb ein halben gulden, thut fl. -.4.6.

Item Ein ungerisch Rots Heublein um zehen kreutzer fl. -.1.12.

Item drey Par Türckisch Stifel, mer ein Par Schuch unnd ein Par Panndtoffel zusammen umb fl. 3.-.-.

Item zwo Türckisch Pünden mit gollt eingewürckten Leisten, eine umb zwen gulden, thut fl. 4.-.-.

Mer Ein schöne Türckische Pünden umb fl. 2.-.-.

Item zwo weiße Türckische Pünden, eine mit gestraimbten Leisten zusammen angeschlagen umb fl .3.-.-.

Item drey schlecht Türckische Pünden, eine umb eim gulden, thut fl. 3.-.-.

Mer Ein Türckische Pünden umb ein halben gulden, thut fl .-.4.6.

Item Ein Türckisch fatscheinlein von farben umb fl. 1.-.-.

Mer Ein schlechts türkisch fatscheinlein umb drei ort, thut fl. -.6.9.

Item Ein Türckisch fatscheinlein unnd ein solches Fatzinetlein zusammen umb fl. 1.-.-.

Item zwen Türckische Pögen mitsambt Köcher unnd Pfeuln, auch zwen Türckische schuch, zusammen umb fl. 2.4.6.

Item Ein ennglischer Poegen unnd Vierundzwaintzig Pfeiln Inn einem futter, zusammen umb fl. 2.-.-.

Item zwo Türckisch Gaißel zusammen umb fl. -.-.18.

Item vier Türckisch schlecht Pögen, zusammen umb fl. 1.-.-.

Item Ein Par Spitziger Panndtoffel mit Messing beschlagen umb zehen kreutzer, thut fl. -.1.12.

2   Item Ein Illuminirt Kunstbuch mit allerley frembten drachten Inn folio unnd Compert eingebundten, umb fl. 6.-.-. (34v)

Item mer Ein Illuminirt Kunstbuch mit allerley frembten drachten Inn folio und Compert eingepundten umb fl. 3.-.-. (35r)

Item Ein Trachtbuch von allerley Teutscher unnd frembter Nation umb fl. 2.-.-. (35r)

Item Ettliche gemehl Türckischer Tracht, in Quarto unnd weiß Compert eingepundten umb ein halben gulden thut fl. -.4. 6. (35v)

References

Arnold, Janet. 1988. *Queen Elizabeth's Wardrobe Unlock'd. The Inventories of the Wardrobe of Robes Prepared in July 1600 [...]*. Leeds: Maney.

Endres, Rudolf. 1983. "Das Schulwesen in Franken im ausgehenden Mittelalter." In *Studien zum städtischen Bildungswesen des späten Mittelalters und der frühen Neuzeit. Bericht über Kolloquien der Kommission zur Erforschung der Kultur des Spätmittelalters 1978 bis 1981*, edited by Bernd Moeller, Hans Patzke, and Karl Stackmann, 173–214. Göttingen: Vandenhoeck & Ruprecht.

Fink, August. 1963. *Die Schwarzschen Trachtenbücher.* Berlin: Deutscher Verein für Kunstwissenschaft e.V.

Fleischmann, Peter. 2008. *Rat und Patriziat in Nürnberg. Die Herrschaft der Ratsgeschlechter vom 13. bis zum 18. Jahrhundert.* 3 Volumes. Neustadt an der Aisch: PH.C.W. Schmidt.

Franke, Birgit, and Barbara Welzel. 2013. "Morisken für den Kaiser: Kulturtransfer?" In *Kulturtransfer am Fürstenhof. Höfische Austauschprozesse und ihre Medien im Zeitalter Kaiser Maximilians I,* edited by Matthias Müller, Karl-Heinz Spieß, and Udo Friedrich, 15–51. Berlin: Lukas-Verlag.

Hayward, Maria. 2007. *Dress at the Court of King VIII.* Leeds: Maney.

Heikamp, Detlef. 1970. "Mexikanische Altertümer in süddeutschen Kunstkammern." *Pantheon* 28: 205–20.

Isphording, Eduard. 1994. "Die Büchersammlung Paulus II. Praun." In *Die Kunstsammlung des Paulus Praun. Die Inventare von 1616 und 1719,* edited by Kathrin Achilles-Syndram, 95–99. Nürnberg: Selbstverlag der Stadt Nürnberg.

Knod, Gustav C. 1899. *Deutsche Studenten in Bologna (1289–1562): Biographischer Index zu den Acta nationis germanicae Universitatis bononiensis.* Berlin: Decker.

Kress, Christoph. 1584. *Reichsstadt Nürnberg XVIII Kress, Nr. 62, Inventar Christoph III Kress, 1584.11.7.* Historisches Archiv, *Germanisches Nationalmuseum.*

Kress, Christoph. Briefe 1575. *Kress-Archiv XXXIV, E, 22, Brief Christoph Kress an seinen Bruder Karl in Herrental, 1575.1.3.* Historisches Archiv, *Germanisches Nationalmuseum.*

Kress, Hans. Briefe 1572–74. *Kress-Archiv XXXIV, C, 31, 40, 48. Historisches Archiv, Germanisches Nationalmuseum.*

Kuhl, Isabel. 2008. *Cesare Vecellios Habiti antichi et moderni: Ein Kostüm-Fachbuch des 16. Jahrhunderts.* PhD dissertation, Universität Köln. Available at: http://kups. ub.uni-koeln.de/2878/

Löcher, Kurt, ed. 1994. *Kunst des Sammelns. Das Praunsche Kabinett. Meisterwerke von Dürer bis Carraci. Kat. Ausst. Germanisches Nationalmuseum, Nürnberg.* Nürnberg: Verlag des Germanischen Nationalmuseums.

Loose, Wilhelm. 1881. "Des Hieronymus Kress Kriegstagebuch 1571 bis 1576." *Mitteilungen des Vereins für Geschichte der Stadt Nürnberg* 3: 37–72.

Madersbacher, Lukas. 1992. *Hispania—Austria: Kunst um 1492. Die katholischen Könige Maximilian I. und die Anfänge der Casa de Austria in Spanien. Kunst um 1492. Katalog zur Ausstellung im, Schloss Ambras in Innsbruck.* Milan: Electa.

Mentges, Gabriele. 2007. "Pour une approche renouvelée des receuils de costumes de la Renaissance. Und cartographie vestimentaire de l'espace et du temps." *Apparence(s)* 1: 1–20.

Mentges, Gabriele. 2013. "Drawing Borders: Perceptions of the Cultural Other in Renaissance Costume Books." In *Fusion Fashion. Culture beyond Orientalism and Occidentalism,* edited by Gabriele Mentges and Gertrud Lehnert, 27–47. Frankfurt am Main: Internationaler Verlag der Wissenschaften.

Mentges, Gabriele. 2015. "Mode, Städte und Nationen: Die Trachtenbücher der Renaissance." In *In Mode. Kleider und Bilder aus Renaissance und Frühbarock. Ausstellung im Germanischen Nationalmuseum*, 144–51. Nürnberg: Verlag des Germanischen Nationalmuseums.

Michel, Eva. 2015. "zu ainer gedächtnüß hie auf erden: Albrecht Altdorfers Triumphzug für Kaiser Maximilian." In *Maximilians Ruhmeswerk. Künste und Wissenschaften im Umkreis Kaiser Maximilians I*, edited by Jan-Dirk Müller and Hans-Joachim Ziegeler, 381–94. Berlin u.a.: De Gruyter.

Mohrmann, Ruth-E. 2003. "Nachlaßinventare—Quellenkritik und Forschungsfragen." In *Volksleben im 19. Jahrhundert. Studien zu den bayrischen Physikatsberichten und verwandten Quellen. Wolfgang Zorn zum 80. Geburtstag*, edited by Peter Fassl and Rolf Kießling, 199–210. Augsburg: Veröffentlichungen der Schwäbischen Forschungsgemeinschaft, Reihe 10, Quellen zur historischen Volks- und Landeskunde, Band 2.

Paresys, Isabelle. 2006. "Images de l'autre vêtu à la Renaissance. Le recueil d'habits de Francois Desprez (1562–1567)." *Journal de la Renaissance* IV: 25–56.

Paulicelli, Eugenia. 2008. "Mapping the World. The Political Geography of Dress in Cesare Vecellio's Costume Book." *The Italianist* 28(1): 24–53.

Paulicelli, Eugenia. 2014. *Writing Fashion in Early Modern Italy: From Sprezzatura to Satire*. Farnham and Burlington: Ashgate.

Petrasch, Ernst. 1991. *Die Karlsruher Türkenbeute. Die "Türckische Kammer" des Markgrafen Ludwig Wilhelm von Baden-Baden. Die "Türckischen Curiositaeten" der Markgrafen von Baden-Durlach. Badisches Landesmuseum Karlsruhe*. München: Hirmer.

Pilz, Kurt. 1932. "Das Gesellenstechen in Nürnberg am 3. März 1561 von Jost Amman." *Zeitschrift für historische Waffen- und Kostümkunde* N. F4 (1932–1934), 74–80.

Rodenbeck, John. 2001. "Dressing Native." In *Unfolding the Orient. Travellers in Egypt and the Near East*, edited by Jane and Paul Starkey, 65–100. Reading: Ithaca.

Rublack, Ulinka. 2010. *Dressing Up: Cultural Identity in Renaissance Europe*. Oxford: Oxford University Press.

Rublack, Ulinka, and Maria Hayward. 2015. *The First Book of Fashion: The Book of Clothes of Matthäus & Veit Konrad Schwarz of Augsburg*. London: Bloomsbury.

Schilling, Michael. 1990. *Bildpublizistik der frühen Neuzeit. Aufgaben und Leistungen des illustrierten Flugblatts in Deutschland bis um 1700*. Tübingen: Niemeyer.

Scholler, Ernst. 1912. *Das Münzwesen der Reichsstadt Nürnberg im 16. Jahrhundert. Ein Beitrag zur reichsstädtischen Wirtschaftsgeschichte*. Nürnberg: Hilz.

Simon-Muscheid, Katharina. 2004. *Die Dinge im Schnittpunkt sozialer Beziehungsnetze. Reden und Objekte im Alltag (Oberrhein 14. bis 16. Jahrhundert). Veröffentlichungen des Max-Planck-Instituts für Geschichte, 193*. Göttingen: Vandenhoeck & Ruprecht.

Smith, Jeffrey Chipps. 1983. *Nuremberg: A Renaissance City, 1500–1618*. Austin: University of Texas Press.

Stolleis, Karen. 1977. *Die Gewänder aus der Lauinger Fürstengruft. Mit einem Beitrag über die Schmuckstücke von Irmtraud Himmelheber*. München and Berlin: Deutscher Kunstverlag.

Taylor, Lou. 2004. *Establishing Dress History*. Manchester and New York: Manchester University Press.

Trauth, Nina. 2009. *Maske und Person. Orientalismus und Porträt im Barock*. Berlin and München: Deutscher Kunstverlag.

van der Woude, Adrianus Maria, and Anton J. Schuurman. 1980. *Probate Inventories: A New Source for the Historical Study of Wealth, Material Culture and Agricultural Development*. Papers presented at the Leeuwenborch conference, Wageningen, May 5–7, 1980.

Vecellio, Cesare. 1590. *De gli Habiti antichi, et moderni di Diuerse Parti del Mondo libri dve* [...].Venice: Presso Damiano Zenaro.

von Frank, Karl Friedrich. 1936. *Die Kressen. Eine Familiengeschichte*. Schloß Senftengg: Frank zu Döfering.

von Kress, Georg. 1895. "*Briefe eines Nürnberger Studenten aus Leipzig und Bologna (1556-1560)*." *Mitteilungen des Vereins für Geschichte der Stadt Nürnberg 11*: 97–172, bes. *133*.

Wardwell, Anne E. 1988–89. "Panni Tartarici: Eastern Islamic Silks woven with Gold and Silver." In *Islamic Art: An Annual Dedicated to the Art and Culture of the Muslim World*, Vol. 3, 95–173. New York: Bruschettini Foundation for Islamic and Asian Art.

Weigel, Hans, and Jost Amman. 1577. *Habitus praecipuorum populorum, tam virorum quam foeminarum singulari arte depicti. Trachtenbuch: Darin fast allerley und der fürnembsten Nationen die heutigs tags bekandt sein Kleidungen [...]*. Nürnberg: Hans Weigel.

Wien KHM 2017. Accessed January 27, 2017. http://www.khm.at/it/objektdb/detail/543 719/?pid=2287&back=1035&offset=33&lv=listpackages-1342&cHash=33578435c 5e527248b6946395faec897

Zander-Seidel, Jutta. 1990. *Textiler Hausrat. Kleidung und Haustextilien in Nürnberg von 1500 bis 1650*. München: Deutscher Kunstverlag.

Zander-Seidel, Jutta, ed. 2015. *In Mode. Kleider und Bilder aus Renaissance und Frühbarock. Ausstellungskatalog. Germanisches Nationalmuseum, Nürnberg*. Nürnberg: Verlag des Germanischen Nationalmuseums.

Section Two

Materiality in motion: Global circuits of fashion

Introduction

As much as things are situated "in" time and place, they move through time and space, and also mobilize time and space. By being worn, carried, taken, given, and received, apparently immobile things become mobile. Through migration, exchange, gifting, or sale, and also through nonconsensual acts such as robbery, theft, and looting, material things are set in motion, entering new places and relationships. Such acts substantially transform the use, status, value, and meaning of things, as previous bonds between people and things are loosened or disrupted and made anew elsewhere. This does not mean that old bonds always or entirely dissolve. Just as an inherited, textile object can form generational ties, a fabric or piece of clothing can continue to entangle locally and globally distanced people and communities. As a part of those practices, things also "move" in a wider sense—for example through affect or arousing "emotion," at a personal level and in the wider historical senses of the word "emotion," tied to "motion" and "movement": as "agitation of mind," "disturbance," or "political unrest" (see *OED*). In this sense, materials can settle and unsettle. The material exchange, migration, and appropriation of things create a juxtaposition of many forms of relationship that drive the heterogenization of cultures (see Jones and Stallybrass 2000). Imported things may become attractive goods specifically for their "difference" or "foreignness," as Chapter 4, on the sixteenth-century collector Christoph Kress, has shown. But, by assigning things new uses and meanings, "foreign" things are also rendered or declared "own" things, so that they are no longer the same as they were where they originated, or where and when they were introduced. Through historical and contemporary case studies, this second section of the book provides insights into some of the histories, material practices and interconnections of locally and globally acting textile and fashion productions considering the examples of eighteenth-century chinoiserie fashion in Europe, golden embroidery in Uzbekistan, "chitenge" dress in Zambia, and fast fashion in China.

Geography has played a crucial role in the way humans have come to learn to envision and map place and distance, and so has, of course, the interconnected world of travel and trade that organizes the movement of human and nonhuman actors across place. Much research has centered on the role of raw materials such as silk, cotton, linen, and wool, as well as finished fabrics as movable goods or commodities in the historical development of markets. In fact, economic considerations give the greatest incentive to get things moving. This includes decision-making about whether an item is for sale and whether or when it can be purchased (Appadurai 1986, 17–29). The historical trade in fiber and cloth advanced a system that defined textiles as an "alternative currency" (Lemire 2005), or as being equivalent to money: "so it should come as no surprise that cloth wealth has enriched the treasuries of many kingdoms and chiefdoms, conferring credibility on political elites along with gold, silver, jewels and exotic shells" (Weiner and Schneider 1989, 2). It would be too limiting, however, to consider the dynamics of textile production as a key driver of the industrialization and globalization processes in economic terms only. It is also the specific materiality of textiles and clothing that showcases local techniques of making or singular patterns of decoration, which are important within the communities of trade and exchange. Textiles and cloth offer unique sensual encounters with a diversity of technological skills and, as such, reveal various forms of knowledge, use, and symbolic value (see also Lehnert and Mentges 2013, 8). The trade and consumption of textiles has led to the establishment of one of the most significant historic trade routes, the "Silk Road" (see Mentges 2005, 36). Spanning more than 5,000 miles, this major network of trails was used as a vast "east-west artery" to transport valuable goods between China and the Roman and Byzantine empires (Kaiser 2012, 15). The routes brought countries and cultures into close contact and mutual exchange. The early worldwide trade in fibers and textiles has not only been crucial to innovations in fashion but also to the development of geographic and global imaginaries.

While we learned that the sixteenth-century patrician, Christoph Kress, traveled from Nuremberg to as far as Bologna, Anne Gerritsen and Giorgio Riello remind us that, in early modernity, the "average European adult man or woman would have spent most of their life within a radius of just a few miles" (2015, 118). To travel from Europe to China and back would have been an undertaking of at least two years (Gerritsen and Riello 2015, 113). For many people who indulged in the "pleasure" offered by material things from foreign countries, this was therefore not by "being there" or by any kind of firsthand experience, but via "armchair" travel and study made possible through the circulation of materials: "The rich and literate became increasingly conscious of the expanding world that surrounded them via the printed media—both books and prints—and the richest prided themselves by collecting expensive artifacts from Asia, Africa and the New World" (Gerritsen and Riello 2015, 118). As Gerritsen and Riello note, it is then through the European import of materials such as porcelain (china) and cotton (indiennes) that the circulation of global commodities and imaginaries expanded across social classes over the course of the seventeenth and eighteenth centuries, and "came to embellish the interiors of rich and poor households alike" (2015, 111–12). In the first chapter of this section, Daniel Purdy examines the fashion of chinoiserie, which he describes as "material images circulating between China and Europe." He traces the eighteenth-century European fascination with the Chinese empire, together with its religion, philosophy, and courtly ritual. Ethnologists view the ability to integrate foreign things as a key driver for cultural change. Purdy provides insights into the interests of European humanists and monarchs and their wish to acquire knowledge about China, referring back to Gottfried Wilhelm von Leibnitz (1646–1716), who saw himself as an intermediary in publishing his correspondence with missionaries in China. At a time when the power of many European courts was being eroded, an empathic relationship with China was created through the import of chinoiserie on materials such as porcelain, silk, and paper, generating a global trade of patterns.

Within Europe the interest in the supposedly exotic was immense and was seen to represent a person's good taste. Drinking tea from a cup made in China, which featured a scene from a faraway world, created a very sensual pleasure of indulging through material objects with a distant place in the comfort of a person's home. As Purdy points out, the special value of foreign things was due to their distance traveled, which, for the transport of fragile materials such as fine porcelain, was not without its challenges, something that only increased their appreciation as a messenger from a distant culture, in a material as well as an imaginary sense. Purdy discusses the processes of remediation and decontextualization as the objects and images that came to circulate as chinoiserie became disconnected from any "original" or former narrative context, exemplifying what in today's context is associated with the dynamics of cultural appropriation. The Chinese manufacturers directed their design development toward the European style and market. Through the processes of dissemination and transformation, things were culturally appropriated at various levels (Ashley and Plesch 2002): through the Chinese tastemakers, through the European consumers, who fitted the Chinese materials, patterns, and objects into their own style, or through the producers themselves, such as the potters in Meissen, Delft or Worcester, who created their own imitations of "China" porcelain, which in turn influenced Chinese manufacturers. As these material images circulated between China and Europe, they facilitated, as Gerritsen and Riello argue, particular visualizations and imaginations of other worlds for producers and consumers: "Each will have interpreted what they saw depicted in his or her own way, and extrapolated a different imagined space from it. The object is what creates the connection, and what makes this a 'global imaginary'" (Gerritsen and Riello 2015, 119). While Purdy argues that the popularity of chinoiserie diminished with the French Revolution, it is an example of a global, or transnational, trading of patterns, and of the kind of decontextualization that fashion and commodity culture foster through processes of appropriation, translation, and transformation. Cultural traces of chinoiserie-like images and objects remain in wide circulation throughout various contexts today. Thuy Linh Nguyen Tu has shown this, for example, in her discussion of "Asian Chic" in late twentieth- and early twenty-first-century fashion design and imagery, specifically in her interpretation of the commodification of "Asianness" within Euro-American fashion as a "symbolic resolution of the dilemma of global interconnectedness" as a way to reassert distance and distinction in the light of cultural anxieties around immigration, outsourcing, and the increasing economic power of China (2010, 102–03).

In her chapter, Christina Moon expands the focus on the mobilization of political power through fashion as she follows the routes of fashion "Made in China" across various "fast-fashion cities"—Los Angeles, Hong Kong, Guangzhou, Shenzhen, and Shanghai. As she notes in her chapter, it is the transformation of China into a manufacturing powerhouse nation, as well as the ties across Chinese and Korean diasporic communities, that made American fast fashion possible. She ties her observations and reflections on the encounter with fashion across these globally connected sites, including places of manufacturing and trade, design schools, and their museums, to historical, political, and infrastructural changes. Through this, she shows how fast-fashion production shapes not only the materiality of clothing and fashion but also migration and urbanization processes together with the material landscape of cities, highlighting how, today, Chinese cities promote design as a strategy to upgrade and rebrand themselves from the "world's factory" to "design studio." In the wholesale market in Shanghai, she describes the merging of global fashion in one item of clothing as she encounters *shanzai*, or knock-off items, that turn the traditional hierarchies of art and design, high and low, original and copy, on their heads, with long-lasting consequences for social distinction strategies. At this point, too, a change of perspective seems appropriate when, on the basis of her observations, she highlights that the commonly perceived powerful "fashion cities," most notably New York, are not actually the center of the world, or the main interface for creative amalgamations.

In the late twentieth and early twenty-first century, the "globalization of fashion" has been especially associated with mass-produced fashion and the renouncement of country-specific variations of fashion and style in favor of globally uniform products. Multinational companies seem to be influencing consumers so that their fashion preferences are converging. And the increasing similarity between some worldwide economies together with the division of labor in textile and fashion production are also fueling this process. Yet, in this sense, the much-used term globalization describes primarily the supranationalist extension of markets. In such an application, the term fails to recognize that there exist well-functioning national and local production facilities that are neither totally separate from "global fashion" nor exclusively bound to "local tradition." Rather, in a context of increasing global interconnectedness, they are dynamic and important pillars of political, social, and national self-assertion. This is shown in the chapters by Lola Shamukhidinova and Karen Tranberg Hansen, who, through their fieldwork in Uzbekistan and Zambia, trace how diverse communities of craftspeople, designers, factory workers, and consumers manage their own fashion networks. The historically and currently emerging products, markets, and social networks are the opposite of a "powerless recipient of an imposed and total hegemony of western styles" (Ivaska 2003, 587). Rather, with their everyday textile and fashion practices, they constitute their own material discourse on questions of cultural, national, ethnic, and/or family identities.

In her chapter, Lola Shamukhidinova traces the history and revival of the old craft technique of golden embroidery in Uzbekistan and how it is tied to the various political changes the region underwent. Uzbekistan, one of the five *stans* (countries) of Central Asia, became an independent nation in 1991, following the breakdown of the Soviet Union. As such, this newfound independence was not the result of an already existing movement toward freedom, but "it occurred rather unexpectedly and unwillingly," posing a significant challenge: "namely to re-define and re-create the Soviet concept of ethnicity to be used in the resulting processes of nation building" (Mentges 2017, 11). Uzbekistan today has a population of ca. 32 million, made up of a large diversity of groups with various cultural backgrounds. As Gabriele Mentges notes, historically the "territorial border demarcations enacted by colonial powers" following a foreign, Western system of establishing national identity, "led to divisions and the fracturing of former territories, family networks and other ways of doing business and creating cultural customs" (2017, 16). With a focus on "fashioning heritage," Lola Shamukhidinova describes in her chapter how textiles are used to overcome the Soviet past and construct a new image of the nation, one that is interwoven with the narrative of Uzbekistan as the natural heir of the Silk Road, as its trade roads passed by several Uzbek cities, including Bukhara, the situated site of her research. In this sense, the revival of textile technologies, such as golden embroidery, is seen as a direct material continuation of the region's historical position at a major crossroads of the Silk Road. And moreover, this material narrative is used as a resource in the process of nation branding, which can be understood, following Mentges, as a "symbol orientated economization" (2017, 12) of culture and society, with the aim of participating in the "global showcase of fashion" (Skov 2011; Mentges 2017, 13). With a reorganization of the craft, traditional political and social hierarchies as well as archaic gender roles are modified as modern processing techniques are integrated. By modernizing the traditional luxury goods into a motif of national fashion and material for the heritage tourism industry, the country is trying to reunify, and to harmonize the numerous national conflicts that extend from the time of Soviet rule to the present.

Karen Tranberg Hansen observes something similar in her chapter, as she describes the "evolution" of chitenge, a printed cotton fabric and women's dress practice in Zambia. Fabric and dress are part of the colonial history, but also, since 1964, when Zambia became independent from British rule, a motif carrier and national dress of state independence. As she states, women in Zambia refer to it as their "traditional" dress, yet this identification is not only entangled with an ongoing process of changing national representations but also with the dynamics of global trade. As the colonial administration did not develop a domestic textile and garment industry in Zambia, chitenge was imported from various countries, including from Japan in the 1930s, though today it is imported primarily from China. Despite the transnational fabric sourcing, as Hansen shows, chitenge is considered *the* national textile emblem, having conquered a place in the Zambian fashion scene by being adopted and refined by local tailors as well as designers. She describes chitenge as an "invented tradition," which Eric Hobsbawn and Terence Ranger understand as practices that imply a certain "continuity with a suitable past" (1993, 1), where such continuity is usually fictitious, a response to the needs of a new situation (1993, 4), such as nation-building processes in postcolonial contexts, as discussed in the example of golden embroidery and the crafting of heritage in Uzbekistan (see Chapter 6). As Hansen notes, chitenge, or the women in chitenge, has withstood the effects of time, as the garment continues to be considered "traditional" since Zambia's gaining independence. But this withstanding of time, does not mean chitenge does not keep undergoing change, including the ways in which it is worn, or in its design—for example, when chitenge cloth is printed with images of cell phones, fusing past and present in its materiality. Indeed, Leslie Rabine reminds us how "tradition" is a concept inherited from colonial discourse (2002, 10). It is a concept tied to the construction of the "other" as static and unchanging outside (Western) modernity. Rabine states in her work on the globalization of African fashion: "Although local fashions mostly are encoded as traditional by their consumers, they are far from embodying the timeless, closed societies evoked by the colonial notions of tradition" (Rabine 2002, 11 cited in Jansen and Craik 2016, 10). Drawing on ethnographic research, Hansen offers insights into the tailoring, retail spaces, and wearers of chitenge in Zambia's capital, Lusaka. She shows how uses and perceptions of chitenge have changed over the course of the past decade, especially as it has become a vital part of the contemporary fashion scene in Zambia, being adopted as an identity-constituting tool by women of a much wider demographic.

"Through the process of neoliberal globalization," Gabriele Mentges notes, "traditional fashion hierarchies between old fashion centers and the periphery have changed considerably, generating new patterns of relations and by implication a new order of fashion cultures and economies" (2017, 13). The chapters in this section by Christina Moon, Lola Shamukhidinova, and Karen Tranberg Hansen make this evident in various ways. Despite the parallels that can be observed between the mobility of material strategies, including organizing self-presentation and creating identity and self-location through nation branding and fashioning heritage, it is clear that the national histories and myths inscribed in fashion, as well as the social lives of people, are specific and take different paths.

References

Appadurai, Arjun, ed. 1986. *The Social Life of Things: Commodities in Cultural Perspective*. Cambridge: Cambridge University Press.

Ashley, Kathleen, and Véronique Plesch. 2002. "The Cultural Processes of 'Appropriation.'" *Journal of Medieval and Early Modern Studies* 32(1): 1–15.

Gerritsen, Anne, and Giorgio Riello. 2015. "Spaces of Global Interactions: The Material Landscape of Global History." In *Writing Material Culture History*, edited by Anne Gerritsen and Giorgio Riello, 111–33. London: Routledge.

Hobsbawn, Eric, and Terence Ranger, eds. 1993. *The Invention of Tradition*. Cambridge: Cambridge University Press.

Ivaska, Andrew. 2003. "'Anti-Mini Militants Meet Modern Misses': Urban Style, Gender, and Politics of National Culture in 1960s Dar es Salaam, Tanzania." *Gender & History* 14(3): 584–607.

Jansen, M. Angela, and Jennifer Craik. 2016. "Introduction." In *Modern Fashion Traditions: Negotiating Tradition and Modernity through Fashion*, edited by M. Angela Jansen and Jennifer Craik, 1–21. London: Bloomsbury.

Jones, Ann Rosalind, and Peter Stallybrass. 2000. *Renaissance Clothing and the Materials of Memory*. Cambridge: Cambridge University Press.

Kaiser, Susan B. 2012. *Fashion and Cultural Studies*. Oxford: Berg.

Lehnert, Gertrud, and Gabriele Mentges, eds. 2013. *Fusion Fashion: Culture Beyond Orientalism and Occidentalism*. Frankfurt am Main: Peter Lang.

Lemire, Beverly. 2005. "Shifting Currency: The Culture and Economy of the Second Hand Trade in England, *c.*1600–1850." In *Old Clothes, New Looks: Second Hand Fashion*, edited by Alexandra Palmer and Hazel Clark, 29–47. London: Bloomsbury.

Mentges, Gabriele, ed. 2005. *Kulturanthropologie des Textilen*. Berlin: ebersbach & Simon.

Mentges, Gabriele. 2017. "Introductory Remarks." In *Textiles as National Heritage: Identities, Politics and Material Culture*, edited by Gabriele Mentges and Lola Shamukhidinova, 9–28. Münster: Waxmann.

Rabine, Leslie. 2002. *The Global Circulation of African Fashion*. Oxford: Berg.

Skov, Lise. 2011. "Dreams of Small Nations in a Polycentric Fashion World." *Fashion Theory* 15(2): 137–56.

Tu, Thuy Linh Nguyen. 2010. *The Beautiful Generation*. Durham: Duke University Press.

Weiner, Annette B., and Jane Schneider, eds. 1989. *Cloth and Human Experience*. Washington DC: Smithsonian Books.

5

Chinoiserie in fashion: Material images circulating between China and Europe

Daniel Leonhard Purdy

Gottfried Wilhelm Leibniz's *Novissima Sinica*, published in 1697, is often cited as the most important philosophical treatise testifying to the European elite's fascination with China at the end of the seventeenth and the start of the eighteenth century (see Purdy and Brandt 2016). Like many others, the German philosopher Leibniz had read the treatises written by Jesuit priests in China (see Strasser 2012). Jesuit missionaries had arrived in China more than a hundred years earlier and quickly integrated themselves into China's administrative elite by adopting their scholarly habits, philosophies, and vestimentary styles (see Figure 5.1), allowing them to gain access to important officials and inner circles. Europeans learned about China through the annual letters, historical treatises, and translations of canonical Chinese texts sent by the Jesuits to European courts (see Mungello 1985; Hsia 2010). These works were eagerly read by scholars, collectors, and aristocrats, including Leibniz, who were drawn to the image of a peaceful and ancient civilization in the Far East (Strasser 2012). Leibniz, who had never traveled to Asia, aspired to become a central intermediary, eager to learn about China and the Jesuits stationed there. By circulating his correspondence with missionaries in Asia publicly, he hoped to provide Europeans with the newest information from China. In his preface to *Novissima Sinica*, Leibniz praised Chinese manners as setting a standard that Europeans could only hope to emulate. He admired China as a ritualized society in which polite ceremonies held great importance.

> So great is obedience toward superiors and reverence toward elders, so religious, almost, is the relation of children to parents, that for children to contrive anything violent against their parents, even by word, is almost unheard of. . . . Moreover there is among equals, or those having little obligation to one another, a marvelous respect and an established order of duties. (Leibniz 1957, 70)

Figure 5.1 Peter Paul Rubens' portrait of Nicholas Trigault, a Flemish Jesuit missionary in China, 1617. The portrait was painted while Trigault visited the city of Antwerp for fund-raising purposes. He wears a Korean cap and the robe of a Chinese scholar. *Photo*: Metropolitan Museum of Art.

With a friendly nod to his Jesuit informants, Leibniz recommended that the Chinese send their own missionaries to Europe: "we need missionaries from the Chinese who might teach us the use and practice of natural religion, just as we have sent them teachers of revealed theology" (Leibniz 1957, 75). After decades of religious wars between Protestants and Catholics, Leibniz believed that the Chinese were exemplary for both their lawful obedience to the emperor and their tolerant manner of thinking about religion.

Leibniz's proposal did not come to pass. Confucian scholars were never sent to proselytize in Europe, largely because Europeans were far more interested in acquiring luxury goods from the Middle Kingdom. Leibniz well understood this fact, for his patron, Duke Anton Ulrich von Brunswick-Wolfenbuettel, had himself brought together one of Germany's largest collections of Asian porcelain and art at his palace, Schloss Salzdahlum. Built just outside the small town of Wolfenbuettel in Lower Saxony, Salzdahlum had been designed in 1688 to emulate Versailles, the grand estate built outside Paris by the French monarch Louis XIV (Marth 2005). The French image of Chinese pagodas, latticed teahouses, pagodas, and Confucian temples was integral to the design of Versailles' pleasure pavilion (Honour 1961, 53), and this was mimicked by Salzdahlum, with, among other things, a Chinese pagoda erected in the gardens (Marth 2005, 585–86). The duke's palace was extolled throughout Central Europe for its Chinese art and porcelain collections, including 8,000 Asian porcelain specimens, along with lacquerware and soapstone sculptures (Querfurt 1710). While an inventory of clothes does not exist, later reports suggest that Chinese garments were available for celebrations, for example, at the wedding ball of the future Prussian monarch Friedrich II to princess Elizabeth Christine, all the principal participants wore Asian costumes (Glaser 1871, 105–7). Because Leibniz was very familiar with the Salzdahlum palace and its collections, it is unlikely that the Jesuits were the only inspiration for his enthusiasm about China. Rather, his patron's dedication to collecting Chinese luxuries from porcelain to silk must also be acknowledged as the material source of Leibniz's understanding of China. While chinoiserie has never received the same intellectual consideration as Leibniz's Jesuit-inspired philosophy, its importance to courtiers was undeniable.

Drawing on recent media theory, in particular the concept of remediation, this chapter examines the European fascination for these Chinese and Chinese-inspired commodities. It will show that chinoiserie, as the fashionable adoption of Chinese styles, demonstrated many of the qualities associated with later fashion culture. It will further show how contemporary theories about fashionable media in a global context can be used to understand the elite culture of European courts at the start of the eighteenth century.

Chinoiserie fashion

Chinoiserie began as craze among European courts to display and enjoy wealth through the importation of Chinese luxury goods such as silk fabrics, porcelain ceramics, and lacquered wood furniture as well as tea, spices, and medicines. Historically, the chinoiserie fashion is commonly divided into two phases: the first being the last decades of the seventeenth century, during the reign of Louis XIV. During this phase, Chinese luxuries were associated directly with the baroque style of architecture and painting that reinforced the monarchical authority of the absolute European prince. The second phase was far more playful and fantastical: it emerged, with its own distinctiveness, after the death of the great French monarch, and it is commonly associated with rococo styles in art. During this second phase, European producers of porcelain and silk developed techniques that could compete with Chinese and Indian manufacturers, making it possible for chinoiserie fashions to eventually reach the middle classes. For example, Dutch weavers (see Figure 5.2) outmaneuvered their French and English competitors by producing cloths that very closely imitated the feel and

Figure 5.2 *Gown à la française* with a chinoiserie pattern. Silk satin with silk and metal thread. Amsterdam, Netherlands (1740–1760). *Photo*: Los Angeles County Museum of Art.

look of Chinese silk (Corrigan et al. 2015, 326). Because the first adoption of Chinese luxuries was so closely linked with specific court cultures, it is important to distinguish between different enunciations of the style. English enthusiasm was perhaps more muted when compared with the major investments in Chinese designs made in France and the Central European courts that followed its lead (Porter 2001). The close connection chinoiserie had with monarchical authority meant that it eventually drew the ire of critical Enlightenment intellectuals and, by the second half of the eighteenth century, chinoiserie in silk, porcelain, and paper attracted all the typical denunciations leveled against courtly luxury: inauthentic, feminine, superstitious, elitist, ornamental, and unrestrained in its silly enjoyment of itself (see Krubsacius 1759; Porter 2010). One of the major criticisms of chinoiserie, both in the eighteenth century and today, is that it distorted and decontextualized Chinese art and objects by placing them within a European courtly setting. Chinoiserie made the foreign harmless by reducing it to triviality, domesticating it, so that it could, for example, be painted on the wall of a neoclassical villa (Hallinger 1996). In a sense, the importation of Asian commodities reversed the Jesuit strategy of adapting to Chinese culture.

Chinoiserie embodies quite visibly the early modern tendency to borrow, reproduce, and transfer images and texts from one material or medium to another (see Ducret 1973; Cassidy-Geiger 1996). Whereas seventeenth- and eighteenth-century adaptations of Classical art and architecture develop with subtle shadings of differences between styles, the outburst of Asian images and materials within the European arts provides more distinct traces of how emulation and elaboration inspired individual works. Understanding fabrics, not only in terms of materials such as cotton and silk but also as media, is by no means unusual in fashion studies. A conference at the Abegg Stiftung in Riggisberg, Switzerland, examined Asian elements in a variety of fashionable media such as "woven silks, embroideries, tapestries, costumes, wallpaper, ceramics and music" (Jolly 2007, 7). Without indulging in the curatorial fantasy of finding an Asian original for every European or American copy, we can detect the media routes that supplied the upper-class fashion for Chinese luxuries, while spotting a few direct connections between images.

The material allure of foreign luxuries

The first impression Chinese silk conveyed was associated with the great distance it had traveled. Its presence in Europe pointed both to its origins hidden in China and its transport across the globe by Portuguese and Dutch merchants. Chinese silk was lightweight with a lustrous color and glossy finish, marvelous material qualities that heightened the wonder at the long passage it had undergone. Starting in the Middle Ages, the fabric had been associated with royal pleasure, with the rank and beauty of the person wearing Chinese silk reinforcing the awe of the fabric's materiality. In Gottfried von Strassburg's thirteenth-century epic tale of adultery, when the Irish queen Isolde wanted to attract her knightly lover Tristan, she lay down in her garden on a bed covered with shiny silk blankets (von Strassburg 1988, 238). The allure of luxury goods is usually linked to the difficulty of their acquisition. However, Chinese silk was not merely expensive, it was a precarious material mystery; its journey was risky beyond what most land dwellers could grasp, and its design dramatically different than anything woven in Europe. Like porcelain or lacquered wood, silk felt dissimilar to anything else one could touch.

The figures embroidered onto fashionable silk often depicted the utopian setting in which they would be used. The idyllic scenes showing Chinese figures in gardens were self-conscious references to the locales that aristocrats sought to emulate in their own pleasure gardens. There was a visual match between the setting painted on a teacup, the figures embroidered onto fashionable robes, and the physical place in which the cup was raised and the robe worn. Chinoiserie paintings taught the European consumer how to indulge in a tea ceremony, for instance. These illustrations of peaceful Chinese gardens provided a *mise en abyme* of fashion's ceremonial location. A typical example of this kind of self-referential, fashionable image was a Meissen coffee pot, decorated with a painting of a wealthy Chinese man holding a tray full of porcelain containers with steaming hot contents. This loop from ornamentation to social guidebook reinforced the spatial circuit that enabled luxury consumption. Through its reliance on images as both ornaments and examples of social ritual, chinoiserie became a complete design principle, extending from utensils and clothes to furniture and the garden, from the smallest item to the entire environment, so that every element fitted into a coordinated ensemble.

While chinoiserie painters such as Jean-Antoine Watteau and François Boucher worked with traditional painterly surfaces and oils, the fashion for China insisted that the material on which images were placed had to be just as strikingly foreign as the visible forms themselves. Form and materiality were combined in the European fashion for Chinese fabrics. For an Asian luxury to succeed as a fashion statement in the European context, it had to not only look like it came from afar but also have the feel and texture of a unique, exotic substance. In many cases, the material surfaces upon which chinoiserie images appeared lent these commodities the quality of media—they seemed to convey a visual and material representation of a foreign culture, even as they performed all the other functions of luxury fashion. As it happened, the three materials most commonly associated with China—silk, paper, and porcelain—were also surfaces on which images could be displayed. As with porcelain, Chinese manufacturers catered to European tastes by embroidering or weaving motifs into silks that were then exported to the West to be tailored into dresses, screens, furniture fabrics, and wall hangings. Emulation flowed in both directions: Chinese painters applied European images to silk and porcelain while European artisans copied images from Chinese novels and ceramics.

From early on, Asian fabrics shared decorative motifs with ceramics. What we today call "remediation" (see Bolter and Grusin 1999) was, in the premodern era, the well-understood tendency for porcelain painters to adapt patterns used in weaving or printing cloth to the surface of their ceramics. In Japan, the blue-and-white designs on Kakiemon porcelain were based on complex textile prints, Ukiyo-e prints, and illustrated books (Berg 1998, 398). Japanese porcelain was itself derived from China, where the integral connection between fabrics and porcelain had already been well established. The T'ao Shuo, a thesaurus of porcelain developed under Chinese emperor Chia-ching (1521–1566), described how porcelain motifs were copied from fabrics:

> Porcelain enameled in colours was painted in imitation of the fashion of brocaded silks, and we have consequently the names of blue ground, yellow ground, and brown-gold ground. The designs used to decorate it were also similar, and including coiling dragons, clouds and phoenixes, kilin, lions, mandarin-ducks, myriads of gold pieces, dragon medallions, pairs of phoenixes, peacocks, sacred storks, the fungus of longevity, the large lion in its lair, wild geese in clouds with their double nests, large crested waves . . . dragons pursuing pearls, lions playing with embroidered balls, water-weeds and sporting fish. These are the names of ancient brocades, all of which the Imperial potters in designing and colouring porcelain have reproduced more or less exactly. (Slomann 1953, 21)

When Europeans began to manufacture goods in emulation of Chinese wares in the early eighteenth century, they adopted this tendency to transfer decorations from one medium to another, even if they did not always rely on traditional Asian materials. As the art historian Hans Belting has noted, this migration of images from one medium to another is hardly unusual in European art history (Belting 2011). For a striking example of how chinoiserie images are transferred between media, we can turn to designs etched into British-made silverware in the eighteenth century that were inspired by Chinese embroidered silk (Williams 2016, 110). The images painted onto the first generations of European manufactured porcelain in the eighteenth century were imitations of illustrations in Chinese manuscripts belonging to the ducal collection in Dresden, Germany. In general, chinoiserie is made possible by the separation of image and text, where images take on their own meaning without being embedded in an explanatory narrative. Art historians today try to situate images in a historical and theoretical frame, but for eighteenth-century decorators, chinoiserie was the result of their inability to read Chinese. This tendency to borrow Chinese images was obvious when European porcelain production first began in Dresden. Painters at the Meissen porcelain manufactory in Germany, such as Johann Gregor Höroldt, copied images without understanding their social context in China, especially if they depicted recognizable domestic scenes (Dennis 1963). In these cases, Chinese figures could be copied and adapted without the painters having to read the language (Cassidy-Geiger 1998, 35). This decontextualization of images from any specific, written account of their context soon became a favored practice across Europe, wherever copies of Chinese commodities were being produced.

Fashionable emulation: The many sources for chinoiserie

The tendency to borrow images from Chinese sources went far beyond porcelain, to include most materials involved in the chinoiserie style. Stacey Sloboda underscores the importance of emulation over originality:

> Images of playing children and slender ladies frolicking amidst vast, "uncircumscribed" landscapes specked with pagodas and temples were not born from European ignorance or imagination of Chinese culture, but rather from a complex and piecemeal network of images, objects, and texts that circulated within and between Europe and Asia. (Sloboda 2014, 34)

Beverly Lemire and Giorgio Riello (2008) argue that the diffusion of Indian and Chinese patterns and fabrics needs to be understood in terms of global trade patterns, suggesting that the older model of Europeans importing Asian luxuries does not accurately describe the diffuse routes and directions fashionable goods took. They further challenge the presumption that Asian societies did not develop their own distinct patterns of fashionable consumption. Their questions raise the fascinating problem of understanding how design patterns on luxury goods circulated across cultures, inspiring new fashionable products in many directions. Astrid Erll (2014) addresses similar queries in terms of media theory, specifically the process of remediation—in which forms from one medium are applied and revised within another. Erll augments the classical communications model (sender: transmission: receiver) to take account of how artifacts are produced, transferred, and then appropriated in a process that can lead to their remediation with a long subsequent afterlife as a collected work of art. In discussing the transmission of objects between Asia and Europe, Erll points out that channels of communication were frequently quite precarious, as seen in the case of ocean voyages. The Dutch East India Company may have dominated its colonies, but sea voyages were always risky. A more important amendment to the classical communication model requires us to recognize and follow the many directions in which messages flow. Not only did the Dutch and Portuguese send manuscripts on several ships with the understanding that they might not all arrive, but foreign influences were also often dispersed in different directions. Therefore, Chinese motifs might be spread across the Pacific to artisans in the Andes as well as to those around Africa or in European centers (Peck 2013).

The history of shipping Chinese products demonstrates that the material quality of an object affects its transportation as well as its long-term survival. Silks and cotton textiles were readily carried on board but were much less likely to survive undamaged as they were passed down through generations of European consumers. Porcelain, while harder as a material, and able to withstand wear and tear better than cloth, was still vulnerable to being smashed either by clumsiness or the violence of war. So, it is no surprise that prints were more easily transported than large oil canvases, yet they may have been treated with less regard once they had arrived.

The process of remediation—in which artifacts are replicated in new material forms—alters the simple transmission model. If a message is copied and revised once it has been received, only then to be transmitted back again, a spiral sequence starts to unfold that calls into question the importance of an "original" transmission (see Erll 2014). As many critics have argued, terms such as "hybrid" imply the existence of some pristine identity that is then mixed, an assumption few would want to make. Certainly, within the markets of the Indian Ocean and East Asia, artisans were already engaged in gathering inspiration from new sources.

Through the widespread circulation of images both as ornaments and as examples of social ritual, chinoiserie became a complete design principle, extending from the smallest implement to an entire environment, so that every element could fit into a coordinated cosmopolitan ensemble. In contrast to canvas paintings in the Chinese manner, chinoiserie commodities in the form of, for example, a calligraphic manuscript, a porcelain tea service, or a silk robe *à la française* offered Europeans the double fascination of foreign images on exotic materials. Lacquered boxes and furniture were likewise marked as Asian by their unique treatment of surfaces.

While the materials of chinoiserie fashion goods were not interchangeable, the images depicted on their surfaces often were. Pictures were regularly transferred from one medium to another, particularly once European manufacturers were able to replicate the production of Chinese materials, such as silk and porcelain in the early eighteenth century. Early Meissen pieces were often decorated with Chinese scenes derived from travel literature or Chinese manuscripts. The sources for Chinese motifs on fabrics were not very different from those that inspired porcelain painting and interior decorations: "If the origin of the designs used for the *chinoiserie* fabrics woven in Holland is explored, it becomes clear that many of the 'Chinese' elements do in fact derive from the travelers' tales which were published with some success in the 17th century" (Colenbrander 2013, 116). While early Jesuit treatises on China had few illustrations, the memoirs of the Dutch traveler, Johan Nieuhof (1655), about a Dutch diplomatic trip to China were filled with almost 150 plates based on drawings made by the author. The Jesuit polymath, Athansius Kircher, published *China Illustrata* (1667) soon thereafter. Without having left his teaching position in Rome, Kircher collected descriptions from his colleagues in Asia and produced a, sometimes fanciful, array of images, including striking scenes of temples with pagan gods. Around 1700, pattern books that showed Chinese ornaments based on these earlier works began to appear and serve as the basic source for artists interested in designing in the Chinese manner (Ulrichs 2007). As the number of books with Western images of China proliferated, so too did the mix-and-match variations in European-designed chinoiserie. As Frederike Ulrichs notes, the original drawings made by Nieuhof were adapted to the expectations of the Amsterdam book market, and then inevitably altered further as they were used in the design of fashionable commodities over the following decades (Ulrichs 2007; see also Standaert 2005). By rearranging illustrations originally intended to convey visual information into purely decorative tables, the correlation between image and reference was soon replaced by questions of taste. Just as baroque compilations about the wider world readily set curious tales from the Americas alongside wonders from Asia, so could visual ensembles place flora and fauna together on the same page without concern for the natural order. Indeed, the great discovery of chinoiserie was how pleasing such disorder could become (Schmidt 2015, 328). The stranger the juxtapositions appeared, the more the viewer's delight grew. What seemed like willful ignorance to learned missionaries back then and cultural critics today was, at the start of the eighteenth century, an aesthetic strategy that gathered together forms and materials in order to revel in their paradoxical convergence in Europe. Without question, chinoiserie reflects the amazement felt by many consumers at the strange diversity available to them, if not to purchase then at least to gaze upon. At the same time, it also reveals how far removed these celebrants of Chinese leisure and luxury were from the country they believed to understand. Anthropological notions of authenticity did not yet oblige consumers to carefully weigh the differences between cultures in order to show their respect and understanding of these distant peoples. So long as China appeared to Europeans solely on mediating surfaces, such as paper, silk, and porcelain, it could remain as imaginations. Empathetic bonds that extended beyond simple representations would emerge only later in the eighteenth century. In time, as publishers offered a greater variety of perspectives on China, the stock figures of chinoiserie became less amusing. And, ultimately, the amusing parallels that chinoiserie proposed between aristocrats and Chinese scholar-officials fell victim to the French Revolution.

Chinoiserie as a fashion insisted and thrived on the otherness of both form and image; as a luxury good, it had to establish itself as alien before it deserved to be incorporated into aristocratic spaces. Of course, the eagerness with which the French monarch and absolutist court adopted Chinese images and materials grew out of their identification with the authority and the leisure of the Chinese emperor and his administrative elite. Chinoiserie images thus vary from the terrifying to the comical, from the august to the idyllic. This coupling of power and pleasure guaranteed that chinoiserie would garner the reprobation and envy of those classes excluded from this circle. While the increasingly large-scale production of chinoiserie commodities raised the promise that ever wider circles of the middle class could share in the leisure and legitimacy afforded by the court's emulation of China's elite, the Enlightenment formulated moral and aesthetic dismissals of chinoiserie that still color contemporary scholarship (see Johns 2016). Chinoiserie was denounced as inauthentic, both in artistic and anthropological terms: the style did not embody the originality of creative genius, a key Enlightenment value, nor did it accurately represent the Chinese people. In either case, the fashion for Chinese ornaments was treated as a distortion. Of course, these arguments required critics to ignore the deliberately comical and grotesque qualities of chinoiserie as a genre.

Chinoiserie as embodied images

Even though silk and porcelain were treated as flat surfaces, comparable to paper, upon which images could be woven and painted, they also created volume and dimension. Porcelain vases were round-shaped and fabrics wrapped the body as loosely hung drapings or as tightly fitted bodices and vests. The fabrics were shaped by the bodies they covered, and thus the material environment of chinoiserie interiors cannot be treated as just a collection of printed surfaces, since they were also implements at the service of the inhabitants. The European fascination for Chinese fabrics did not translate into alterations of the cut and design of fashionable clothes. When Jesuit missionaries in China adopted the garb of scholar-administrators who served the court in Beijing, they accepted a very different relationship between dress and body. This different look might hint at liturgical gowns, which surprised Europeans whenever a missionary returned, as shown in Rubens' portrait of Nicholas Trigault on a trip to Europe to raise funds (see Figure 5.1). Chinese fabrics were integrated into existing European conventions about how the costumes were supposed to envelope the body. As Kimberly Chrisman-Campbell notes, "the fundamental outer garments—the three-piece suit for men and the three-piece ensemble of dress, petticoat, and stomacher for women—remained the same from the early to the late eighteenth century" (2013, 17). For formal events, the robe *à la française* remained the canonical design for women at the French court; chinoiserie simply introduced new patterns. As Johannes Hallinger argued, chinoiserie in the eighteenth century was enframed or even "tamed" within long-established European traditions of decoration (Hallinger 1996). Thus, new Chinese figures and patterns might be continuously introduced, but they were usually placed within a familiar, often classical, architectural framework. Much of the same could be argued for clothes: Asian fabrics did not alter the strictures of formal wear. At most, the loose shape of some Asian garments served as the template for private robes. For example, the men's banyan dressing gown (see Figure 5.3), worn in private, allowed for a more relaxed comfort inspired by the caftan (Jolly 2007, 10).

The gown shown in Figure 5.2 was produced in Amsterdam after restrictions on importing silk woven in China were enforced in England and France. The dress pattern features the stereotypical figures of a rococo idyll set somewhere in China: the figure of a Confucian scholar, a Chinese lady resting under an umbrella, fantastical pagodas, imagined country huts, dragon birds, and immensely overgrown flowering plants (Colenbrander 2013, 118; Takeda and Spilker 2013, 58). The images are of unnatural, disproportionate sizes, so that

Figure 5.3 Man's at-home robe (banyan); robe from the Netherlands dated 1750–1760, made from Chinese textile, silk satin, and silk plain weave (*damassé*) dated 1700–1750. *Photo*: Los Angeles County Museum of Art.

the bird is much larger than the garden house. David Mitchell suggests that such shifts in scale may have prompted many "bizarre" patterns (Mitchell 2007, 30). The images on the gown suggest a leisurely setting even though the robe *à la française* was designed for formal ceremonies. Even though the decorative images seem to not synchronize with the gown's design, we must understand that even leisure in a garden was carefully ritualized. The dress enacts a formal relationship with the body that is contrasted to some degree by the interpreted, idyllical Chinese figures on the fabric.

Just as courtly spaces formed a continuum of ritualized behavior, the interior decor of chinoiserie rooms formed a gradation of stylized commodities centered around the body. Georg Simmel may have been the first to develop a spatial sociology of the body and its decoration, but the courtiers at Versailles were clearly aware of how proximity to the private body of the king was, in itself, a sign of social status (Elias 1979). After a survey of French and English collections,

Mitchell suggests that chinoiserie was used as a decorative principle primarily in more intimate rooms, such as the bed chambers (Mitchell 2007). Mimi Hellman brilliantly explains how the entire ensemble of a chinoiserie boudoir revolved around the body and its pleasures:

> It should be clear by now that social seduction in eighteenth-century France was impossible without furniture. Objects were like extensions of the body, part of a wardrobe that, correctly worn, could turn the activities of elite existence into dances of artful persuasion. The wardrobe analogy is really very apt, for the way in which furniture simultaneously valorized the body and controlled its conduct is closely related to the aesthetic and social impact of clothing. (Hellman 2006, 23)

We could add, of course, the gardens to suggest that the style was associated more with bodily repose and leisure than with the august formality of court ceremony. Mitchell (2007) goes on to suggest that there was no gender distinction in the Continental taste for chinoiserie, even though English commentators tended to consider the collection of such finery a feminine preoccupation. In response to the discrepancies between English and Continental chinoiserie, Michael Elia Yonan suggests that we ought not look for a single, unified style but instead "conceptualize multiple and overlapping *chinoiseries*, each with different configurations, in order to address its fullness and complexity" (2004, 657). Such an approach would allow distinctions between chinoiserie in Dresden and in London, thereby avoiding the very English assertion that Augustus II the Strong was effeminate because of his fascination with Japan, an argument that Jonas Hanway put forward in his travel description of Dresden, wherein he mocks porcelain by associating it with Catholicism, femininity, absolute monarchy, secrecy, and superstition (Hanway 1753).

If we compare the earnest representations of China in the seventeenth century with the playful figures decorating material culture in the middle of the eighteenth century, we can recognize different phases of chinoiserie. There was a self-conscious difference between the missionary effort to assimilate into the elite Chinese culture that Leibniz so admired and the European elite's adoption of Chinese figures in its own fashionable dress. Whereas Rubens' portrait of the missionary Nicolas Trigault (Figure 5.1) depicts the attempt to blend into Chinese dress norms, the portrayal takes that relationship as the basis for its own signification. If Trigault's dress signifies European assimilation into China, the robe *à la française* (see Figure 5.2) represents a second level of connotation that seeks to incorporate the missionary attitude back into European fashion. The figure of the Chinese scholar appears as an ornament on a European garment rather than as an idealized image of how to dress differently (Hallinger 1996). To understand the affected self-consciousness of late chinoiserie, we might revive Roland Barthes' hierarchy of connotations described in *The Fashion System* (1983), for it helps explain how the Jesuit strategy of accommodating Chinese culture through dress is subsumed within the second-order signification of chinoiserie. This second order of connotation entails a reversal in the original order of signifier to signified. To put structuralist semiotics into historical terms, the two manners of dress reflect a shift in the cultural dynamic between China and Europe: whereas the missionary in Chinese robes seeks to introduce European culture to China through conformity, chinoiserie adapts this earlier fascination with China into a sign within its own syncretic fashion. The figure of the learned Chinese scholar wearing robes is no longer an ideal to emulate but rather a signifying image. Chinoiserie reincorporates the earlier European awe and respect for Chinese culture back into its own court rituals.

Whereas romantics and modernists would characterize such second-order reflections as ironic, in the early modern period they were perceived as theatrical and comical. Thus, many chinoiserie figures share their space with stock *commedia dell'arte* characters, for these Italian comedians were a popular mode for depicting and laughing along with self-conscious posturing. Chinoiserie ends at the point when Chinese gowns have become a staple costume in theater and recognizable design in fashion. In other words, when they have lost their strangeness.

As a living fashion, chinoiserie faded away at the late eighteenth century, when romantic artists began to emphasize the importance of originality and authenticity. As a style that was based upon the endless circulation of the same images copied from a handful of illustrated books, chinoiserie was eventually displaced by new styles that claimed to speak in a more authentic voice. The aristocratic tendency to recycle and resuscitate the same self-congratulatory images came to a sudden stop with the French Revolution. Among the many victims of this political upheaval was the old court's fascination with China as an "exotic" empire.

References

Barthes, Roland. 1983. *The Fashion System*. Translated by Matthew Ward and Richard Howard. Berkeley: University of California Press.

Belting, Hans. 2011. *An Anthropology of Images: Picture, Medium, Body*. Translated by Thomas Dunlop. Princeton: Princeton University Press.

Berg, Maxine. 1998. "Manufacturing the Orient, Asian Commodities and European Industry 1500–1800." In *Prodotti e Techniche D'Oltremare nelle Economie Europee Secc. XIII-XVIII*, edited by Simonette Cavaciocchi, 385–419. Florence: Le Monnier.

Bolter, Jay David, and Richard Grusin. 1999. *Remediation: Understanding New Media*. Cambridge: MIT Press.

Cassidy-Geiger, Maureen. 1996. "Graphic Sources for Meissen Porcelain: Origins of the Print Collection in the Meissen Archives." *Metropolitan Museum Journal* 31: 99–126.

Cassidy-Geiger, Maureen. 1998. "Gestochene Quellen für frühe Höroldt Malerein." *Keramos* 161: 3–38.

Cassidy-Geiger, Maureen, ed. 2007. *Fragile Diplomacy: Meissen Porcelain for European Courts, ca. 1710-63*. New Haven: Yale University Press.

Chrisman-Campbell, Kimberly. 2013. "Fashioning and Refashioning European Fashion." In *Fashioning Fashion: European Dress in Detail 1700–1915*, edited by Sharon Sadako Takeda, 15–33. Munich: Delmonico Books.

Colenbrander, Sjoukje. 2013. *When Weaving Flourished: The Silk Industry in Amsterdam and Haarlem, 1585–1750*. Amsterdam: Aronson.

Corrigan, Karina H., Jan van Campen, Femke Diercks, and Janet C. Blyberg, eds. 2015. *Asia in Amsterdam: The Culture of Luxury in the Golden Age*. New Haven: Yale University Press.

Dennis, Jessie McNab. 1963. "J. G. Herold and Company: The Art of Meissen Chinoiserie." *Metropolitan Museum of Art Bulletin* 22(1): 10–21.

Ducret, Siegfried. 1973. *Keramik und Graphik des 18. Jahrhunderts*. Braunschweig: Klinkhardt & Biermann.

Elias, Norbert. 1979. *Die höfische Gesellschaft*. Darmstadt: Luchterhand.

Erll, Astrid. 2014. "Circulating Art and Material Culture, A Model of Transcultural Mediation." In *Mediating Netherlandish Art and Material Culture in Asia*, edited by Thomas Dacosta Kaufmann and Michael North, 321–28. Amsterdam: Amsterdam University Press.

Glaser, Adolf. 1871. "Die Hochzeit Friedrichs des Großens auf dem Lustschloß Salzdahlum." *Westermann's Jahrbuch der Illustrierten Deutschen Monatshefte* 31: 105–07.

Gleeson, Janet. 1998. *The Arcanum, The Extraordinary True Story*. New York: Warner Book.

Hallinger, Johannes Franz. 1996. *Das Ende der Chinoiserie*. Munich: Scaneg.

Hanway, Jonas. 1753. *An Historical Account of the British Trade over the Caspian Sea with a Journal of Travels from London through Russia into Persia; and back through Russia, Germany and Holland*. London: Sold by Mr. Dodsley.

Hellman, Mimi. 2006. "Interior Motives: Seduction by Decoration in Eighteenth-Century France." In *Dangerous Liaisons: Fashion and Furniture in the Eighteenth Century*, edited by Harold Koda and Andrew Bolton, 15–23. New York: Metropolitan Museum of Art.

Hoffmann, Friedrich H. 1980. *Das Porzellan der europäischen Manufakturen*. Frankfurt am Main: Propyläen.

Honour, Hugh. 1961. *Chinoiserie, The Vision of Cathay.* New York: E. P. Dutton.

Hsia, Ronnie Po-chia. 2010. *A Jesuit in the Forbidden City: Matteo Ricci 1552–1610.* Oxford: Oxford University Press.

Johns, Christopher M. S. 2016. *China and the Church: Chinoiserie in Global Context.* Berkeley: University of California Press.

Jolly, Anna. 2007. "Introduction." In *A Taste for the Exotic: Foreign Influences on Early Eighteenth-Century Silk Designs*, edited by Anna Jolly, 7–10. Riggisberg: Abegg Stiftung.

Krubsacius, Friedrich August. 1759. *Gedanken von dem Ursprunge, Wachsthume und Verfalle der Verzierungen in den schönen Künsten.* Leipzig: Bernhard Christoph Breitkopf.

Leibniz, Georg Wilhelm. 1957. *The Preface to Leibniz' Novissima Sinica.* Translated by Donald F. Lach. Honolulu: University of Hawaii Press.

Lemire, Beverly, and Giorgio Riello. 2008. "East & West: Textiles and Fashion in Early Modern Europe." *Journal of Social History* 41(4): 887–916.

Marth, Regine. 2005. "Herzog Anton Ulrich-Museum in Brunswick." In *Japanese Collections in European Museums*, vol. 2: *Regional Studies*, edited by Josef Kreiner, 585–88. Bonn: Bier'sche Verlagsanstalt.

Mitchell, David M. 2007. "The Influence of *Tartary* and the Indies on Social Attitudes and Material Culture in England and France, 1650–1730." In *A Taste for the Exotic: Foreign Influences on Early Eighteenth-Century Silk Designs*, edited by Anna Jolly, 11–43. Riggisberg: Abegg Stiftung.

Mungello, David. 1985. *Curious Land: Jesuit Accommodation and the Origins of Sinology.* Wiesbaden: Franz Steiner Verlag.

Nieuhof, Johan. 1655. *Het Gezantschap der Neêrlandsche Oost-Indische Compagnie, aan den Grooten Tartarischen Cham, den tegenwoordigen Keizer van China.* Amsterdam: Amsterdam University Press.

Peck, Amelia, ed. 2013. *Interwoven Globe: The Worldwide Textile Trade, 1500–1800.* New Haven: Yale University Press.

Porter, David. 2001. *Ideographia: The Chinese Cipher in Early Modern Europe.* Stanford: Stanford University Press.

Porter, David. 2010. *The Chinese Taste in Eighteenth-Century England.* Cambridge: Cambridge University Press.

Purdy, Daniel, and Bettina Brandt. 2016. "Introduction." In *China in the German Enlightenment*, 1–19. Toronto: University of Toronto Press.

Querfurt, Tobias. 1710. *Kurtze Beschreibung Des Kürftl. Lust-Schlosses Salzdahlum.* Braunschweig: Zilligern.

Rajewsky, Irina O. 2005. "Intermediality, Intertextuality, and Remediation: A Literary Perspective on Intermediality." *Intermédialités* 6: 43–64.

Schmidt, Benjamin. 2015. *Inventing Exoticism: Geography, Globalism, and Europe's Early Modern World.* Philadelphia: University of Pennsylvania Press.

Sloboda, Stacey. 2014. *Chinoiserie: Commerce and Critical Ornament in Eighteenth-Century Britain.* Manchester: Manchester University Press.

Slomann, Vilhelm. 1953. *Bizarre Designs in Silks, Trade and Traditions*. Copenhagen: Ejnar Munksgaard.

Sonntag, Hans. 1993. *Die Botschaft des Drachen: Ostasiatische Glückssymbole auf Meissener Porzellan*. Leipzig: E.A. Seemann.

Standaert, Nicholas. 2005. "Seventeenth-Century European Images of China." *China Review International* 12(1): 254–59.

Strasser, Gerhard. 2012. "The Impact on the European Humanities of the Early Reports from Catholic Missionaries in China, Tibet and Japan between 1600 and 1700." In *The Making of the Humanities*, edited by Rens Bod, Jaap Maat, and Theijs Weststeijn, 185–208. Amsterdam: Amsterdam University Press.

Takeda, Sharon Sadako, and Kaye Durland Spilker, eds. 2013. *Fashioning Fashion: European Dress in Detail 1700–1915*. Munich: Delmonico Books.

Ulrichs, Friedericke. 2007. "Johan Nieuhof's and Olfert Dapper's Travel Accounts as Sources for European *Chinoiserie*." In *A Taste for the Exotic: Foreign Influences on Early Eighteenth-Century Silk Designs*, edited by Anna Jolly, 45–56. Riggisberg: Abegg Stiftung.

Von Strassburg, Gottfried. 1988. *Tristan and Isolde*, edited by Francis Gentry. New York: Continuum.

Williams, Elizabeth A. 2016. "A Gentlemen's Pursuit: Eighteenth-Century Chinoiserie Silver in Britain." In *Materializing Gender in Eighteenth-Century Europe*, edited by Jennifer G. Germann and Heidi A. Strobel, 105–20. Farnham, England: Ashgate.

Yonan, Michael Elia. 2004. "Veneers of Authority: Chinese Lacquers in Maria Theresa's Vienna." *Eighteenth-Century Studies* 37(4): 652–72.

6

Tradition in fashion: Golden embroidery and the crafting of heritage in Bukhara

Lola Shamukhitdinova

The golden embroidery production of Bukhara, one of the largest ancient cities in Uzbekistan, has historically played an important role in the economic, political, social, and private life of Central Asian society. The material culture of golden embroidery has been preserved through the donation of textiles to and the collection efforts of museums. But as a textile technique, the knowledge and skill of golden embroidery has also been handed down through families and communities, as with other living traditions such as oral traditions, performing arts, social practices, rituals, and festive events. This chapter will discuss the social importance of golden embroidery and how its connection to the community has evolved and changed over the last two centuries. It is important to note that the shift in status of golden embroidery, as a valued craft practice, correlates with substantial political and economic changes in Bukhara and in Uzbekistan as a whole. The suppression and demise of the craft, followed by its revitalization through a recent newfound fashionable status, mirror the tumultuous political history of the region as an emirate (1785–1920), a Russian protectorate (1873–1917), a Soviet republic (1920–1990), and, finally, an independent nation (1991–today). Following this historical trajectory, the chapter focuses on the various shifts in the structure of the craft business. These shifts include the evolution of golden embroidery as a craft historically dominated by male practitioners to a craft practice more recently dominated by female practitioners. Further, the chapter highlights the role of golden embroidery in the image making of national identity and the recent negotiation of its role within the development of a heritage and tourist market in Uzbekistan. As a newly independent state, the Uzbek government carefully considers how its national image is presented to global audiences. This is an image that attempts to fuse the multitude of textile practices and traditions from across Central Asia into a coherent identity as materialized in modern Uzbek fashion design (Mentges 2012, 221). Therefore, to contextualize the historical research of golden embroidery, this chapter draws on contemporary interviews with hereditary golden embroiderers and also analyzes contemporary craft production sold in the bazaars and shops of Uzbekistan.[1]

Golden embroidery: Between Khanate, Protectorate, and Soviet republic

Today, a great portion of the ancient Silk Road, a ramified network of trade routes that connected China and Central Asia with Europe from 120 BCE through 1450s CE (Uhlig 1986, 11), is situated in modern Uzbekistan. As one of the largest cotton exporters and the fourth largest silk producer in the world, Uzbekistan considers itself the legitimate heir of the Silk Road (Kalter and Pavaloi 1997, 9). The longevity of the Silk Road made a significant contribution to the cross-cultural development of the region and the promotion and development of trade in local textile crafts, including golden embroidery. Meticulously described in the Bible for its prominence in Aaron's ephod (Exodus 28: 2–43), golden yarn embroidery is an ancient art that derives its name from the use of gilded metallic or metallic-looking thread. As used in the construction of the first High Priest of the Israelites' elaborate holy garment, "[t]his ancient craft, because of its magnificence and its price, was reserved for a long time for Temples, Kings, and Pontiffs" (De Saint-Aubin et al. 1983, 15). Golden embroidered clothes were particularly valued for their use of gilded threads and the visible demonstration of wealth through materials, design, and production skills. In Central Asia, golden embroidery was used in the court of Tamerlane (1370–1405) and continued to develop during the Khanate of Bukhara (1500–1785) and the Emirate of Bukhara (1785–1920). Numerous artifacts from the feudal period are kept today in the collections of Uzbek and Russian museums, including the State History Museum of Uzbekistan in Tashkent, Bukhara State Architectural Art Museum-Preserve and its branch in at Sitorai Mokhi-Khosa Palace, and the Kunstkamera in St. Petersburg, Russia.

The Emirate of Bukhara was an autocratic state, ruled by a hereditary monarch (emir) in accordance with Muslim religious law and customs. It hosted a population of two to three million people (Becker 2004, 27), with seventy thousand to one hundred thousand people inhabiting the capital of Bukhara.

During the emirate period, golden embroidered clothes served to display feudal power and rank at court; much of the golden embroidered menswear, including footwear, belts, headdresses, and decorated horsecloths, were produced solely for the emir (Rahimov 2006, 22–49). High officials could wear certain types of embroidered court clothes if the clothes were received as a present from the emir, with the general population allowed to wear fewer kinds of embroidered clothes (Goncharova 1986, 8). In the Emirate of Bukhara (1785–1920), the craft of golden embroidery was called *zarduzi*, and was considered a special feature of Bukhara city. There were one or two palace workshops as well as private manufacturing workshops. Between 1885 and 1911, around twenty to twenty-five of these private golden embroidery workshops existed, whereby the production of official court clothes was allowed only in the case of an urgent order made by the emir (Goncharova 1986, 15). Highly skilled embroiderers in the emir's palace workshops, as with the best court jewelers and tailors, could receive court ranks (Peshcherova 1955, 277).

The palace workshops employed between twenty to forty craftsmen and were supervised by an *usto-kor* (master), elected by the craftsmen and approved by the *kushbegi* (first minister). The *usto-kor* was responsible for all processes in a workshop, including fulfilling orders, ensuring the quality of the work, and distributing the work materials. However, the distribution of the gilded threads, the most valuable material in the workshop, was performed by the *mirzoli-kalebatunchi*, who also supervised the hiring and dismissal of craftsmen (Goncharova 1986, 14). Other notable positions were the specialists, who prepared tambours, and the draftsmen, followed by ordinary masters (*halfa*) and pupils (*shogird*).

By 1917, more than 300 golden embroiderers were united in a professional guild in Bukhara. The guild was led by a *bobo*, a person responsible for general religious and moral questions, and an *aklsakal*, a person responsible for production, technology, and sales. As with other textile crafts, golden embroidery had its own spiritual patron and protector of the guild, Saint Hazrati Yusuf. The *risola* (written regulations) of the guild contained the mythical history of the craft, technical instructions, and the rituals and morals regarding the order and maintenance of the workshops and the conduct of its members. Guild members were closely connected to each other, economically as well as socially: they visited each other on significant occasions such as family celebrations and funerals. Most of them lived in the southwest part of Bukhara, where many private golden embroidery workshops were located. Within the guild system, the *aksakal* oversaw and resolved various economic and household problems: he obtained and distributed the court orders between workshops, allocated labor, settled conflicts, collected the finished products, and organized the sale of products (Goncharova 1986, 10). The regional importance of the craft and its guild encouraged the establishment of a local craft school, which taught distinctive design compositions and motifs, and developed a local professional vocabulary for the production processes and technology.

The craft of golden embroidery in Bukhara developed as a men's craft, paternally passed down through generational lines. Women were involved only occasionally and were usually assigned the task of completing semi-finished products (Goncharova 1986, 9–16). This rendered the labor of women in the production of embroidery invisible. Male hegemony was strengthened by the fact that women were forbidden to participate in the guild as well as by the popular belief that the threads' sheen would dim when touched by a woman. According to anthropologist Olga Gorshunova's research on the gender roles of Uzbek women (2000, 23), during this time a woman was defined primarily by her reproductive, childbearing function, and her role within the family was limited to household activities. Thus, unlike other forms of embroidery, golden embroidery was entangled in reinforcing gender roles within a patriarchal society and state and in visualizing the power and wealth of the emirate.

In 1868, the emirate lost a war with Imperial Russia, which was competing with the United Kingdom for colonial aspirations in the region. As a result of the defeat, the emirate became a Russian protectorate in 1873 (Becker 2004, 35–51). After the 1917 revolution in Russia, the Emirate of Bukhara was conquered by the Russian Bolsheviks and replaced with the Bukhara People's Republic. Between 1924 and 1929, the new Soviet government established five new socialist republics in Soviet Central Asia: Kazakhstan, Uzbekistan, Turkmenistan, Kyrgyzstan, and Tajikistan, by which most of the Bukhara territories were incorporated into Uzbekistan (Kamp 2002, 266). During this period, it is possible to trace the material influence of various cultures through the development of new design motifs and compositions that were inspired by the golden embroidery seen on Russian Orthodox Christian vestments (Peshcherova 1955, 282), drawings, and motifs found on Russian industrial textile fabrics, and the designs of popular imported Chinese porcelain.

The main base materials for golden embroidery were different kinds of velvet as well as local silk and semi-silk fabrics. The metallic threads that were used before the second half of the nineteenth century came from India and Iran, after which they were sourced from Russia. Two main types of threads, *kalebatun* and *sim*, were used by Bukharan craftsmen. *Kalebatun* was made of silver thread twisted on silk thread. To achieve a golden color, the silver threads were then gilded. *Sim* was a thin flattened silver or gilded thread. The main instruments of embroiderers were tambours (*kochub*) in different sizes, a small tetrahedral stick (*patilya*) for thread tension, a thimble, and needles (Goncharova 1986, 18–21).

The official palace workshops that produced golden embroidery existed until the overthrow of the Bukhara Emirate and its subsequent transition into a Soviet republic in 1920. Applying Marxist-Leninist theory to the craft's political economy, the craftsmen could position themselves as exploiters or exploited. As owners of the workshop they could be exploiters or, as victims of the capitalist system, they could be exploited, blurring a clear or fixed political position (Krebs 2011, 71). During the first decades of Soviet rule, golden embroidery production was strongly reduced. It was declared decadent and bourgeois (Krebs 2011, 132). Most of the Soviet government's sanctions were not directed at the craftsmen but at their customers, particularly the court and the businessmen to whom their production was addressed (Krebs 2011, 72), and the golden embroiderers, being employees of the court, were pressed to find other work, such as paving streets (Krebs 2011, 132).

In the 1930s, the first golden embroidery *artel* (a cooperative association of handicraftsmen and artists) in Bukhara was created, and women became openly involved in the work for the first time (Fakhretdinova 1972, 65). The involvement of women was a result of the political and ideological processes in Central Asia, organized by the Soviet government and the *hujum* (the attack) movement for the unveiling of women (Kamp 2002, 263–78). These efforts broadened the scope of women's work beyond the family, and local women became increasingly involved in social labor. However, during this time golden embroidery also began to lose its prestige, following the demise of its most influential customer, the court of the emir. The metallic threads used in golden embroidery were gradually substituted with gold-looking imitation threads. Ethnologist Melanie Krebs notes that golden embroidery and ikat production were valued as crafts associated with the court because they were made by men (Krebs 2011, 167). But gradually, from the 1930s, the golden embroidery craft ceased to be associated with men and was socially degraded to the category of women's craft.

Golden embroidery and its link to art tradition dramatically changed under the new political conditions. To appeal to a new clientele from the broader community, the embroiderers repurposed old designs and patterns to create a new simplicity and clarity of ornamentation (Fakhretdinova 1972, 66). Whereas varied and numerous styles flourished during the emirate period of the 1920s to 1930s, production shifted to a smaller assortment of gift items such as skullcaps, scarves with an embroidered forehead band, collar trimmings, and other accessories for women (Goncharova 1986, 8). In the 1940s, the demand for gold embroidered items slightly increased, mostly for skullcaps, with new patterns reflecting the impact of the Soviet government. An example of this is the "hero" motif, in which the main element of composition is a five-pointed star associated with the image of the highest award for courage and heroism in the Soviet Union. Such motifs thrived since stylized zoomorphic motifs, such as a peacock, are not allowed in Islamic art (Fakhretdinova 1972, 121).

In 1938 due to the efforts of the artel, a golden embroidery craft factory was opened in Bukhara. The present-day factory is now a joint-stock company. In 1962, the factory obtained new premises, where more than 400 golden embroidery masters—most of whom were women—worked (see Khakimov 1999). In the 1970s, a new kind of golden embroidery emerged: some of the products were monumental wall panels and theatre curtains with decorative motifs from modern life. The design of these objects was usually entrusted to professional artists (Khakimov 1999, 88). Motifs include *panno bairam* (holiday), with a round composition of peasant figures used to celebrate the harvest holiday, *pakhta* (cotton), with a composition of cotton bolls, *panno Ismoil Somoniy makbarasi* (the image of the historical monument of Samanid mausoleum) (see Artmuseum.uz 2016), and *anor* (garnet), with pomegranates (Temirova and Pulatova 2015, 119–25).

According to one of the embroiderers who still works in this factory, Mariam Rahimova (2013), during the 1980s and 1990s, the factory mostly served the Ministry of Foreign Affairs, fulfilling state orders for national souvenirs, curtains for theatres, and large wall decorations. After many years, the craft of golden embroidery was once again used as an instrument of state presentation. Krebs notes that the social and fundamental breaks that transformed the Bukhara Emirate into a Soviet republic led to changes in customers' demands and preferences. At the same time, although state-owned institutions changed, the gold embroidered goods and products continued to serve the representation of political power (Krebs 2011, 139).

Embroidering a new tradition (1991–2017)

After the fall of the Soviet Union in 1991, Uzbekistan became an independent state seeking to establish a national identity. The deep, historical meanings associated with textile crafts played an important role in shaping the national identity and were economically and socially supported by the Uzbek government, through low taxes and preferential leasing of rooms for workshops, and by different international institutions such as United Nations Educational, Scientific and Cultural Organization (UNESCO), Central Asia Crafts Support Association (CACSA), the British Council, and Asia Theological Association (ATA) (Shamukhitdinova and Adelt 2013, 7). Consequently, traditional textile crafts that had seen a reduction during the Soviet period enjoyed a new renaissance, and it became fashionable and respectable to be a traditional craftsman. Further, in the difficult economic climate after the fall of the Soviet Union, when the Soviet industrial integration system necessitated the closure of many factories, traditional crafts such as golden embroidery offered the opportunity for many people to survive, especially in the rural areas where the crafts originated. In newly independent Uzbekistan, the popularity of golden embroidery spread throughout the population. This was partly due to the increased accessibility of the craft due to the substitution of gold-looking synthetic threads for actual gold or silver threads. Nevertheless, golden embroidered objects, even with synthetic substitute threads, have not lost their reputation and are still associated with special occasions to this day (Krebs 2011, 140). At family and state ceremonies, government institutions promoted the heritage of textile and craft traditions as a contemporary public expression of national identity (Adams 2010, 356), encouraging the crafts as an important attribute to and asset for modern, young Uzbek design. However, according to sociologist Lise Skov, small national fashion labels are more "orientated toward international validation rather than domestic power" (Skov 2011, 139).

Crafting heritage in Bukhara

Interviews with the skilled workers at the golden embroidery factory, Zarduz, in Bukhara, as well as with small business embroiderers of *kishlak* (village) *Kalon* in the Bukhara region, provide insights into the contemporary business organization of golden embroidery as a heritage craft. Mariam Rahimova began her work at the factory in 1981 when she was eighteen years old. In the eighth grade, she decided to be a professional embroiderer and took part in the informal golden embroidery circle during her free time. During the last few years of her formal education, Rahimova's parents allowed her to attend night school so that she could learn the craft professionally. Today, Rahimova has worked at the Zarduz factory for more than thirty-five years, making her an expert in golden embroidery. She has participated in almost all of the large, important orders, many of which have become part of valuable collections of Soviet decorative applied arts and are now national property. Large items of golden embroidery are accomplished by collective creativity and teamwork, exhibiting the considerable labor required from the process of embroidering. The production process also necessitates many other types of work that enriches the product's quality, including the cut of the items to be embroidered, the design and composition of the embroidery, the preparation of base materials for embroidery, cutting out the patterns for ornaments, and setting the tension of the fabric on a tambour. Thus, all of these factory production segments share responsibility in achieving the products' high-quality craftsmanship (see Figure 6.1).

Rahimova explained that, after Uzbekistan became an independent state, the factory participated in numerous national and international exhibitions and fairs, receiving awards for its unique products, such as thematic and decorative panels, wall decorations, and carpets that often showcase images of prominent people, state leaders, historic buildings, and national symbols. The factory also established commercial connections with countries in Europe, the Middle East, the Americas, and Africa. Today many products are ordered by the Council of the President, the ministries of Uzbekistan, and Uzbek embassies abroad, as well as by theatres and concert halls. The factory also produces all kinds of men's and women's robes and gowns, skullcaps, and smaller souvenir products. The workers occupy a large, light room filled with rectangular tambour frames and large tables. The factory continues the tradition of using two methods of embroidering: *zarduzi-*

Figure 6.1 The golden embroidery process in Zarkon factory, Bukhara (2013). *Photo*: Lola Shamukhitdinova.

za-minduzi, entirely covering the fabric, and *zarduzi-gul-duzi*, embroidering flower designs to a cut-out pattern made from cardboard (previously the cut-out pattern was made from leather). The most difficult kinds combine golden and silk embroidery in very complex compositions. During the time of our research visit, there were more than a hundred women and girls working at the factory, including outsourced workers. Rahimova asserted that even today it is a special honor when embroiderers enter the rank of the professionals (masters) of this craft.

An interview with a skilled handicraftswoman, Vasilya Umurbekova (2013), clearly elicits how the work of small business embroiderers differs from that of a handicraftswoman descended from several generations in Kalon near Bukhara. For Umurbekova, the production is mostly oriented toward the local market or dependent on individual orders. Kalon is one of several villages in the Bukhara region where handicraftsmen, sometimes even the entirety of the village's inhabitants, are engaged together in golden embroidery craft. Almost all family members, and sometimes even neighbors, get involved in the family-run business. The men of the family supply the embroiderers with the required materials and tools and bring the finished pieces to sellers in the market. The time and place for selling are stipulated by the administration of the market. Every Monday in the specifically allotted place on the market square, a craftswoman or someone from the family sells skullcaps behind the family's own counter. The same day, new materials and tools for further production are purchased. The majority of women are busy with embroidery, with two or three responsible for drawing and cutting the ornaments from cardboard for embroidery, and two or three busy with the cutting and sewing of products. Many of the skilled craftswomen learned their craft either during childhood or sometimes after marriage, when they stopped working outside the home and began staying home to look after their small children. The products made in Kalon include skullcaps, women's wedding gowns, men's wedding and gift robes, vests, wall decorations and covers, pillow covers, covers for teapots, headbands for women (*peshonaband*), embroidered details of women's national dress (*peshkurta*), national fans (*bodbezak*), cases for eye glasses, and purses or handbags. During the interview, Umurbekova explained that the customers' demand and design preferences for traditional items change from time to time, prompting customization of designs for the local market based on the trends reported by the sellers. Sometimes Umurbekova would develop a new design in a traditional style or modify an existing style in a new way. She does not care about a special name for the new styles, simply calling them a "fantasy of embroideries." Aside from her engagement in the family craft business with her daughters, her primary occupation is teaching at the rural school. She learned to embroider seven years ago from her mother, who learned the skills from her grandmother. Umurbekova grew up among craftspeople. She described how the women of Kalon, after they had finished their duties at home, would gather in one of the houses to embroider. While they worked, they sang songs and told interesting stories while always keeping their children nearby under their supervision. After her classes at the teaching institute ended, Umurbekova would hurry home to join the handicraftswomen, and gradually golden embroidery became more than just her hobby. Following her graduation from the teaching institute, she continued to be engaged in embroidery. Once married, she stayed at home for several years and continued embroidering: "It was very convenient when I was constantly at home. I did the household chores and looked after children. After the children grew up, my daughters began to help me. I had more time and I went to work at the school as the teacher." The primary income of Umurbekova's family comes from the craft business. Her daughters learned the craft from her, and she would like it if they continued with the craft. Now the profession of "golden embroidery" can also be learned in the Republic College of Design in Tashkent. She never participated in craft exhibitions and does not have any awards or honors, but as she says, the reward is "the gratitude of those who buy our products."

The two main forms of craft organizations, the craft factory and individual craft production (including small, family-based businesses, the informal cottage industry, and home-based production), have different clients, serve different markets, and have different specialisms, but all use the same traditional techniques and instruments. Reestablished as a respectable and fashionable traditional craft, Bukharan golden embroidery has become widespread throughout Uzbekistan over the last ten years. Given its demand and popularity, golden embroidery now ensures that one can earn a good, stable income from this craft. The support of international organizations fostered the development of golden embroidery centers in almost all regions of Uzbekistan, even in places where they were historically underdeveloped or did not exist—for example Surkhandarya, the Kashkadarya, and the Fergana Valley (Tashkent 2005). Of course, this boom also helped to reduce the unemployment of women, especially in rural areas. According to a report of the Asian Development Bank (2014), many women in Uzbekistan earn income through small, family-based, handicrafts businesses, and the informal cottage industry, or home-based production, are important factors in contributing to the family's earnings. However, it also leaves women without the social protection, such as pensions, maternity leave, sick leave, or holidays, typically offered by formal employment.

After 1991, the fashion design industry was supported by the Uzbek government and media as an important actor in crafting a new national image. This led to the creation of Tashkent Art Week, numerous design competitions, festivals, and grants, and to the establishment of a National Institute of Art and Design. After Oscar de la Renta, in 2005, and Gucci and Dries van Noten, in 2010, presented collections inspired by the ikat textiles from the Uzbek culture, there was a new push to use local textile crafts in Uzbek fashion. Modern Uzbek fashion design refers to craft traditions by citing and applying ornaments, colors, and fabrics of Central Asian traditional dress cultures. Cultural historian Gabriele Mentges notes that "this phenomenon of revitalization is often addressed as 're-orientalization,' (Leshkowich and Jones 2003, 1–49) i.e. adopting and playing with old Oriental stereotypes, which, in the case of Uzbekistan, date from the time of the Tsarist colonialism" (Mentges 2012, 217). Thus, traditional textile crafts and new fashion design have become strong markers of the new Uzbek national identity. Golden embroidery has been widely used as a favorite decorative method for international haute couture fashion collections, as well as by the local population as by the modern woman for festive or special occasion clothing and accessories. Typically, local women select the fabric and dress design, cut it out at the dressmakers, and then give it to golden embroidery masters. Golden embroidery is also frequently used for stage costumes for national shows and performances during state festivities (see Figure 6.2). Therefore, a national Uzbek image fuses traditional textile crafts with modern fashion design to create the image of a coherent Uzbek identity, made visible through personal dress practices as well as national performances and events (Mentges 2012). This illustrates M. Angela Jansen and Jennifer Craik's idea that non-Western fashions are far from static, but rather are powerful tools in an ongoing negotiation of continuity and change, of tradition and modernity, and of local developments and global influences (2016, 3–4).

Since the time of the Silk Road, luxury textiles, especially silk ikats or gift robes made from ikat or golden embroidery, were appreciated as gift objects because of their high value. There were, and still are, many Central Asian traditions that are accompanied by the donation of robes: acceptance into school, dedication to master craftsmen, and family festivities such as marriage and circumcision. The donation of a robe to the guest of honor, such as teachers, honorees of the anniversary, national sportsmen, and honorable international politicians is still interpreted as a token of gratitude and favor, and remains a tradition in all areas of Uzbekistan. In Soviet times, the robe was usually made from silk, velvet, or cotton, but now there is demand for custom golden embroidered robes. Until the

Figure 6.2 The opening of the fashion show and national dress contest during Tashkent Art Week (2013). *Photo*: Lola Shamukhitdinova.

mid-1990s, gift robes were only presented to men. In 2002, at the celebration of the anniversary of one of Tashkent's higher education institutions, for the first time, I witnessed the female head of the institution being publicly presented with a female variant of a claret velvet robe without sleeves, traditionally decorated with the golden embroidery. Gift robes, varying in price and quality, can now easily be found on the Uzbek market. More recently, wedding salons have begun to offer embroidered clothing for the bride and groom.

Bukhara as a craft tourism destination

Bukhara's historical center was listed as a UNESCO World Heritage Facility in 1993. The tourism market of Uzbekistan has grown considerably over the last decade, supported by an improved government visa policy and the development of a tourism infrastructure. It is now "one of the best examples of well-preserved Islamic cities of Central Asia of the tenth to the seventeenth centuries with an urban fabric that has remained largely intact" (UNESCO World Heritage Center 2017). Bukhara has attracted mostly cultural tourists (Kim 2013, 92–97). Golden embroidery craft contributes to the international image of "Golden Bukhara," the most often-used epithet for the city. The tourism industry naturally encourages souvenir production, since cultural tourists, who usually hold greater cultural knowledge and interest, prefer original, handmade souvenirs. Among the best-selling items are traditional textile craft products (see Figure 6.3), which represent the culture of the region and seamlessly combine arts with crafts. In 2013, souvenir research conducted in a folklore market in Old Bukhara found a growing demand for golden embroidery products among tourists (Pulatova 2013, 95–102).

Everything that is connected with the golden embroidery craft as a specific marker of Bukhara culture is involved now in an orbit of tourist interests. Even subsidiary materials used by golden embroiderers, such as the patterns that are cut out from cardboard and the special scissors *kaychi-ushtur-gardan*

Figure 6.3 Skullcaps sold at the bazaar in old Bukhara (2013). *Photo*: Lola Shamukhitdinova.

(camel's neck) for cutting out patterns, have been turned into souvenirs. Both are examples of functional, "authentic" objects that have been transformed from their original use and function into a souvenir that will act as a memory for a tourist. At times, the increased demand for craft souvenirs, caused by the rapid development of tourism, enacts a pressure on production that results in low-standard, hastily made products (Shamukhitdinova 2017, 153–77). Some advanced handicraftsmen and sellers in the tourist market in Old Bukhara have transformed their shops into salons to create a peculiar mix of a showroom and workshop. They commonly speak European languages, even if at a basic conversational level, in order to do more business. Such changes in crafts performance can be interpreted as examples of how the rising importance of heritage industries in a globalized world reinforces and communicates a national image.

Conclusion

During the last two centuries, due to the historical and political tumult in the Bukhara region, a number of substantial changes occurred in the organization and production of golden embroidery. These changes included different forms of business organization, changes in the clientele and desired products, and a significant shift in the material used, for example, substituting gilded thread with gold-looking thread. However, the technique and patterns did not change as dramatically. Under the influence of Russian colonialism, and later Soviet political and ideological processes in Central Asia, golden embroidery shifted from a male-dominated to a female-dominated craft. After the country gained independence in 1991, textile crafts became an important tool for establishing and marking a new national identity. Following a period of suppression, golden embroidery has now reverted to being seen as a respectable, fashionable, traditional craft. Uzbek fashion design, supported by the government and media, became an important influencer and promoter of the new national image through its referencing and experimenting with traditional textile crafts. The contemporary craft business is usually organized into two forms. The first is an informal cottage industry or home-based production business, oriented to the local market and tourism market. The second form of a craft factory is rarer as it produces mostly unique representative products for the state, institutions, and special exhibitions. However, both these forms illustrate how golden embroidery remains an important craft and tool to symbolize and indicate social status as well as national and cultural identity. After Uzbekistan gained independence, the craft entered the sphere of mass production for the local population and the increasing numbers of foreign tourists. However, the mass production of the craft has led to issues with the quality of golden embroidery production. Nonetheless, the craft of golden embroidery has been successfully utilized to preserve the regional heritage of the craft through its design, patterns, and technology, as well as the inherited traditions and practices of golden embroiderers, supported by oral family history and local textile practices. This has ensured that the craft remains associated with the Bukhara region and can be evaluated as a cultural marker of "Golden Bukhara."

Note

1   The chapter draws on field research conducted as part of the project "Modernity of Tradition: Uzbek Textile Heritage as Cultural and Economic Resource," funded by The Volkswagen Foundation, directed by Professor Gabriele Mentges at TU Dortmund University (from 2010 to 2012 and 2013 to 2015).

References

Adams, Laura. 2010. *The Spectacular State: Culture and Identity in Uzbekistan*. Durham and London: Duke University Press.

Asian Development Bank. 2014. "Uzbekistan: Country Gender Assessment. Gender and Development / Central and West Asia." Accessed June 16, 2017. https://ww w.adb.org/sites/default/files/institutional-document/42767/files/uzbekistan-coun try-gender-assessment.pdf

Becker, Seymour. 2004. *Russia's Protectorates in Central Asia: Bukhara and Khiva, 1865–1924*. Cambridge: Harvard University Press.

De Saint-Aubin, Charles Germain, Nikki Scheuer, and Edward Maeder. 1983. *Art of the Embroiderer*. Boston: Los Angeles County Museum of Arts and David R. Godine Publisher.

Fakhretdinova, Dinara. 1972. *Dekorativno-prikladnoe iskusstvo Uzbekistana [Decorative and Applied Art of Uzbekistan]*. Tashkent: G. Gulom.

Goncharova, Polina. 1986. *Zolotoshveynoye iskusstvo Bukhary. [Golden Embroidery Art of Bukhara]*. Tashkent: G. Gulom.

Gorshunova, Olga. 2000. "*Obraz zhizni sovremennoj uzbekskoj zhenshchiny: po materialam Ferganskoj doliny.*" [*"Way of Life of the Modern Uzbek Woman: On Materials of the Fergana Valley "*]. PhD dissertation, Institute of Ethnology and

Anthropology of Nicholas Miklukho-Maclay of the Russian Academy of Sciences, Moscow.

Jansen, M. Angela, and Jennifer Craik. 2016. *Modern Fashion Traditions: Negotiating Tradition and Modernity through Fashion*. London: Bloomsbury Academic.

Kalter, Johannes, and Margareta Pavaloi. 1997. *Uzbekistan: Heirs to the Silk Road*. New York: Thames and Hudson.

Kamp, Marianne. 2002. "Pilgrimage and Performance: Uzbek Women and the Imagining of Uzbekistan in the 1920s." *Nationalism and the Colonial Legacy in the Middle East and Central Asia* 34(2): 263–78. http://repository.uwyo.edu/history_ facpub/?utm_source=repository.uwyo.edu%2Fhistory_facpub%2F13&utm_mediu m=PDF&utm_campaign=PDFCoverPages

Khakimov, Akbar. 1999. *Atlas of Central Asian Artistic Crafts and Trades*. Vol. 1, Uzbekistan. Tashkent: Sharq.

Kim, Alexandra. 2013. "Analysis and Perspectives of Tourism Development in Uzbekistan." *Revista AGALI Journal* 3: 87–101. http://www.agaliasociacion.org/es/r evista3

Krebs, Melanie. 2011. *Zwischen Handwerkstradition und globalem Markt: Kunsthandwerker in Usbekistan und Kirgistan*. Berlin: Klaus Schwarz.

Leshkowich, Ann Marie, and Carla Jones. 2003. "Introduction: The Globalization of Asian Dress: Re-Orienting Fashion or Re-Orientalizing Asia?" In *Re-Orienting Fashion: The Globalization of Asian Dress*, edited by Sandra Niessen, Ann Marie Leshkowich, and Carla Jones, 1–49. Oxford and New York: Berg.

Mentges, Gabriele. 2012. "The Role of UNESCO and the Uzbek Nation Building Process," In *Heritage Regimes and the State*, edited by Regina F. Bendix, AdityaEggert, and Arnika Peselmann, 213–26. Göttingen: Universitätsverlag Göttingen.

Museum of Applied Arts of Uzbekistan/Artmuseum.uz. 2016. "Embroidery in Gold." Accessed March 2, 2017. http://www.artmuseum.uz/en/gold_sewing.html

Palmer, Edwin H. et al. 2011. *The Holy Bible, New International Version containing the Old Testament and the New Testament*. Grand Rapids: Zondervan.

Peshcherova, Elena. 1955. *Buharskie zolotoshvei [Bukhara Gold Embroiders]*, Vol. XVI, 282. Moscow and Leningrad: Kunstkamera Collection.

Pulatova, Sabokhat. 2013. "Folklore market in Old Bukhara." In *Modernity of Tradition: Uzbek Textile Culture today*, edited by Gabriele Mentges and Lola Shamukhitdinova, 95–102. Münster: Waxmann.

Rahimov, Rahmat. 2006. "Bukhara-Petersburg: The Silk Road for the House of Romanovs (Historical and Cultural Portrait of the Kunstkamera Collections)." In *Oriental Dreams: Russian Avant-Garde and Silks of Bukhara*, edited by Efim Anatol'evič Rezvan, 22–52. St. Petersburg: Kunstkamera.

Rahimova, Mariam. (Name of interviewee anonymized). 2013. Interview by Lola Shamukhitdinova. October 21, 2013.

Shamukhitdinova, Lola. 2017. "Uzbek Skull Caps: A Popular Headwear between Traditional High Quality and Touristic Souvenir." In *Textiles as National Heritage: Identities, Politics and Material Culture*, edited by Gabriele Mentges and Lola Shamukhitdinova, 153–77. Münster: Waxmann.

Shamukhitdinova, Lola, and Svenja Adelt. 2013. "Die Wiederbelebung zentralasiatischer textiler Handwerkstechniken im Prozess der Nationsbildung in Usbekistan." *Zentralasien-Analysen*, 23(72): 2–6.

Skov, Lise. 2011. "Dreams of Small Nations in a Polycentric Fashion World." *Fashion Theory* 15(2): 137–56.

Tashkent. Fragments of Culture. 2005. Cultureuyz.net "Stenograph of the Colloquium 'Arts of Uzbekistan at the present stage of socio-cultural development.'" Accessed June 16, 2017. http://cultureuz.net/index.php/analitica/208-first-1

Temirova, Matlab, and Sabokhat Pulatova. 2015. "The Patterns of Bukhara Region Skullcaps" ["Uzory primenyaemye v tyubetejkah buharskogo regiona"] *Perspektivy uzbekskoy tekstilnoy kultury: traditsii i innovatsii [Perspectives of Uzbek textile culture: traditions and innovations]*, edited by Halimahon Alimov, Gabriele Mentges, and Lola Shamuhitdinova, 119–26. Tashkent: O'zbekiston.

Uhlig, Helmut. 1986. *Die Seiden-Strasse: Antike Weltkultur zwischen China und Rom.* Bergish Gladbach: Bastei-Lübbe.

Umurbekova, Vasilya. (Name of interviewee anonymized). 2013. Interview by Lola Shamukhitdinova. March 10, 2013.

UNESCO World Heritage Center. 2017. "Historic Center of Bukhara." Accessed March 2, 2017. http://whc.unesco.org/en/list/602

7

"Our dress": Chitenge as Zambia's national fabric

Karen Tranberg Hansen

When women in Zambia tell you that their "chitenge" outfits are "traditional," they are talking about an invented tradition that keeps evolving as a result of changing inspirations from across the African continent and beyond. It is "our wear" they say, and, indeed, as this chapter demonstrates, chitenge is deeply embedded in an ongoing history of changing national representations and global trade. Chitenge ("vitenge" in some regions of Zambia) is one of several colorful printed cotton fabrics, including wax prints and "kanga," which are worn widely in several countries in Africa (Gott et al. 2017). They are often called "African prints," with a designation that turns history on its head (Steiner 1985). Produced in Europe since the middle of the nineteenth century, if not earlier, these fabrics have become Africanized, imbued with meanings whose significance arises from the particularities of time, location, and context (Sylvanus 2016). This chapter explicates the case of dress in Zambia, a former British colony in the southern part of the African continent, where the term chitenge identifies both a fabric as well as a dress practice, thus merging upon women's bodies the agentive medium of the fabric and the dress practice.

How, given its multiple origins, can we view chitenge as traditional dress in Zambia? Reflecting on the significance of textiles in Africa and inspired by his long-term observations, art historian, John Picton, considers it no longer acceptable to contrast the "traditional" with the "contemporary" (Picton 1995, 11). "The reality is," he explained two decades ago, "that traditions entail histories . . . and that in arts as in politics, religion, and so forth, all manner of traditions are contemporary with each other, coexisting, often mutually reflexive, each with its particular temporal status and functional locus" (Picton 1995, 11). Writing recently about the developing African fashion scene, Victoria Rovine does not use the term "traditional" to refer to the fundamental status of a textile, a garment, or an image. Instead, she uses the term for styles or media that make connections with, or evoke, local culture and history (Rovine 2015, 18–19). Such views do not involve a search for historical origins but rather entail explorations of the consequences of their transformations, as I do here for the case of chitenge.

Contributing to the growing body of scholarship on fashion in Africa (Gott and Loughran 2010; Hansen and Madison 2013; Rabine 2002; Rovine 2015; Sylvanus 2016), this chapter traces the evolution of chitenge wear in the wake of Zambia's independence in 1964 and subsequent shifts in chitenge fashions against a backdrop of changing trade regimes, wide-ranging global commercial networks including China, and socioeconomic and political upheavals.[1] Describing the domestic, regional, and external sourcing of chitenge fabric, the fashioning of chitenge outfits by different generations of tailors, and more recently, designers, I examine how chitenge has withstood the effects of time in a dress universe strongly influenced by Western wear.

The national fabric

In 1964, when Zambia became independent from British colonial rule, the nascent nation presented itself symbolically to the world with a newly designed coat of arms (see Figure 7.1). The new republic's heraldic imagery features a shield with black-and-white wavy lines, representing white water cascading over black rock at the Victoria Falls, with a fish eagle on top and a crossed hoe and pick underneath. The eagle stands for freedom, the hoe and pick for farming and mining. To the left and right of the shield are a man and a woman, the man dressed in a bush jacket and shorts, and the woman wearing a length of fabric tied at the waist, and a top with a square bustline, a yoked neck, and puffed sleeves. She is adorned with beads and an ivory bracelet. They both wear sandals. At their feet are symbols of the country's natural resources: a maize crop, a mine headframe, and a zebra. And at the bottom is a narrow horizontal banner with the political motto, "One Zambia, One Nation," uniting the country's many ethnic groups into one polity, Zambia (Hansen 2000, 78).

When the ministerial consultative committee for the independence celebration in 1964 asked Zambian artist Gabriel Ellison to design a coat of arms for the new nation, the artist proposed that birds or wild game be bearers, arguing that human bearers were unlikely to withstand the effects of time (Gabriel Ellison interview, Lusaka, September 12, 1997; cited in Hansen 2000, 78). However, the

Figure 7.1 Coat of arms, the Republic of Zambia.

committee insisted on human figures as bearers. Considering several suggestions for the dress of the bearers, the consultative committee members settled on dress styles that were common during the two decades prior to independence. The all-male committee members agreed more easily on the male bearer's dress than that of the female bearer.

Subsequent developments indicate that Gabriel Ellison was partly right in her argument. The coat of arms has indeed been subject to criticism for its colonial associations, particularly with the male bearer's bush suit. Adult African men who worked in lowly jobs for the colonial administration commonly wore shorts as did many grown-up African men who served in the private households of white employers. Despite its history, the bush suit of colonial vintage soon became required wear for men in official jobs in the new nation but with an important twist: men now wore long trousers rather than shorts. Called a *safari suit* in Zambia, in eastern and southern Africa, this suit was often referred to as a *kaunda* with reference to Zambia's first president, Kenneth Kaunda, for whom a safari suit was standard wear throughout his lengthy presidency (1964–1991).

Aside from the missionary-inspired top with puffed sleeves and yoked neck, the woman's dress style on the coat of arms is charged with fewer colonial associations than the man's bush suit. It depicts a dress practice that since independence has come to be interpreted as traditional. When Zambia became a one-party state in 1972, a commemorative stamp, also drawn by Gabriel Ellison (Figure 7.2), was issued. Featuring three women in chitenge wear, the stamp effectively helped to turn chitenge into an emblem of Zambian women's dress.

During the 1960s and 1970s, Betty Kaunda, the wife of Kenneth Kaunda, together with members of the ruling party's women's league, played a prominent role in promoting chitenge dress as "respectable" at a time when miniskirts were all the rage for younger women (Hansen 2004). Conflating dress practice with women's "proper roles" as wives and mothers (Schuster 1979, 160–65), they

Figure 7.2 Zambian women wearing chitenge. Postage stamp drawn by Zambian artist Gabriel Ellison (1972). *Photo*: Karen Tranberg Hansen.

helped popularize the chitenge suit, an ensemble of a skirt or a wrapper and a top, that became increasingly more elaborately tailored and often accessorized with a folded headscarf in the West African manner. During the Second Republic (1972–1991), invitations to government events recommended such "national" or "traditional" attire: safari suits for men and chitenge dress for women.

Sourcing and production

Recognizing the small size of the local market and applying "empire preference" to imports from other British colonies, the colonial administration never developed a domestic textile and garment industry in Zambia. And major manufacturers of African prints in Europe did not produce textiles specifically targeting this region as, for example, the Dutch firm Vlisco did for West and East Africa. Scholarship has focused particularly on the West African destination of these fabrics (Steiner 1985), yet the Vlisco archives demonstrate that fabrics with different designs also were produced for traders on the East African coast from 1884 onward (Picton 1995, 28). During the 1930s, when Japan was a major exporter of cloth, apparel, and household objects, some kitenge fabrics from Japan reached Zambia from the Belgian Congo (Kitaguwa 2006, 161–62), while Europe, India, and America served as other sources of fabric. Dominating the print fabric market in East Africa from 1950 to 1981, Japanese manufacturers worked with local trading houses and residents to canvas women's tastes and create new kanga designs (Ryan 2016). Furthermore, there has likely been an informal trade in printed fabrics from a variety of sources. The memories of elderly Zambians and photographs may still hold traces of such fabrics.

At independence in 1964, questions about clothing consumption and textile and garment production became both culturally and economically important to the new nation, since independence meant, among other things, producing what previously had been imported. The establishment of two government-supported textile manufacturing factories, Kafue Textiles of Zambia and Mulungushi Textiles, during the late 1960s and early 1970s were an outcome of these developments. Privately owned weaving and spinning plants opened up as well, and small-scale garment production grew. The two textile factories initially produced both chitenge fabrics and ordinary clothing. Over the course of subsequent years, production rose and fell, corresponding to the imposition of import restrictions during most of the 1970s and 1980s and the restrictions' removal in the early 1990s, when the market was opened up (Guille 1995).

Uncompetitive on global markets, both Kafue and Mulungushi closed before the turn of the last millennium, when market liberalization allowed an increase in the importation of textiles and clothing (Hansen 2000, 83–86).[2] Today, the main source of chitenge fabrics in Zambia is China, the biggest supplier for most of Africa (Sylvanus 2016). What is more, chitenge is also a sought-after commodity for long-distance Zambian "suitcase traders," who travel to the Democratic Republic of Congo and Tanzania to purchase domestically produced textiles that are popular with Zambian customers.

There are two main types of African prints: the costlier wax prints that are printed on both faces of the fabric, and the lower-priced fancy or roller prints, that are printed on one face only (Picton 1995, 24). Chitenge (kitenge in East Africa and the Congo) is a roller printed fabric. Consumers evaluate it in terms of fabric quality and design, as well as in terms of price. The colorful imagery includes symbolic and geometric motifs, depictions of human beings, animals, mythical figures, and masks—in lots of different designs. Some designs copy existing fabrics and graphic art. Diverse aspects of changing everyday life appear on chitenge fabrics, among them shoes with stiletto heels, sunglasses, and new forms of technology such as cell phones. There are also commemorative chitenge fabrics with both political and religious motifs.

When a woman intends to source chitenge fabric, she has quite a variety of options, ranging from commissioning chitenge manufactured in the Democratic Republic of Congo from a suitcase trader to shopping at a market venue that specializes in fabrics. Between these two options, Zambia's capital Lusaka has also several large urban markets with open and covered stalls, displaying African print fabrics, and outdoor vendors with piles of chitenge on the ground. The oldest of these markets is located in the part of the city reserved for African trade during the colonial period and still often referred to as the "second-class" trading area in the present day. Many traders of Indian and Pakistani background have their retail premises here.[3] A few sell only fabrics, while many offer a mix of fabrics, garments, and household objects, most of which are made in India and China.

In these Lusaka shops and in other areas where fabrics are sold, the fabrics are generally displayed on shelves lining the walls and hung from lines under the ceiling. In the more exclusive stores, chitenge is only sold at its full length (ca. 5.5 meters or approximately 6.5 yards), sufficient for a two- or three-piece outfit, while smaller shops may sell cuts of 2 meters (approximately 2.5 yards), the standard length for a wrapper. When a potential customer wishes to scrutinize a fabric, a shop assistant either has to bring a sample from the shelves or remove it from the line of hanging fabrics with the use of a long pole. As this approach does not readily encourage the customer to touch and rub the fabric to assess its quality, it is not surprising that women are fond of shopping in open air and market stalls where they can actively engage with both the fabric and the vendor. Touch is an important part of fabric selection. If a fabric contains "too much" starch, for example, the customer knows that it is of poor quality and that the starch will wash off when laundered, making the fabric difficult to fold and leaving it with a worn look. In effect, fabric quality contributes to the sensuous experience of wearing chitenge and the embodied materiality of chitenge dress practice.

Chitenge fashions

For everyday use today, many women in Zambia wear chitenge fabrics as wrappers and plain dresses. At home and when they go shopping, women often tie a chitenge wrapper around the waist on top of a plain dress or skirt. They carry their infants in a piece of chitenge on their back. Because chitenge fabric is multipurpose and worn in both town and country, it is unlikely to be replaced entirely by Western-styled garments. The increased availability in recent years of chitenge fabrics with attractive designs at affordable prices has helped to make chitenge wear part of many more women's wardrobes than was the case in the 1970s and 1980s. Office workers and teachers often dress in chitenge to go to work, as do bank clerks on their "free dress" day. Above all, chitenge outfits are worn very widely at formal visits and social occasions such as weddings and kitchen parties (bridal showers), where mature women who have the figure to wear them proudly display their latest chitenges.

With change as the hallmark of fashion everywhere, chitenge wear takes center stage on the fashion scene in Zambia. Detaching fashion from its conventional association with the Western-dominated international fashion industry, chitenge dress practice demonstrates an additional dimension of fashion, namely its individuality and efficacy that play out in the performative quality of embodied dress practice (Hansen 2013b, 4–6). Here, the materiality of the fabric and the body play together. As I explained earlier, tailored chitenge dresses became popular in the 1960s as "national dress." Over time, chitenge outfits have incorporated changing style elements from across Africa, influenced in particular by clothing trends from the Democratic Republic of Congo and West Africa and, in turn, spreading regionally in southern Africa (Sizaire, Mwembu, and Jewsiewicki 2002).

During the mid to late 1980s, chitenge outfits were plain skirts or wrappers worn with tops adorned by contrasting ribbons around necks and sleeves. Tie-dyed cloth, made by women from Ghana and Nigeria who taught Zambian women the technique, also became common. Chitenge was tailored into loose garments, including trouser and top combinations, with West African-styled embroidery around the necks, sleeves, and edges. During the early 1990s, the trouser and top combination changed to skirts and tops of chitenge or tie-dyed fabric with marked waistlines, peplums, elaborate, built-up sleeves supported by interfacing, and with collars, necklines, and fronts embellished by contrasting fabric, buttons, ruffles, or smocking. There were several types of skirts, including pencil skirts, plain wrappers, and double wrappers (for an example, see Figure 7.3). During the mid-1990s, tight pencil skirts reaching below the knee with a long slit in the front became known as "Tshala Muana," the name of a popular singer in the Democratic Republic of Congo. The late 1990s saw a style inspired by West African dress and referred to as "Nigerian *boubou*," named after the French term for the big robes men wear in Francophone Africa. It consisted of huge gowns of single-colored fabric, damask, or damask imitations, with

Figure 7.3 Women dressed for a party: one (*left*) in tailor-made office wear, and three in chitenge outfits (the second woman from the left wears a "Nigerian *boubou*,") Lusaka (2002). *Photo*: Karen Tranberg Hansen. Previously published in: Hansen (2017).

embroidery in contrasting colors. Elaborate head ties completed the look. By the turn of the millennium, popular chitenge outfits comprised short-sleeved blouses and full-length skirts, one particular style was called *donafish* and had a bottom flounce reminiscent of a mermaid's tail.

Going to the tailor

Zambia's postcolonial fashion scene centered on tailors, small stores, and boutiques as well as on entrepreneurial suitcase traders. Going to a tailor to place an order for a garment is a long-standing dress option in Zambia, especially in the not-so-distant past, due to the limited choice and drab clothes for sale in the government-owned department stores during the era of the one-party state (1972–1991). Most tailors then were men, as many still are, though more and more women have since joined their ranks.

If small-scale tailoring in markets, alleyways, and storefronts is dominated by men, there is another setting in which many women have become involved in the tailor's craft. Home-based production, often with hired tailors of both sexes, is a sideline activity organized by women who work away from home, but also by some who pursue design full-time. Such operations may take place in the home or in servants' quarters in homes in medium- to high-income residential areas. Some of these women entrepreneurs go to office buildings soliciting orders. In the second half of the 1990s, most of their output consisted of women's two-piece office wear and chitenge outfits.

When a prospective client wishes to commission a chitenge outfit, she can call on local and foreign tailors (from the Democratic Republic of Congo, Ghana, and Nigeria), many of them men, as well as designers, who are mostly (but not exclusively) women. Throughout the 1990s, for example, I commissioned my chitenge outfits from two male tailors, beginning with a small-scale corridor tailor of Malawian background and then turning to a man from the Democratic Republic of Congo—who had worked from his downtown, alleyway atelier with six women tailors in Lusaka since the 1980s, if not earlier. On the advice of a friend, herself a former clothing vendor, in the present millennium I have called on a woman tailor, again of Congolese background, who worked with four to six women tailors in an atelier located in a never-completed downtown office building. I have also bought ready-made chitenge outfits from displays in arcades, alleyways, and markets, in spur-of-the-moment decisions, attracted by the styling of the outfit as well as its color combination and design.

How do people attribute meaning to dress in Zambia? Going to the tailor offered rich insights into one phase of the meaning-making of clothing. Participant observation in tailors' workshops enabled me to see how tailors and their clients reached decisions about design and style, to investigate how tailors created and developed style, and to ask clients about their decision to go to the tailor rather than to formal stores or secondhand clothing markets. Some tailors show albums featuring photographs of their own styles. Others display old pattern books, and European or South African fashion magazines, while still others use simple drawings. Many customers bring garments or photos of dresses they want to have copied, or they describe what they want the tailor to create. Since the turn of the millennium, Nigerian and Ghanaian posters of women's tailored outfits in African print fabrics have been on display in many tailor shops, adding regional inspirations to a thoroughly Africanized dress practice (Gott 2010, 24).[4]

Tailors have played an important yet somewhat unappreciated role in the making of fashion conscious consumers (Hansen 2013b). Satisfying both needs and desires, tailors' creations help to fabricate dreams. Tailors sew anything from school uniforms to party wear, and they also mend or alter *salaula* (secondhand clothing). Many tailors produce chitenge outfits that continue to develop in new directions. Some tailors produce job lots for established boutiques, while others make chitenge dresses "on order" for suitcase traders who in turn sell them in Zimbabwe and South Africa. There, the production of African print dresses is not very widespread, and in fact, in the mid-1990s, such dresses were known in the south as "Zambia." Perhaps throughout the entire southern African region, as Leslie Rabine suggested to be true in Kenya, such "global African dress signifies not tradition but modernity . . . [that constructs] an elusive and ambiguous . . . national identity" (Rabine 1997, 163).

Today, in addition to tailors, dress shops, boutiques (some of which are in newly developed shopping malls), and secondhand clothing markets offer an abundance of clothing choices for all income groups—choices that were unknown in Zambia's controlled economy prior to the turn of the 1980s. No longer facing currency restrictions, apparel entrepreneurs fly to London, New York, Dubai, Hong Kong, Bangkok, and other long-haul destinations to purchase clothing, shoes, and accessories for resale in a growing number of exclusive shops as well as in private arrangements. Suitcase traders, catering to less upscale consumers, travel across the region to South Africa, Botswana, Tanzania, the Democratic Republic of Congo, and West Africa, as well as to Mauritius, India, and China, buying more affordable apparel and textiles, some on commission for established traders and the rest to resell to traders in city markets or from homes and offices. Chitenge is one of the commodities they source in this way.

Designers and new style creations

The design scene is the most recent twist on the ever-changing appreciation of stylish dress in Zambia, as it is in many other countries in Africa (Delhave and Woets 2015; Rovine 2015; Grabski 2009). In the mid-1990s, downtown Lusaka had several production units with boutique-style outlets, operated by well-educated women, often married to wealthy men. Such women were able to travel abroad, where some had taken design and fashion courses. They concentrated on producing "high quality fashion garments for high-income clients who prefer imported clothing from London, Paris, and New York" to what they perceived as cheap, local wear, including chitenge (Kasengele 1998, 96–98). But when I began to explore the fashion and design scene in 2007, the preferences for Western wear were being challenged. Seasonally changing and creatively styled chitenge outfits had begun to take center stage alongside other dress inspirations in fashionable women's wardrobes.

Several upscale shopping malls have opened in Lusaka since 1997. New consumption spaces, clothing stores, and boutiques appeal to urban residents with money to spend. Against this backdrop, two processes have helped fuel the growth of a more vibrant fashion design scene. First, the production potential of the new designers has been greatly improved by the ready availability of imported sewing machines, dress fabric, and sewing notions in recent years. Second, and above all, their exposure to a global world of fashion and styles has expanded and along with it, the scope for local dress entrepreneurship. The internet and social media have opened up networks of previously unimaginable interchange, spanning the globe.

There is now a formal fashion circuit, complete with organizers, promoters, models, and photographers. Dress entrepreneurs view themselves as designers and label their own clothing lines, among the recent and carefully watched are Debbie Chu, Dodo Wear Design, Fay Designs, Kamanga Wear, and Kutowa. The first organized Zambia Fashion Week unfolded in Lusaka in October 2005 and has taken place subsequently every year except for a brief hiatus between 2009 and 2011. Alongside this, other fashion shows and competitions have flourished, with new events and venues cropping up each year. In 2014, for example, a group of fashion professionals established the Zambia Fashion Council to promote locally produced fashion.

Most of these designers are women, although there are a few men as well. Among them are people of several national and cultural backgrounds, that is, not all of them are black Zambians. What they all share is a keen sense of style acquired from diverse experiences and exposures that do not always include formal training. Many of these designers, as I noted above, do not sew themselves but hire tailors, mostly men but also women, to carry out the basic tasks. A few put out their work for completion by tailors. Many operate from their own or their parents' homes or from rented premises. They use several sewing machines, mostly their own but, at times, these can be rented too. These can include specialized equipment such as chain- or lock-stitch sewing machines, as well as machines for embroidery and knitting. Some designers had several industrial sewing machines as well as old-fashioned treadle and hand-operated machines. Consider Angela Mulenga, for example, whose production of the Queen's Wear label, started by her mother, takes place in a tiny workshop in one of downtown Lusaka's older shopping venues, the Central Arcade, using four industrial machines and one embroidery machine. Angela employs four male tailors, of whom the oldest began working for Angela's mother several years ago.

Who are the clients? For a while, My Choice, an upscale boutique in Lusaka's Manda Hill shopping mall, sold some garments produced by the new designers. In 2014, Zambia's first designer boutique featuring locally created fashion, Vala Local Design House (*vala* meaning wear in the Cinyanja language in Zambia), opened in a strip mall for commissioned sales of the clothes by local designers. This new emporium was the brainchild of the Zambia Fashion Council. The new crop of style entrepreneurs also designed clothes for beauty pageants and *Face of Africa* contestants.[5] In 2009, a group of them designed part of the wardrobe for the Zambian participant in the Miss Universe contest held in Brazil. Designs produced for such events have ripple effects, initiating a chain of referrals. Women of means call on these designers to get special dresses made, particularly for kitchen parties (bridal showers) and weddings. Many designers have a special clientele of women in high-level jobs and public positions: these women are well known throughout Zambian society and regarded as trendsetters when it comes to fashion.

The new designers operate in a fashion arena where tailors continue to be important. Consider Sylvia Masebo, who is in her forties, and was member of Parliament and minister for local government and housing from 2005, and used two local designers and a Nigerian tailor. A flamboyant dresser, depending on whether she was visiting her local constituency or seated in Parliament, she mixed Western-styled and chitenge wear, often with hats or folded headdresses.

"I have a lot of *dukus* [headdresses] which I usually do myself,"[6] she said in an interview, "it is just that I am captured [in photographs in the media] more in Western hats as opposed to African." She loves jewelry, which she carefully pairs with every outfit as well as matching shoes and bags. When traveling abroad, Ms. Masebo makes sure to dress in "African outfits" as a representation of who she is and where she comes from. "Fifty percent of my clothes are Western while the others are African . . . I do not wear Zambian or Nigerian or Kenyan, I wear African because that's who I am" (Post 2005).

Fabric, dress, and body works

Chitenge, as I noted at the outset, identifies both a fabric and a dress practice thus merging on women's bodies the agentive medium of the fabric with dress practice. I can think of no better illustration of this argument than a faux pas committed by the mayor of Livingstone, John Mukosho, at the 51st Local Government Association of Zambia's annual conference in July, 2007. The minister of local government and housing, Sylvia Masebo, whom I introduced earlier, attended the Livingstone conference, as did other government representatives. In his address, the Livingstone mayor said that Masebo was a very beautiful woman and that she was "evergreen" because of her dressing. He continued: "I would like to congratulate the ever-beautiful Masebo for the appointment to the chair of the SADC [Southern African Development Community] local government desk," and then went on to suggest that "no wonder the people in Chipata [Masebo's constituency] refer to you as the evergreen woman." At that point vice president Rupiah Banda intervened, reprimanding Mukosho that it was against protocol to overpraise Ms. Masebo. Before he officially opened the conference, the vice president advised Mukosho: "If I were you, I would not do that because even myself as vice president, I cannot say those things. You should just look, don't comment" (Chirwa, Kapekele, and Sichalwe 2007).

This exchange invites explanation. Protocol aside, Mayor Mukosho's comments on good-looking Masebo translated some Tonga or Leya terms (languages spoken in the Livingstone area) into rather awkward English. The translation captures the meaning of shiny or bright as a characterization of a person, *mukozi ujo nio veka* [from the adjective *kubeka* for shiny], meaning "she is [looks] bright [shiny/shimmering]."[7] This is the "evergreen" of Sylvia Masebo, a person whose presence, including her dress and accessories, lights up the room and who has a special aura around her in particular contexts. Regardless of whether it followed protocol or not, Mukosho's captivating characterization of Sylvia Masebo's dressed form goes to the heart of widespread understanding of the performative dimension of fashionable dress in Zambia and its affecting sensibilities. At that moment and in that context, the materiality of her dress and accessories embodied Sylvia Masebo's entire *gestalt* as a fashionable woman (Eicher and Roach-Higgins 1992, 13).

Conclusion

Today in Zambia, adult men wear suits and not big robes as more commonly seen among men in West Africa or on the East African coast. Adult women's wardrobes hold Western-styled garments, which they wear when at work in schools, banks, and offices. For festive occasions and special events, women may dress in elaborate chitenge outfits. Once considered as appropriate for mothers and grandmothers, today chitenge wear is a part of fashionable Zambian women's wardrobes, demonstrating the material role of fashion in the experience and expression of a proud cultural identity (Hansen 2017). Although most chitenge fabric today is imported from China, it nonetheless constitutes the emblem of women's dress in Zambia. Developing within changing political, economic, and cultural contexts with its multiple origins and ever-changing styling, chitenge continues to be considered "traditional."

Contrary to Gabriel Ellison's earlier mentioned concern about the human bearers in her national coat of arms design in 1964, the woman in chitenge wear has indeed withstood the effects of time. This chapter has demonstrated how women's dressed bodies have appropriated chitenge fabric to make, or change, a sense of gender identity and place in the world since independence in Zambia. The sensuous experience of wearing chitenge makes the fabric act together with women's bodies. What is more, propelled by the aesthetic sensibilities of a new generation of Zambian creative designers, chitenge fashions have been developed in new directions with inspirations from many angles. And yet, so-called "traditionally built" women continue to proudly display their dressed bodies in chitenge as occasional and special events wear. Young women, who used to complain that chitenge outfits made them look "old" (Hansen 2000, 204), are increasingly attracted to the new creatively styled chitenge fashions. Today's young designers work to change the way Zambian women dress by adding a new edge to chitenge, allowing it to become everyday wear in the wardrobes of young, upcoming professional women with disposable incomes (Kutowa interview 2014). A twenty-one year old designer with a background in business administration with whom I had discussed design and dress practice had no doubt that *chitenge* would stand the test of time (interview July 2009).

Notes

1 This chapter draws on my previous work on markets and dress in Zambia (Hansen 2000) as well as on explorations of the developing fashion scene in Lusaka, undertaken in 2007, 2009, and 2014 (Hansen 2014).

2 There have been several unsuccessful efforts to revive these industries.

3 Many of these traders live in the residential area adjacent to their retail establishments in an area reserved for persons of "Indian" background during the colonial period. The area has a mosque and a Hindu Hall.

4 The internet may be opening up new style options, which I have not explored.

5 The Face of Africa competition sponsored by the South African satellite network M-Net takes place once a year. It features stunning-looking young women aged between seventeen and twenty-four, who have been selected from fourteen countries across Africa to compete for international modeling contracts. The 2010 winner was from Zambia.

6 Dukus is a misspelling of the plural form of duka, from the Afrikaans term *doek* for scarf or headwear. The widespread use in Zambia of terms like *boubou* and *duka/duku* without specific place reference testifies to the generalization of dress inspirations into a "[pan]-African" style.

7 Translation and explanation by Tonga-speaking Violet Muchilimba Banda.

References

Chirwa, Joan, Mutale Kapekele, and Noel Sichalwe. "Banda Rebukes Mayor for Saying Masebo is Beautiful." *Maravi* (blog), July 17, 2007. Accessed May 31, 2017. http://maravi.blogspot.it/2007/07/banda-rebukes-mayor-for-saying-masebo.html

Clarke, Towani, designer of *Kutowa*, 2014. "Interview" in Lusaka by Karen Tranberg Hansen. September.

Delhave, Christine, and Rhoda Woets. 2015. "The Commodification of Ethnicity: Vlisco Fabrics and Wax Cloth Fashion in Ghana." *International Journal of Fashion Studies* 2(1): 77–97.

Eicher, Joanne B., and Mary Ellen Roach-Higgins. 1992. "Definitions and Classifications of Dress: Implications for Analysis of Gender Roles." In *Dress and Gender: Making and Meaning*, edited by Ruth Barnes and Joanne B. Eicher, 8–28. Oxford: Berg.

Gott, Suzanne. 2010. "The Ghanaian *Kaba*: Fashion that Sustains Culture." In *Contemporary African Fashion*, edited by Suzanne Gott and Kristyne Loughran, 11–27. Bloomington: Indiana University Press.

Gott, Suzanne, and Kristyne Loughran, eds. 2010. *Contemporary African Fashion*. Bloomington: Indiana University Press.

Gott, Suzanne, Kristyne Loughran, Betsy D. Quick, and Leslie Rabine, eds. 2017. *African Print Fashion Now! A Story of Taste, Globalization, and Style*. Los Angeles: Fowler Museum, University of California at Los Angeles.

Grabski, Joanna. 2009. "Making Fashion in the City: A Case Study of Tailors and Designers in Dakar, Senegal." *Fashion Theory* 13(2): 215–42.

Guille, Jackie. 1995. "Southern African Textiles Today: Design, Industry and Collective Enterprise." In *Technology, Tradition and Lurex: The Art of Textiles in Africa*, edited by John Picton, 51–54. London: Lund Humphries Publishers.

Hansen, Karen Tranberg. 2000. *Salaula: The World of Secondhand Clothing and Zambia*. Chicago: University of Chicago Press.

Hansen, Karen Tranberg. 2004. "Dressing Dangerously: Miniskirts, Gender Relations, and Sexuality in Zambia." In *Fashioning Africa: Power and the Politics of Dress*, edited by Jean Allman, 166–85. Bloomington: Indiana University Press.

Hansen, Karen Tranberg. 2013a. "Introduction." In *African Dress: Fashion, Agency, Performance*, edited by Karen Tranberg Hansen and D. Soyini Madison, 1–11. London: Bloomsbury.

Hansen, Karen Tranberg. 2013b. "Fabricating Dreams: Sewing Machines, Tailors, and Urban Entrepreneurship in Zambia." In *The Objects of Life in Central Africa: The History of Consumption and Social Change, 1840–1980*, edited by Robert Ross, Marja Hinfelaar, and Iva Pesa, 167–85. Leiden: Brill.

Hansen, Karen Tranberg. 2014. "Dressed Bodies, Everyday Fashion Practices and Livelihoods: Perspectives from Africa." In *Haute Africa, People Photography Fashion*, edited by Christophe De Jaeger and Ramona Van Gansbeke, 189–206. Tielt, Belgium: Lannoo Publishing.

Hansen, Karen Tranberg. 2017. "From Grandmother's Dress to the Fashion Runway: *Chitenge* Styles in Zambia." In *African-Print Fashion Now! A Story of Taste, Globalization, and Style*, edited by Suzanne Gott, Kristyne Loughran, Betsy D. Quick, and Leslie Rabine, 160–61. Interleaf H. Los Angeles: Fowler Museum, University of California at Los Angeles.

Hansen, Karen Tranberg, and D. Soyini Madison, eds. 2013. *African Dress: Fashion, Agency, Performance*. London: Bloomsbury.

Kasangele, Mwango. 1998. "Differentiation among Small-Scale Enterprises: The Zambian Clothing Industry in Lusaka." In *African Entrepreneurship: Theory and Practice*, edited by Anita Spring and Barbara E. McDade, 93–106. Gainesville: University of Florida Press.

Kitaguwa, Katsuhiko. 2006. "Japanese Competition in the Congo Basin in the 1930s." In *Intra-Asian Trade and the World Market*, edited by A. J. H. Lantham, Heita Kawakatsa, and Katsuhiko Kitaguwa, 155–67. New York: Routledge.

Mulenga, Andrea, designer of *Queen's Wear*, 2009. "Interview" in Lusaka by Karen Tranberg Hansen. July.

Picton, John. 1995. "Introduction. Technology, Tradition and Lurex: The Art of Textiles in Africa." In *Technology, Tradition and Lurex: The Art of Textiles in Africa*, edited by John Picton, 9–30. London: Lund Humphries Publishers.

Post. 2005. "Trendsetters." December 2, 2005.

Rabine, Leslie W. 1997. "Not a Mere Ornament: Tradition, Modernity, and Colonialism in Kenya and Western Clothing." *Fashion Theory* 1(2): 145–68.

Rabine, Leslie W. 2002. *The Global Circulation of African Fashion*. New York: Berg.

Rovine, Victoria L. 2015. *African Fashion. Global Style: Histories, Innovations and Ideas You Can Wear*. Bloomington: Indiana University Press.

Ryan, MacKenzie Moon. 2016. "Designed by Resident Indian Traders, Consumed by East African Women: Japanese Dominance in Imported Kanga Cloth Production, 1950–1981." Paper presented at conference on Dressing Global Bodies: Clothing, Cultures, Politics and Economies in Globalizing Eras, c. 1500–1900s. University of Alberta, Edmonton, Canada, July 7–9, 2016.

Schuster, Ilsa M. G. 1979. *New Women of Lusaka*. Palo Alto: Mayfield Publishing.

Sizaire, Violaine, Dibwe dia Mwembu, and Bogumil Jewsiewicki, eds. 2002. *Femmes—Modes—Musiques: Memoires de Lubumbashi*. Paris: L'Harmattan.

Steiner, Christopher. 1985. "Another Image of Africa: Toward an Ethnohistory of European Cloth Marketed in West Africa, 1873–1960." *Ethnohistory* 32(2): 91–110.

Sylvanus, Nina. 2016. *Patterns in Circulation: Cloth, Gender, and Materiality in West Africa*. Chicago: University of Chicago Press.

8

"Made in China": Material meanderings of fast-fashion cities

Christina H. Moon

The "jobber market" in downtown Los Angeles has become, over the last decade, a central hub for fast fashion, proliferating the design and distribution of fashion-forward clothing at affordable prices to an American mass market. In a ten-block area, hundreds of Korean families operate small mom-and-pop businesses of over 6,000 clothing labels, in what is known as "private label" businesses. The labels in these clothes will be switched out and replaced by the labels of American department stores, retail outlets, and brands that purchase and sell this clothing to the mass market. Fast fashion's emergence within this neighborhood, and its quick production, is reliant on the intergenerational dynamics of these Korean families, whereby divisions of labor and skills between an older and younger generation bring together decades of knowledge and experience in garment production and market trends (see Moon 2014). The majority of the fast-fashion designed in this district is materially sourced and laboriously made in China. In fact, within Los Angeles, nearly all fast-fashion retailers who sell their designs to American department stores and retail stores regularly travel to cities such as Guangzhou and Shanghai in China, often twice a month. They maintain business contacts and buy clothing at fast-fashion wholesale markets in these cities. In addition, they check in on orders that they have put into production at manufacturing factories across southern and inner China. Understanding the material and labor practices of Korean fast-fashion families in Los Angeles requires the tracking and understanding of complex global supply chains of fast-fashion production across multiple sites. As fast fashion demands us to follow intermediaries, agents, and jobbers to Asia, it becomes important to understand the context and role of countries, particularly China, in the coordination and complex webs of material sourcing, technological capacities, labor for assembly, notions of creativity, and the role of cities in the making of a new fashion order.

I had the opportunity to travel to southern and northern China in 2015 with a research group called "Spatial Politics of Work: Working Group on Economies and Societies," which is part of the India China Institute at The New School in New York. The group's mission is to bring together a multi-/interdisciplinary understanding of the relationship between design and labor across cities in China, India, and the United States. This trip provided me with an introduction to the fashion landscape of China with which these Korean "fast-fashion families" are working. I am guided by fashion studies scholarship on the history and development of fashion industries across China, particularly within the last decade, and this includes the work of Chu (2016), Clark (2012), Finanne (2005), Skov (2002), Tsui (2009), and Tu (2009). I argue that the production of fast fashion in China plays a significant role not only in shaping the materiality of fast fashion, but also in the urbanization and material development of Asian and American cities. Starting off in Los Angeles, this chapter weaves through my impressions of and encounters with materiality across Guangzhou, Shenzhen, and Shanghai, cities that have emerged as major fast-fashion centers or capitals in Asia and globally. In my narrative, I detail global encounters that highlight the relationship between meandering through a city and the materiality of fashion. Inspired by Walter Benjamin's essay "One Way Street" (1985), I show how such material encounters with fashion reflect the legacy of garment industrialization in cities, the communities of innovation, creativity, and labor, who produce fast fashion, and the emergence of state objectives to promote and cultivate economies toward fashion and away from garment manufacturing.

China on my mind

Everyone always has China on the mind, at all hours, in the Los Angeles jobber market. When speaking to vendors, everyone seems to always have a sense of what time it is "over there." They know what time factories are open for business, when workers will be off on holiday, when the work will get done. In Los Angeles, the end of the work day is marked by preparations made for the start of the next work day, which is just about to begin in China. At 6 p.m. in Los Angeles, faxes as well as WeChat, WhatsApp, Kakao, and Skype messages direct orders to agents, vendors, sources, and factories in preparation for the start of their 24-hour work day. Timing is crucial to every aspect of the making and wearing of fast fashion, from how quickly the trends come and go, to how quickly it can be made, to how quickly it can get to the store and onto someone's body.

Throughout the district, nearly every cardboard box full of fast fashion, waiting on sidewalks to be put on the back of some truck, reads "Made in China." At the largest fast-fashion trade show in North America, Korean vendors, who make up the majority of booths, are wary of white businessmen walking the floor slowly with older Asian women trailing behind them. They tell me that these women are patternmakers from China, who were flown in from the factory floor itself, so that they can take a closer look at all the different varieties and kinds of designs that these Korean-American mom-and-pop shop labels make and sell. The Korean vendors tell me that they themselves travel to China often, twice a month from Los Angeles, to carry out business that is entirely culturally set up for them. With a young Korean Chinese agent or guide, Korean jobbers are taken to certain wholesale fast-fashion markets, factory sites, material sources, and neighboring cities or villages with specialized labor. Korean jobbers stay in hotels where the services are provided in both Korean and Mandarin, where even the food is prepared in Korean or Korean Chinese style. These services are streamlined packages that cater to the many Korean manufacturers of the diaspora, working in garment industries from around the world, producing fast fashion in China. Intermediary agents, traders, quality control agents, factory managers, all kinds of human liaisons may turn out to be relatives or friends, or friends of friends, or just plain old contacts from vendors in the Los Angeles market—the crucial cultural in-betweens, who speak both Korean and Mandarin, to create the ties of trust needed in this complex fast-fashion global supply chain. Throughout the 1990s, in the local Los Angeles district, almost everything was produced in Los Angeles itself, or in Mexico, or in Central or South America, supported by the North American Free Trade Agreement (NAFTA) and General Agreement on Trade and Tariffs (GATT) trade relations and Korean diasporic connections to South America. With the introduction of China into the World Trade Organization (WTO) in 2001 and the expiration of the Multi-Fibre Arrangement (MFA) on January 1, 2005, almost everyone in the Los Angeles jobber market began to produce in China through the 2000s (Moon 2014). Today, the local Los Angeles market and the fast-fashion markets of China are inextricably intertwined.

Lace at 30,000 feet in the air

It is the summer of 2015, and I am headed to Hong Kong from New York City. The airplane ride from John F. Kennedy airport to Hong Kong takes approximately sixteen hours, and it somehow feels a relief to sit on an airplane with so many people who look like me, Asian. To read on the plane, I have with me Stefan Al's illustrated guidebook on the *Factory Towns of Southern China* (2012), some journal articles on the history of apparel manufacturing in China, including Ching Kwan Lee's *Gender and the South China Miracle* (1998), Keller Easterling's book on *Extrastatecraft* (2014), which tells the history of export processing zones and zonal technologies. These texts provide me with some context for the conditions that propelled southern China through the 1970s and 1980s into the manufacturing powerhouse of a nation it has become known for in the last two decades. This is, in fact, what made American fast fashion possible throughout the 2000s—the capacities of clothing production throughout Asia: Korea, Taiwan, and Hong Kong from the 1950s onward, and China from the 1980s until now. From 1978 onward, the decollectivization of communes and socialist work units released a massive supply of surplus rural labor in China, evidenced by the migration of entire rural populations into urban areas of the south, alongside the influx of foreign capital (Lee 1998). It is estimated today, that nearly 260 million migrant workers (nearly 25% of the entire population) work in this "world's factory." Many are women working in cities such as Guangzhou, in factories set up for export processing and production for American and European consumption, in fields that were once farms. Diasporic links between Hong Kong and mainland China helped develop agricultural lands in which factories could be set up with joint investment, capital, four walls, and some machines alongside a constant "supply" of young, healthy women willing to work for low wages in export processing zones where state laws and civil rights were suspended (Lee 1998; Ngai 2005). I think back to the time when the labels on my own clothing as a child read "Made in Taiwan," "Made in Hong Kong," or "Made in Korea." These days, my clothes only have labels that state "Made in Bangladesh," "Made in Poland," and "Made in China."

Halfway through my plane ride, the young woman sitting next to me in our two-seater row strikes up a conversation. I learn that she is a manager and sales representative for a lace factory, in which she has been working since graduating from college. Its mills are located in Shaoxing City, Zhejiang Province, and she had come to New York City to find ways to connect the mills to American fashion companies on Fifth and Sixth Avenue. She pulls out lace samples from her purse. We look through them together, and I feel their textures. I look at the lace closely and am reminded of the lace in my own wedding dress, collected in a vintage shop in France by a fashion design friend who made the dress for me. I think of the lace of the Korean family I interviewed in Los Angeles—for its first decade in the United States in the 1990s, lace was the family's livelihood at a time when "fast fashion" did not exist and when one could live off of one material and trend for years. Lace, this material that was once made of linen, silk, and gold, drawn in the earliest European paintings by Hans Mering, hand-stitched in spidery webs of intricacy, and mathematical in its patterns and shapes, is the materiality of collective expression. And here it is, as a sample piece out of the purse of a woman originally from a northeastern city of China and sitting next to me on this plane, stirring a memory, a memory of the material of a family's livelihood.

The woman shows me photos on her phone of lists of company rosters found in the lobbies of garment district industry buildings in New York. During her two-week visit, she tells me she went to the most well-known industry buildings in the district—545, 575, 1411, etc.—which hold the headquarters of the most famous American clothing companies. I think how bold it was of her to just show up, making her way past security guards and into these buildings—there are so many mythical fashion tales of some random designer or sales agent showing up out of the dark to make a pitch, without appointment, and landing a sale. But the New York fashion industry—no matter how it is broadcast to the world through the Internet, social media, and television shows—is insular and exclusive, and an introduction or connection often goes so much further.

She asks me if I will visit the most famous fast-fashion wholesale markets in Guangzhou and Shanghai. I tell her that many of the Los Angeles manufacturers I interview make trips to do business there, and she tells me that the more high-end, quality designs of fast fashion are Korean-dominated and made. Funny that what she describes as high-end in China is often considered "low quality and cheap" in the United States. She then asks me if Parsons School of Design students would perhaps want free samples of the lace to somehow incorporate into their student collections. After all, she states, one day, one of these New York students might run a big design firm—fashion requires one to always look ahead.

The very materiality of the lace in front of us seems to conjure up all kinds of dreams and desires—weddings and the feminine body, yet also of making it big, of one day perhaps supplying a famous well-known New York brand or company, the connection of a Parsons faculty, a relationship between a lace mill as far away as Shantou, China, to the fashion companies in buildings of the New York garment district. When I got home to New York weeks later, I googled the name of the lace company for which she works. K. G. S. Lace is an eighteen-year-old-factory that is listed in Alibaba and employs up to one thousand people in a list of a thousand other lace mills. I think of the texture of lace in my hands, its intricate patterns and webs—a kind of metaphor for webs of networks that could bring together the global encounter by two strangers—one from a mill city and the other from a fashion capital—on opposite ends of the world, in flight 30,000 feet up in the air.

Design, machines, and borders

At Hong Kong Design Institute, which has a student body of 7,000 students, I meet with the dean of design, who tells me of the importance of design programs across China. He points out that most universities in China have developed and cultivated design departments—that design is a part of the "national economy" and "future of China." There are design departments at universities, "incubating" design institutes, design labs, and design centers. The dean tells me how he has helped to establish the Fashion Fund Foundation, a nongovernmental organization (NGO) that "grooms and incubates designers into an international platform," with the university working to represent local Hong Kong design brands in fashion weeks held at global fashion capitals such as Paris, Tokyo, and Beijing. He aims to bring local design talent to New York Fashion Week to court international press and buyers. In this fashion world and system, cultural recognition among cities, their hierarchies, and global positioning have material and economic consequences for national and local economies in their pursuit of cultural prominence and recognition.

Yet just forty years ago, the state apparatus of economic policy maintained a completely different message. Under Deng Xiaoping's 1982 reforms of "one country, two systems," foreign investment and international trade emerged in a system of coexistence between capitalist and communist modes of production, dramatically shaping the culture and economic policy of China today. Focused on the development of South China, which was given degrees of autonomy and flexibility in soliciting foreign investment and trade, the first five Special Economic Zones (SEZs) of Shenzhen, Xiamen, Shantou, Zhuhai, and the entire province of Hainan that emerged during the 1980s (Easterling 2014) became the manufacturing hubs for emerging fast-fashion industries. Though the industries that were developed included electronics, hardware, and furniture, foreign capital aimed to invest and develop labor-intensive export manufacturing industries that would largely include clothing and textiles. The next four decades saw the development of the garment factories and industrial zones of South China, where diasporic communities from Hong Kong played a significant role in developing and migrating garment manufacturing to Guangdong, Shenzhen, and the Pearl River Delta (Brooks 2015)—where Koreans now buy or produce American fast fashion. Today, however, municipal governments across Chinese cities are attempting to "rebrand" themselves, moving away from the nickname of "the world's factory" to "the world's tech lab" or "design studio," be it in fashion, electronics, graphic arts, or design, in an effort to "upgrade" local and national economies and provide GDP growth outside manufacturing (Chumley 2016). Today, Hong Kong is a city less well known for manufacturing than it was throughout the 1980s, but instead it is a hub for trading agents, intermediaries, and designers developing local brands for production in the coastal and inner regions of mainland China.

At a different design school, Hong Kong Polytechnic, I am standing in a facility that houses the machinery of the textile, fabric, weaving, dyeing, and assembly process involved in the making of clothing. This giant room is filled with every kind of imaginable loom that may have existed within a 150-year history, including Jacquard looms the height of the ceiling, used for silk embroidery. These looms were built so that silk could compete with the mainstream European cotton of the Industrial Revolution. In this room of looms and machinery, students have access to a history of not only changing technologies in textile and garment production, but also of woven fabrics, decorative patterns, intricate textures, and blended colors in all kinds of imaginative combinations—these are the tangible, material outcomes of technology. Here, numbers, math, equations, and codes for patterns magically transform into fabric.

A fashion design professor accompanies me to an adjacent exhibition gallery to meet its curator and view the final collections of the senior thesis show. The walk from these two spaces of design, labor, and technology—from looms to fabrics to design collections—reminds me of Walter Benjamin who, thinking of photography, wrote, "the physiognomic aspects of visual worlds which dwell in the smallest things, meaningful yet covert enough to find a hiding place in waking dreams, but which, enlarged and capable of formulation, make the difference between technology and magic visible as a thoroughly historical variable" ([1931] 1999, 512). These material worlds that dwell in the smallest things, in the magic of the warp and woof, the colors, and intricate patterns, uncannily capture the cultural and familiar sense of a certain era within the fabric itself. A closer examination reveals the tugs and pulls of machinery—

Figure 8.1 Spools of thread to make textiles, Hong Kong (June, 2015). *Photo*: Christina Moon.

not so much magic but a narrative of machine technology—that people have built to make more efficient "labor," "productivity," and quantifiable "outcomes," archived within this giant room in a Hong Kong design school.

The fabric's patterns, weaves, colors, and textures are dizzying. I head to the Lok Ma Chau, Fumin Lu, train station to get myself across the border to the mainland, the southern city of Shenzhen, where I am to meet my research group. This train station is a control point that connects via a pedestrian footbridge to Futian Port, an immigration port of entry to the People's Republic of China. Crossing the border means a long walk over a covered footbridge that hovers over a dry riverbed, as if I am in Juarez, Mexico, making my way over the Rio Grande River back into El Paso, Texas, close to the border city in which my in-laws once lived. Mostly women walk this footbridge alongside me, carrying with them clothing and fast fashion, cigarettes, milk powder, diapers, liquor, and counterfeit phones from Hong Kong into mainland China. What is the meaning and materiality of these things? As gifts, as commodities, and as gestures, with new shifting values, aesthetics, and identities of their own, how does our understanding of them transform upon the crossing of a border above a dried riverbed? In *Passport Photos* (Kumar 2000), Amitava Kumar asks how identities, subjectivities, and selfhood shift once confronted by an immigration officer— our faces read for truths as our passports are denied or stamped. Though I am above a dried riverbed in China, I keep thinking back to the arroyos of the Rio Grande at the United States-Mexico border. The photographer Richard Barnes captured pictures of the Sonoran Desert at the border of Arizona, of a dried riverbed flowing not with water but discarded clothing. Fast fashion in every imaginable color, feature, and design is caked with dry desert dust, abandoned by owners who used the dried riverbed to change into a fresh set of clean clothes. Once across the border, the undocumented hope to pass as everyday citizens, in clothing that carries their new identities: these migrants hope for their sense of belonging and American dreams to take hold.

The pyramids and an urban village

Entering the Shenzhen Special Economic Zone (SEZ), I feel as if I am entering a corporate park, or a university campus, or perhaps even a gated community/factory site. China's export economies had been propelled toward industrialization and modernization by the late 1970s, and Shenzhen has always been the country's most proud experiment and showcased success story. Here, I notice I have access to Google and Facebook despite China's stringent censorship apparatus and laws. Inside the SEZ, I make my way to a reception for an exhibition opening hosted by the Victoria and Albert Museum "outpost" located in Shenzhen. On one side of the street are newly built modern buildings with large billboard-sized photos of famous Western architects, accompanied by all the language of progress and modernity that one might see in California's Silicon Valley. This city has been, from the 2000s onward, a site for urban experimentation for the world's greatest architects, with every project involving investment in all forms of civic infrastructure. There are newly built subway systems, highways, canals, airports, and public parks designed by architects and urban planners from around the world. These architectural futures are heavily intertwined with images of luxury malls and industrial parks, where the most fashionable European, American, and Chinese luxury brands can be found. Yet the awesome massiveness of the city along with its superstar architectural skyline reflects, too, the financial speculation and uneven/unregulated development of the city—the huge warehouses of factory-run barracks for migrant workers found at the base of these new buildings are evidence of the mass labor and social inequality embodied in this site. Throughout Shenzhen are also fashion-centered industrial parks such as Dalang Fashion Valley, garment manufacturing areas repurposed and rebranded. The city government now urges local garment makers to "upgrade" and develop their own brands and products.

Baishizhou village, a cramped neighborhood village located a fifteen-minute drive from the Shenzhen Futian central business district plaza, is representative of the more than 200 urban villages, inhabited by garment workers, which are disappearing in Shenzhen. These urban villages—villages within a megacity—house millions of migrant workers who work across the city, in factories or in thousands of small workshops, to assemble clothing and electronics for American and European consumption. Baishizhou is one of the densest neighborhoods in the world (Figure 8.2). With 150,000 migrant worker residents per 0.23 square miles of mixed-use residential space, a population density more than twenty times the city average, developers such as Hong Kong-based LVGEM aim to demolish it, replacing it with 59.2 million square feet of fashion shopping malls, high-rises, and hotels. At Handshake 302 Gallery, our research group sits on the floor of a typical migrant worker's rented room—a room that would sleep four to five people. We are a group of seven and have spread out on the floor newspapers to eat lychees. We look up at the walls and see murals painted by the children of migrant workers. Next door, to the right and left of us, are the rooms of the migrant workers themselves who make the everyday material culture of our everyday lives. How is fast fashion understood from this perspective—in the home of the migrant worker who lives and works in the "world's factory"? What dreams of fashion does this *dagongmei* working girl feel?

Figure 8.2 Exterior of migrant residence in Baishizhou village (June, 2015). *Photo*: Christina Moon.

A copy of a copy of a copy

Shanghai has become China's high fashion capital, hosting Shanghai Fashion Week, and the headquarters of the world's most renowned luxury brands. A friend of a colleague guides us through an old fabric market across the street from The Bund, the most historic part of the city's center, and then on to the neighborhood of Tianzifang, an arts and crafts enclave that developed from a traditional residential area into a revitalized, gentrified, fashionable tourist spot. Down the tiny alleyways are small fashion boutiques selling products of "nostalgia for old Shanghai" —beauty and skincare products, lipsticks, and nail polish—with the images of Shanghainese women found on advertisements and movie posters from the 1920s. These were Shanghai's golden glamour years—the image that allows it to claim itself as the most fashionable center in all of China. The beauty products here have less to do with the actual product itself. As our Shanghainese friend tells us, this is about packaging: a little tourist souvenir one can take home from old Shanghai. As the fast-fashion vendors of Los Angeles often remind me, New York is not the center of the fashion world. They tell me they get their trend ideas from the fashion and beauty markets of Seoul and Shanghai, thus shifting my geopolitical fashion worldview.

In an adjacent neighborhood near the French Concession, the apartments on tree-lined streets rent for the same sky-high prices found in London and New York. Curiously, the walls of the entire neighborhood are covered in posters depicting cartoon drawings and figures that exclaim: "Don't go selling your fruit or wares on the sidewalks of the streets here!"; "Don't use or blow your horn to let neighbors know what good deals they are getting on their fruit!"; "Don't go hanging your laundry throughout the neighborhood. We don't want to see your clothes blowing in the wind!" The city government has a stake in transforming these "unruly" streets into the tidy, gentrified, fashionable neighborhood they wish it to be. Small, fashion-centered storefronts (see Figure 8.3) become fancy boutiques that sell knock-off copies of high-end designer clothes (or clothes from the factory floors themselves)—and they are not cheap. One window states that the boutique sells "Alexander Wang, Alexander McQueen, Ann Demeulemeester, Balmain, Balenciaga, Comme Des Garçons, Givenchy, Jil Sander, Junya Watanabe, Lanvin, Mugler, Peter Pilotto, Rick Owens, Sacai, Stella McCartney, Toga, The Row." I am amazed that this high-end fashion world could materialize within this one little shop in Shanghai. I meet with a Taiwanese American architect living in Shanghai, who is working for an American firm in China. We make our way to Qipalu market, the largest wholesale fast-fashion market in northern China, located in Shanghai. When we arrive, I feel the familiarity of the downtown Los Angeles jobber market, or Dongdaemun wholesale market in Seoul, South Korea where the Los Angeles vendors first originated. Every advertisement or sign in Qipalu is in both Korean and Chinese. The fast-fashion Korean networks I study are very much visible and at play here. The market

Figure 8.3 Storefront of a boutique in Shanghai (June, 2015). *Photo*: Christina Moon.

is bustling and I feel a sense of déjà vu, this familiarity of corporate-mall-like-look-but-as-if-underground-in-a-subway-passage-with-cheap-goods-and-too-bright-lighting. These market spaces are so individualized and particular, yet completely familiar and homogenous. I feel that I am in multiple cities, across different continents, from the United States to Asia—I find it all fascinating.

Standing in the first-floor basement of one wholesale market department store, I think about the work of the Italian economist, Gabi Dei Ottati (2009), who investigated the Chinese networks revitalizing an ailing garment manufacturing industrial district in Prato, Italy. In a city of just 200,000 inhabitants, over 50,000 of the population represented Chinese migrant workers who had, by the late 2000s, established at least 5,000 firms ranging from fabric dyers, fabric tailors, and fashion designers to garment manufacturers and wholesaler distributors of finished products—all with the "Made in Italy" label. My companion, the architect, tells me about the film *Gomorrah*, made in 2008 and directed by Matteo Garrone, in which mobsters buy a shoe factory in Prato, and how in reality the Chinese are buying up the Italian-made machinery and technology to use for production in China.

Each stall in the Qipalu market, typical of many of the wholesale fast-fashion clothing markets across Asia, represents *one entire factory*. The more high-end the clothing, the bigger the stall, or "showroom." This is evidence that they represent not just singular factories but trading companies that represent multiple factories. The factories of garment and shoe production are themselves located in "second" and "third" tier cities, which are two to three hours by car from Shanghai. I pick up a shoe, displayed in the basement (which is always where the shoes are), feel it, and turn it over. It is digitally printed on terrycloth, has sequins in parts, and contains within it many allusions to various logos—Michael Kors, Calvin Klein, Tory Burch, and Chanel. These logos—all slammed into one shoe—make the shoe a catch-all for a range of high- to low-end fashions. The architect tells me: "This is how *shanzai* happens. This is where it begins. It's a game of telephone and if we keep on going, we can see how far it might go into the supply chain, into the second and third tier cities that are its beginning and end." With *shanzai*, one does not know if it is "real" or "fake," "serious" or a "joke." *Shanzai* is the merging of many different elements and features of brands, combining design, labor, and technology together in a singularly creative and unintentional manner, a critical comment on corporate aesthetics. "OK" may stand in for "CK," "The South Place" replaces "The North Face." The apples of the Apple logo may shrink to become very small polka dots on a button-down shirt. I find it all so funny and satirical, yet without any irony to it. Here we are at the very bottom of the fast-fashion global supply chain—and yet we can look at all this creativity that is unintentionally critical of the American corporation. I cannot help but marvel at the different technologies represented in these "copies of the copies of the copies of the copies." The sequined patterns, the bedazzled and the bejeweled, and the digitally manufactured or hand-stitched, that can be spatially mapped out in its labor and technology across specialized laboring communities in this city and beyond. How might the aesthetics, design features, and materials—and the fast-paced appearance and innumerable varieties—of fast fashion as "designed innovations" materially capture not only changing consumer tastes but also the socially coordinated network ecologies of shared resources, local knowledge, and sets of expertise across the production chain across inter-Asian cities? How does the design of a piece of clothing spatially and materially map inter-Asian sites that offer different technologies, small-scale craft labor, and mass-scale cut-and-sew assembly in the making of fast fashion? How is design matched with these highly complex, flexible, industrial processes, fragmented across cities and regions in a market-driven environment of multiple spatial and temporal organizations? In the wholesale fast-fashion markets of Los Angeles, Guangzhou, Shanghai, and Seoul, one can find an array of designed material forms that reflect such fascinating amalgamations of design practice, materials, technical skills, handicraft techniques, mass-scale labor practices, and use of advanced technologies.

Outside the market at the end of the day, past the tattoo parlors and hair salons, where young rural workers from factories doing business at the market get their "identity souvenirs," only to go back to their villages and show off their visit to Shanghai, workers emerge from the small sewing factories. As they walk past me, I look at their fashions and styles—most of the T-shirts exhibit large, graphically printed nonsensical English words. I am told that "nostalgia" is an odd word here in China. Many of these women workers grew up with mothers and fathers who wore uniforms—their workers' outfits: "No one got their fashion from their moms—this is all new. That's why the most powerful memory of the changes right now is happening through clothing." Many of the Chinese I meet tell me "there is nothing but progress" among those who grew up during the Cultural Revolution. They see the changes in those migrant workers who now live in the cosmopolitan city and who sew and wear fashion: "If you were born after 1951, you were born after the world was getting better. The industrialists who are in their 40s and 50s—those who started these companies, such as La Chapelle—and their contemporaries have made something of themselves. Their children are the *fuerdai* 富二代—the second generation rich."

"Made in China"

Hanging in the main hallway of the Shanghai library is a large, old scroll depicting ancient Chinese scholars—older men with beards—sitting at tables with books and engaged in the act of writing. At Donghua University, home to what is considered the best fashion design program in Shanghai, there is a large, old, cast metal engraving, depicting women from an earlier time spinning at their looms, standing with bolts of fabric, and taking the measurements of each other's bodies. The curators of the university's textile museum take me through their collection of items from China's modern period from 1840 to 1949. By that time, Western fabrics, patterns, and clippings were already challenging traditional, local weaving techniques as machine-made women's wear emerged with new kinds of patterns, colors, and cuts. Materials and textiles went from heavy and fitted fabrics to lighter ones. In an exhibition of royal garments and embroideries, along with illustrations and drawings from those time periods, I find boxes of silk threads from the late 1800s, labeled "Made in China." The boxes are over one hundred years old and have beautiful graphics and text printed in both English and Chinese. I get lost in the thread colors—so bright, glowing, even luminous— these "Made in China" threads whose colors no longer exist (Figure 8.4).

The dresses displayed are handmade but also involve machine-made trims and details. I look closely at the twentieth century, early cotton stockings by

Figure 8.4 "Made in China" on the selvage of fabric, early twentieth century, displayed at the Shanghai Museum of Textiles and Costume at Donghua University. *Photo*: Christina Moon.

"Nanyang Hosiery," and stare at the children's wear, with embroidered comets for boys and small scissors and rulers for girls. An original illustrated print of "Going to the Derby at Shanghai" published by *Harper's Weekly* in New York, June 14, 1879, is hung on the wall, a scene of cosmopolitan Shanghai. There is an entire section titled "Fabrics and Logos of the Early 20th Century" displaying the first cut pieces of the fabric bolt or selvage that would be trimmed off before buyers bought their yards of fabric. Printed large are the characters for "Made in China." The encounter with this mass-industrialized material product is an obvious but surprising moment for me. It makes me think about globalization and the global encounters of culture, not just in this moment among fast-fashion wholesalers and jobbers in China today, but over one hundred years ago, and how the material webs of clothing and fashion spin together people, places, and times.

In what ways do the lives and work of those mentioned in this chapter complicate the assumed directions and global flows of design and production in today's global fashion industry? Diasporic communities have played a constitutive role in the global circuits of fashion, and, as in the United States, they play a significant role in the fast-fashion wholesale clothing markets of South China (where most of the world's manufacturing of clothing takes place) and Shanghai. Never before has fashion been so materially accessible in variation and diversity in both the realms of production and consumption. Asia plays a significant role in making this possible in manufacturing, promoting its fashion culture economies and industries as deindustrialization processes began to take place. The establishment and cultural recognition of a fashion economy has real consequences on the hierarchy of cities, foreign investment, growth of GDP, and the rise of new middle classes as consumers. These cities and fashion economies in China have a powerful impact on cities in the United States, where communities of material production shape the creation of value. By studying the materiality and design of fashion, I hope to show how the material object embodies an incredibly complex, highly skilled, innovative, and industrialized process, resulting in material products that blur the lines between design and copy, authors and imitators, across cities that intimately tie the United States and Asia.

References

Al, Stefan. 2012. *Factory Town of South China: An Illustrated Guide*. Hong Kong: Hong Kong University Press.

Brooks, Andrew. 2015. *Clothing Poverty: The Hidden World of Fast Fashion and Second-Hand Clothes*. London: Zed Books.

Benjamin, Walter. 1985. *One-way Street and Other Writings*. Translated by Edmund Jephcott. New York: Verso.

Benjamin, Walter. (1931) 1999. "Little History of Photography." In *Selected Writings*, Vol. 2, edited by Michael W. Jennings, Howard Eiland, and Gary Smith, 507–30. Cambridge: The Belknap Press of Harvard University Press.

Chu, Nellie. 2016. "The Emergence of 'Craft' and Migrant Entrepreneurship along the Global Commodity Chains for Fast Fashion in Southern China." *Journal of Modern Craft* 9(2): 193–213.

Chumley, Lily. 2016. *Creativity Class: Art School and Culture Work in Postsocialist China*. Princeton: Princeton University Press.

Clark, Hazel. 2012. "Chinese Fashion Designers: Questions of Ethnicity and Place in the Twenty First Century." *Fashion Practice: The Journal of Design, Creative Process and the Fashion Industry* 4(1): 41–56.

Dei Ottati, Gabi. 2009. "An Industrial District Facing the Challenges of Globalization: Prato Today." *Journal of European Planning Studies* 17(12): 1817–35.

Easterling, Keller. 2014. *Extrastatecraft: The Power of Infrastructure Space*. New York: Verso.

Finanne, Antonia. 2005. "China on the Catwalk: Between Economic Success and Nationalist Anxiety." *The China Quarterly* 183: 587–608.

Kumar, Amitava. 2000. *Passport Photos*. Berkeley: University of California Press.

Lee, Ching Kwan. 1998. *Gender and the South China Miracle: Two Worlds of Factory Women*. Berkeley: University of California Press.

Moon, Christina. 2014. "The Secret World of Fast Fashion." *Pacific Standard*, March 17, 2014. Accessed January 10, 2017. https://psmag.com/economics/secret-world-slow -road-korea-los-angeles-behind-fast-fashion-73956

Pun, Ngai. 2005. *Made in China: Women Factory Workers in a Global Workplace*. Durham: Duke University Press.

Skov, Lise. 2002. "*Hong Kong* Fashion Designers as Cultural Intermediaries: Out of Global Garment Production." *Cultural Studies* 16(4): 553–69.

Tsui, Christine. 2009. *China Fashion: Conversations with Designers*. London: Berg.

Tu, Thuy Linh Nguyen. 2010. *The Beautiful Generation: Asian Americans and the Cultural Economy of Fashion*. Chapel Hill: Duke University Press.

Section Three

Materiality and embodiment

Introduction

Many fashion theories revolve around the connection between clothing and identity (see for discussion Davis 1992; Entwistle 2000). They come to the conclusion that clothing and fashion play a constitutive role in the process of identity formation as they act with mental and material-aesthetic force in the identification of human beings according to categories such as gender, class, ethnicity, age, etc. The way humans select, assemble and wear clothing is part of an embodied process of acculturation, which creates and is equally determined by the cultural situation in or for which people present themselves (Entwistle 2000; Barthes [1967] 1990). That is, the modifications and techniques of the body (Mauss 1973; Craik 1994), made possible by fashion and clothing, are highly structured. They are creative, performative acts, through which people construct and experience their being-in-the-world, even if getting dressed in their everyday lives often happens quite habitually and intuitively. We come to know exactly what is appropriate for the job, for leisure, for an evening event, or a job interview. Intangible rules of behavior, which we start to learn at an early age, show us the way through the material-aesthetic possibilities of the world of clothing and fashion.

As Aida Bosch puts it, following Helmuth Plessner, human experience is constituted by the merging of mind and matter, as humans make sense of life and relate to the world in both (distanced) reflexive and (immediate) corporeal ways (Bosch 2012, 66). Eventually one has to assume that materiality forms the first stage of intersubjective perception. People inevitably pay attention to and make sense of one another's appearances. Hence, as part of sensual and aesthetic experience, the process of fashioning and refashioning the body can be understood as particularly suited for joining together the various ambivalences and contradictions that are part of cultural and social life: merging simultaneously rhythm and variation, structure and creativity, ethics and sensuality (Bosch 2012, 66). In this sense, bodily, sensual, and aesthetic experiences through the material can provide orientation in an otherwise overwhelming variety of sensual stimuli.

Hence, clothing, as well as other practices such as dieting, exercising, or shopping, can be understood as material forms of social behavior and meaning-making. They are material, not least since our human actions are inherently tied to the body, and because, in the radius of the body, there are always some kinds of objects involved that (should) say something about the social mode in which we are (or want to be). For example, carrying a roomy, short-handled bag in the "arm-crook hook," in order to hold in one hand a coffee-to-go and, in the other, a mobile device that connects mind and body with the world beyond its immediate surroundings, as one rushes along the street. Based on such a body-dress performance, one can form hypotheses about hypermodern urban life and its dynamics and organization, including human modes of communication, movement, and nutrition. The objects that are used to dress and accessorize the body (including the coffee cup) not only communicate something about status, but define and "redefine the relationship between people, space and time" (Charpy 2015, 201). Manuel Charpy has pointed out how the historical development of accessories such as "folding hats, umbrellas, suspenders with springs were all means of fixing gestures" and highlighted how the "clothing reform across the industrialized world at the end of the eighteenth century was accompanied by a mutation of gestures and postures" (2015, 201). Objects such as clothes and accessories, including technological devices, do not only act as signs or social indicators, but they are "tools" and "instruments" that shape and change us, including how we move, stand, and relate to our environment.

Following Jennifer Craik, the nexus of fashion and identity marginalizes other notable facets of fashion as "poor seconds" (2009, 135), especially if the body is not adequately acknowledged. The design sociologist, Joachim Fischer, stated in this context that it should not just be a question of why people pay such attention to the design of their coverings and surroundings, from dressing the body to architectural spaces. With an emphasis on bodies or *Körper* in a wider sense, it is important to also consider the bodies and surfaces of the various things and artifacts that make up the designed, material world, such as the mobile or the static bodies of cars (*Fahrkörper)* and buildings (*Baukörper)*, as much as the clothes, facial expressions, "facades," or make-up of the human bodies that move within it (Fischer 2012, 92). Putting together one's look and altering the "surface" of the body through various arrangements of clothing make it possible to create maximum sensual attention for the body. And such material acts also point to the social, since the act of dressing and dealing with materials consists of legitimizing, modifying, thwarting, or subverting conventions. For example, synthetic leather can challenge our perceptions of functionality, value, authenticity, artificiality, availability and sustainability, sexuality and morality, and, quite succinctly, human sensibility and body feeling—as well as modify such perceptions, depending on the cultural situation. It requires the existence of the material in order to be able to initiate such sensual evaluations. As with all materials, the relatively new example of synthetic leather is interwoven with the states, actions, and characteristics of the historical and social world, as it is shaped in a particular, material way in a specific moment. Going back to Susan Kaiser's term of "material subjects" and the knitted "pussy hat" in relation to time and place, an object's evaluation depends on which material, in what kind of design, as well as how and when it comes together with the subjects. This constellation, in turn, also shapes social figurations through shared aesthetic experiences (DeLong, Wu, and Bao 2007). This urges us to draw attention to the historical-situational reciprocity of specific material clothing and fashion cultures in relation to human experiences. It is therefore important and productive to keep an eye on the complicated and dynamic connections of materiality and embodiment.

The three chapters in this section focus on the relations between human bodies and fashion materials, which the authors consider in various contexts: from personal investment in designer fashion, to metal yoga, to the growing market of sports clothing and athleisure fashion. Leyla Belkaïd-Neri highlights the realm of clothing consumption in relation to design and uses a case study of five women in the United States to explore how items of dress from various 3.1 Phillip Lim collections are used, worn, and invested with personal meaning on the part of the wearers. Through interviews and observation, she pays attention to the corporeal responses and emotional experiences of the physical and sensual properties of garments, and makes clear that clothes are not only objectifications at a particular stage of production but also throughout their whole social and material life. However, in considering the "self-creation practices," narratives, associations, and imaginings of the wearer, Belkaïd-Neri also highlights the agency of the designer in considering fashion design as a "transformative operation able to shape material culture and to participate in social interactions." As she states, we know that designers use fashion as a screen for their ideas and thus influence the wearers. How this screen is used on the part of the wearer, which sets of emotions and sensory impressions in turn unfold with their clothes in everyday life, remains largely unknown. By asking what relationships are made between the wearer, their fashion objects, and the designer, she draws out "heterogeneous logics of practice" as they occur at the "crossroads of the imaginaries of various consumers and an established designer who has created some of their fashion artifact." Moreover, by illuminating the close relationship between the sensibilities of the body and the sensual materialities of dress, she also teases out the implicit and corporeal interactions between humans and material culture, which is often—as it is corporeal and a kind of tacit knowledge—difficult to verbalize (see Bosch 2012, 61).

In his exploration of metal yoga, Otto von Busch expands the perspective on the connection between materiality and embodiment by drawing on Karen Barad's (2003) agential realism and concept of intra-action and Manuel DeLanda's (2016) theorizing of assemblage to rethink fashion as an "alchemic assemblage" of dress, body, and emotions—as happening "*in* the flesh . . . *in our bodies.*" In his chapter, he traces the practice of contemporary metal yoga in a Brooklyn music venue back to the development of yoga in India in the context of colonialism, as well as to alchemy and the rebellious "left-hand path" attitude and aesthetics of black metal music and style. He thus describes how metal yoga merges seemingly different practices, creating a new experience of fashion, music, body, and movement; and how, through their amalgamation of different lifestyles, ideologies, and philosophies, they affect a "deeper alchemic change of matter and flesh" that "feels good." Conceived in this way, fashion is not only a "draping over the skin" but also an embodied experience that energizes and empowers, which *moves* in a way similar to music.

While von Busch highlights the appropriation of yoga and its merging with metal music as a form of rebellious empowerment in his chapter, he also alludes to the wider popularity of yoga practice, which is bound up with a thriving market of both yoga-specific and other sports studios and their corresponding clothing genre, which is the subject of the third chapter in this section. In this chapter, Jennifer Craik follows the historical migration and material transformation of sporting gear from its original functional context, as a uniform clothing item used in the military "training of mind and body," to a new fashion "biosphere." In her tracing of the evolution and expansion of sports clothing into everyday contexts as a global trend, she demonstrates the mobility of contextual clothing concepts and what kind of effects arise with such crossover. As she notes, activewear is the fastest growing sector in the fashion and clothing industry. Its success has to do with the innovation of new materials and the desire for comfortable, multifunctional clothing that is suitable for many different situations, as the clothes transfer to the non-sportive wearer in everyday contexts and become established new wearing zones. Yet Craik also describes how the new activewear, or so-called athleisure wear, adheres to a specific set of bodily and mental associations, such as fitness, discipline, and sportiness. Hence, athleisure clothes, marketed under the mantra of "feeling premium," can also be understood in a material-discursive sense as tied to the "labor of self-improvement" and the idealization of fitness. The particularities of materials, fibers, and fabrics, as well as patterns and prints are especially important in creating new atmospheres in social interludes. That is, the physical properties of this fashion—its lightness, its elasticity, its visibility, its overall performative qualities—create new human-space-material constellations and raise questions about changing perceptions concerning the human body and lifestyle. In this respect, once again, a special accentuation can be found, demonstrating the significance of the physical material feel and appearance of clothing.

The materiality and design of clothing is not finished at the stage of industrial fabrication but ultimately extends into the everyday use through practices of repurposing and assemblage, for example, when clothes intended for sports are worn and carried into lecture rooms and airplanes. In everyday life, the cultural production of material worlds continues through heterogeneous practices and forms of embodiment. As the chapters show, fashion and dress as material practice is also a kind of mental screen for individuals and groups. As Danielle Bruggeman and Aurelie van de Peer put it so pointedly in their discussion of the material-discursive qualities of fashion: "Fashion means and fashion matters" (2016, 20). Human bodies, fashion material, the space, and the social environments around them are in continuous exchange: material qualities and design patterns impress on the body and affect bodily feelings, emotional feelings, and activities, as well as the meaning-making processes that, all together, co-constitute the experience of social life.

References

Barad, Karen. 2003. "Posthumanist Performativity: Toward an Understanding of How Matter Comes to Matter." *Signs: Journal of Women in Culture and Society* 28(3): 801–31.

Barthes, Roland. (1967) 1990. *The Fashion System*. Translated by M. Ward and R. Howard. Berkeley: University of California Press.

Bosch, Aida. 2012. "Sinnlichkeit, Materialität, Symbolik. Die Beziehung zwischen Mensch und Objekt und ihre soziologische Relevanz." In *Das Design der Gesellschaft:*

Zur Kultursoziologie des Designs, edited by Stephan Moebius and Sophia Prinz, 49–70. Bielefeld: transcript Verlag.

Bruggeman, Danielle, and Aurelie Van de Peer. 2016. "Long Live the (Im)material: Concept and Materiality in Viktor & Rolf's Fashion." *International Journal of Fashion Studies* 3(1): 7–26.

Charpy, Manuel. 2015. "How Things Shape Us: Material Culture and Identity in the Industrial Age." In *Writing Material Culture History*, edited by Anne Gerritsen and Giorgio Riello, 199–221. London: Routledge.

Craik, Jennifer. 1994. *The Face of Fashion: Cultural Studies in Fashion*. London: Routledge.

Craik, Jennifer. 2009. *Fashion: The Key Concepts*. Oxford, New York: Berg.

Davis, Fred. 1992. *Fashion, Culture and Identity*. Chicago: Chicago University Press.

DeLanda, Manuel. 2016. *Assemblage Theory*. Edinburgh: Edinburgh University Press.

DeLong, Marilyn, Juanjuan Wu, and Mingxin Bao. 2007. "May I Touch it?" *Textile* 5(1): 36–49.

Entwistle, Joanne. 2000. *The Fashioned Body: Fashion, Dress and Modern Social Theory*. Cambridge: Polity Press.

Fischer, Joachim. 2012. "Interphänomenalität. Zur Anthropo-Soziologie des Designs." In *Das Design der Gesellschaft: Zur Kultursoziologie des Designs*, edited by Stephan Moebius and Sophia Prinz, 91–108. Bielefeld: transcript Verlag.

Mauss, Marcel. 1973. "Techniques of the Body." *Economy and Society* 2(1): 70–87.

9

Sensorial cosmologies: Fashion design and the embodied practices of the wearer

Leyla Belkaïd-Neri

The way women and men internalize and externalize the properties of the garments they wear in their everyday lives, either in small-scale communities or in industrial consumer societies, has been addressed through the prism of different anthropological insights. Whereas, in nonindustrialized cultures, the making of clothing is often collective, participatory, and ritualized, in capitalist industrialized societies, the production of apparel is usually separated from the consumption of it. Therefore, in critiques of capitalist cultures, the Marxist definition of commodity fetishism has crystallized the image of fashion as an endless source of superficial, frivolous, and ephemeral novelty. At issue is the widely diffused idea that materialism is culturally depleting, especially if enhanced and fed by modern fashion practices. Douglas and Isherwood (1979) have been among the first to argue that commodities allow the making and the marking of social exchange in every society. The hypothesis that consumption is a key medium of culture has been developed further by Daniel Miller (1987), who emphasized how the ritualistic use of commodities is integral to culture, rejecting the pessimistic approaches to modern consumer practices, which see consumption as opposed to sociality, collectivity, and cultural diversity. These perspectives on consumption have indeed revealed recurrent similarities between the endless personalization of commodities by consumers in industrialized societies and the ritual appropriation of craft artifacts in nonindustrialized ones. They have actively contributed to a progressive shift in the anthropological interpretation of fashion production and consumerism. Nonetheless, the social practices and intentions of the designer who determines the forms and functions of the fashion artifact with the aim of anticipating the habits, movements, and sensorial perceptions of the consumer-wearer are too often omitted. The intricate relationship between the bodily, sartorial, and social practices of consumers as subjects, and the identities, intentions, and projects of the designers who define the material, morphological, technical, and stylistic features of the clothing these subjects wear is rarely questioned.

This chapter synthesizes some results of an ethnographic research study based on fieldwork conducted in New York City and Los Angeles in 2013. The research deals with fashion design as a transnational arena for the formation of otherness through the analysis of the experiences, creative practices, and production of Chinese American fashion designers born in Asia. It scrutinizes the creative work of a group of diasporic designers to explain the coherences and dissonances of the identity logics and mnemonic processes that impact their subjective performances. It also addresses the incorporation of the innovations fashioned by the designers in the lifestyles, appearances, sensorial perceptions, and bodily behaviors of a panel of female wearers. I have focused on 3.1 Phillip Lim, the brand of New York-based designer Phillip Lim, because the wider diffusion of his products made it easier to find subjects owning and using garments of this label. The selected informants are not active in the ready-to-wear industry and do not personally know Phillip Lim or anyone working in his studio. Word of mouth has helped in finding subjects in possession of one or more pieces of the designer's label in both New York and Los Angeles. Out of the fifteen women initially identified as potential users, nine participated. They represent a wide range of social and ethnic backgrounds, ages (from 27 to 52), and sizes (from 0 to 10). The variety of their owned clothes is also significant: many typologies of fabrics and forms as well as seasons and collections (from fall 2005 to spring 2013) were represented. I conducted semi-structured interviews whereby I met the women in a place of their choice, in tune with their usual practices as wearers of the designer's pieces.

This multisited ethnography addresses the unexplored intricacies that feed the constitutive and mutual relationship between the fashion designer and the wearer of the objects he has designed. In this chapter, I examine the corporeal responses, the physical performances, and the sensorial, aesthetic, and emotional experiences of five women who have integrated pieces of Phillip Lim's 3.1 collections in their everyday habits and social life.[1] Drawing on participant observation and interviews, I will attempt to approach the designer's agency from the standpoint of the self-creation practices of the wearers and transcend the dualism of subjects and objects, to shed new light on fashion design as an activity that consists in making culture through the active diffusion of artifacts endowed with the power to assimilate and influence the way people experience the world.

The social life of a designer's production

I like to wear vintage stuff. My shorts already had something warm and lively when I bought them at the flea market . . . maybe they had already been like that new. Because . . . honestly, they are perfectly conserved, and the lining is so beautiful . . . Nothing is too tight, but I feel as if I was supported . . . They are part of me. It's hard to imagine that another person has worn them before me.

Kee is a Korean-American ceramic artist and art instructor in her thirties. She found her 3.1 Phillip Lim shorts in the middle of a bundle of clothes at the Brooklyn Flea market in 2010.[2] Her brown woolen shorts have belonged to at least one other person before being involved in her personal life. The career of this object seems a little bit more tumultuous than that of the other clothing artifacts studied during my fieldwork in New York. No one knows the former episodes of its social life. The exchange, appropriation, and recontextualization of the garment might have occurred more than once between 2007 and 2010. Because "things change their meanings through their life cycles and according to the way they are used and appropriated and in the manner in which individuals and groups identify themselves with them" (Tilley 2006, 71), the unknown journey in space and time of Kee's shorts, following the transfer from one owner-wearer to the other, situates objectification as a technique of the self (Warnier [1999] 2005, 144). By objectification, I mean the process of mutual construction that links subject and object together. The designer's clothing is an objectification throughout its unpredictable social life rather than a production-based objectification.

The narratives of the wearer's practices illustrate how the "intrinsic perceptual qualities of objects express their sensory history, and how this salience can motivate and animate their exchange and shared consumption" (Seremetakis 1994, 134). The social biography of the fashion object therefore follows its corporeal, spatial, and social recontextualization from the moment of its conception by the designer and their team to the mobile incorporation into the bodily behavior and everyday life of one or more subjects in political and social space. Indeed, the analysis of contemporary consumption in determined environments bridges the idea of recontextualization and the concept of objectification. Daniel Miller argues that "the possibilities of recontextualization may vary for any given object according to its historical context, or for one particular individual according to his or her changing social environment" (1987, 175). The fashion designer anticipates the variety of possible recontextualizations of the garment he/she imagines, sketches, prototypes, and shares with the rest of the world. Yet, their empirical vision is never broad enough to embed the infinite potential uses it can provide once worn by a myriad of active people.

Because it had previously been part of someone else's social, bodily, and sensorial experiences, Kee's 3.1 Phillip Lim shorts have been recontextualized, but she admits she can hardly consider that they have belonged to the intimate life of another woman. They constitute a malleable second skin that is difficult to imagine detached from one's own body, actions, perceptions, and sensations[3] because "we are constituted by our clothing" (Miller 2005, 42). It is worth questioning the extent to which the social vision and design processes negotiated in Phillip Lim's studio impacted the ulterior perceptions and uses of thousands of anonymous wearers, such as Kee and the other women interviewed during my fieldwork.

Narratives of material subjectivations

Because I am a small size, Phillip Lim's sizes are perfect for me. I don't need to have my jacket altered by a dressmaker. I guess this is the Asian characteristic of his style that comes out because he knows how to dress the small sizes like me and give them an "allure" . . . this anyway speaks to me. So, I chose this jacket that didn't speak to me at the beginning, but that I actually find absolutely sublime and always wear. . . . At the first sight, it's just a kind of tuxedo jacket, and then . . . it is completely floating. It's not shoulder-padded. Details are in the buttons and in the cut of the collar. . . . I wear it all the time. I save it. I came to the point that I use my jacket sparingly so that it doesn't look too worn. I love this jacket because . . . it's true that I have a relationship with clothes that is quite discrete. Sometimes, I can play with clothing, but I like timelessness, that's what I like. You can wear that jacket at a cocktail reception, you can wear it for a dinner, you can wear it for a wedding, you can wear it to go to work, you will always look right. . . . There is always this touch of elegance, of femininity. It is structured, but not too much . . .

A French national in her mid-forties, Claire is a manager based in New York. She owns more than twelve 3.1 Phillip Lim pieces, bought at different moments of her life and in different countries. Among them, seven size 0 silky draped pants of various colors hold a special place in her wardrobe. On the day of the interview, Claire wears a pair of bright orange, draped trousers, purchased on shopbop.com in 2013, with a fluid, black jacket found in 2010 at the flagship store of 3.1 Phillip Lim in New York. The interviewee stresses the use of each object in a wide range of social contexts. The jacket can equally be worn to work or at a wedding ceremony. The interview reveals its exceptional level of adaptability. Similarly, the silky pants, not mentioned in this short quote, are deployed to bike in the city, to go to the opera, or to jog when Claire travels without her gym clothing. The flexible use of the designer's pieces describes a long-term and easygoing relationship with clothing: an extension of the self that contradicts the widespread idea of fashion production as an alienating force.

The redefinition of contemporary fashion design as a transformative process that shapes material culture and facilitates social interactions requires the simultaneous observation of the intimate lives of subjects and clothing objects. In *We Have Never Been Modern* ([1991] 1993), Bruno Latour emphasizes that the centrality of what he states is the other aspect of history: how the objects make the subject, because each subject is constituted by objects as much as objects are constituted by the subject. This dual perspective is also constitutive of Daniel Miller's thoughts when he establishes that "in short, we need to show how the things that people make, make people" (2005, 38). The narratives of the consumers who unveil their intimate ties with clothing items designed and produced by Phillip Lim emphasize the role of the fashion object as a matrix of subjectivation (Warnier [1999] 2005, 118). The concept of subjectivation is used here following the theoretical axiom of Michel Foucault who questions how human beings transform themselves into subjects (1994, 579). That is, at the same time that subjects control their own actions, they are also transformed into the subjects of a "master," which means governed by a power or an environment that dominates the subjects and imposes rules and constraints upon them. Foucault aimed to produce a history of the modes of subjectivation in Western culture to explain the subject's techniques of the self and the interaction that operates between the self and others. The subjective experiences of the wearer are embedded with the subjectivation of the designer who acts upon other subjects and their social bonds by fashioning their clothing as material culture.

Style and the creative cosmos of the wearer

When I put on this T-shirt last summer, it was very hot in New York . . . It was like today, sun all around. . . . My tee lets the air pass through. I float in it, it's very nice. . . . It has a special shape, so I prefer to wear it with a very short skirt

or with shorts. I prefer to show my legs, otherwise I would look like a potato
sack! Even if you can see some of my body under my arms, that doesn't bother
me. I find it modest . . . I don't feel indecent, the rest of the tee is so. . . . The style
is young and sporty, but also very feminine because of the flowers. Well, I really
love the floral print, maybe because I'm Japanese . . . The little flowers on the New
York City layout are very beautiful and I believe it is metaphoric in several senses.
There is a hidden ecological message I think. A criticism of globalization also . . .
Sometimes I think that it represents me, Setsuko from Japan, who lands like a
butterfly or a bee in the middle of Central Park and who blooms like a flower.

Born in Tokyo, Setsuko is a young Japanese artist, who now lives and works
in the Meatpacking District in Manhattan. In the above interview excerpt, she
effuses her interpretation of the black, graphic letters that cover the whole front
of her white sleeveless cotton T-shirt: the imposing letters of "New York City"
are interrupted by small green leaves and colorful flowers randomly printed on
the surface (Figure 9.1). The artist highlights the heteroglossia of this hybrid
motif and interprets it as a denunciation of our planet's massive disruption where
natural vegetation can hardly coexist with the dark asphalt that asphyxiates the
streets of urban metropoles. The print also recalls her native country, Japan,
and its millinery art of floral patterns. The encounter between the flowers and
the name of the global city resonates like a metaphor for the Japanese woman's
personal trajectory: she sees herself as a flower blossoming in New York. Setsuko's
personal style and perception of her body's features and appearance, as well as
her interpretation of the print's meaning, are indicators of the dynamics induced
by the design of Phillip Lim. Her experience of the new T-shirt is the evidence of
a dynamic process of objectification.

The connections between the metaphorical evasions, mythologies, and
imagination of the consumer who integrates the object into her life and the
intentions and aesthetics of the designer who has fashioned the object, give
birth to style. Thus, style does not correspond to a coherent totality. Setsuko's
style is the consequence of a heterogeneous constellation of ethos, perceptions,
and projects. The words used by the young artist state that the fashion artifact
she wears is not consumed but rather experimented materially, corporeally,
sensorially, and emotionally. She "subjectivizes" herself by her use of a garment
created, shaped, and made by a designer who does not personally know her but
who has imagined a form, aesthetic, and texture that lets her reinvent her own
perceived world. Setsuko feels free to identify herself with the spring flowers
spread on the surface of the huge letters that compose the name "New York City."

Figure 9.1 Setsuko's personal style and creative cosmos, wearing her Phillip Lim T-shirt with "New York City" print. *Photo*: Leyla Belkaïd-Neri.

The fact of knowing that Phillip Lim has Asian roots probably encourages her to attempt such a narcissistic exegesis of the print.

Setsuko narrates her own life through her clothing. She drafts the outline of the personal history of a young Japanese painter who comes to New York to develop her artistic skills and emerge on the international scene of contemporary art. Therefore, she establishes a singular style to set up her identity and morphology. As explained by Susan Kaiser, "for some individuals, style becomes a critical and creative strategy for negotiating new truths and subjectivities. That is, it becomes a vehicle not only for being, but also for becoming" (2001, 83). Even though the T-shirt is embedded in the productive and mediatic system of fashion, without which it would not have existed, it participates in the staging of the self, performed by the wearer, and stimulates her identity negotiations. The stylistic translation made by Setsuko determines the creative dimension of the cosmopolitical experience that takes form throughout the dialogic relationship between the body and the fashion object. This complex articulation participates in the redefinition of the designer's spectrum of action.

A decommodified fashion object

Over the years, I have been drawn to things that are really more comfortable to sit in because of the driving in Los Angeles. We are often seated in Los Angeles . . . My Phillip Lim pants keep their beautiful look after I have been seated in the car for two hours, while other fabrics wrinkle and would have a bad look. I have clothing which wrinkles from the moment I sit in the car. Their shape is ruined as soon as I stand up . . . I stay a long time in my car, you know. That's why I think that the 3.1 Phillip Lim style works really well for the women in Los Angeles.

Eleonora is a tall lady of English and Danish descent in her early fifties. She interrupted her career as a classical dancer following her marriage. Mother of three teenagers, she is active in charitable associations for the promotion of living arts in the Los Angeles area. She describes accurately the details of her 3.1 Phillip Lim long, fluid, silky pants and their warm ochre color.[4] She also explains how she has opted on purpose for a bigger size to feel more comfortable and avoid sweating (Figure 9.2). The sweat accumulated between her thighs when she is seated is a source of unease and shame for Eleonora. She suffers from this problem even when wearing a skirt. The shape, material, and size of her 3.1 Phillip Lim pants seem to provide an ergonomic solution to this uncontrollable issue. Its incorporation into her bodily practices and daily activities helps her to envision a more comfortable posture in the car. Indeed, "new clothing makes possible or inhibits new practices, habits, and intentions; it invites new projects" (Miller 2005, 193).

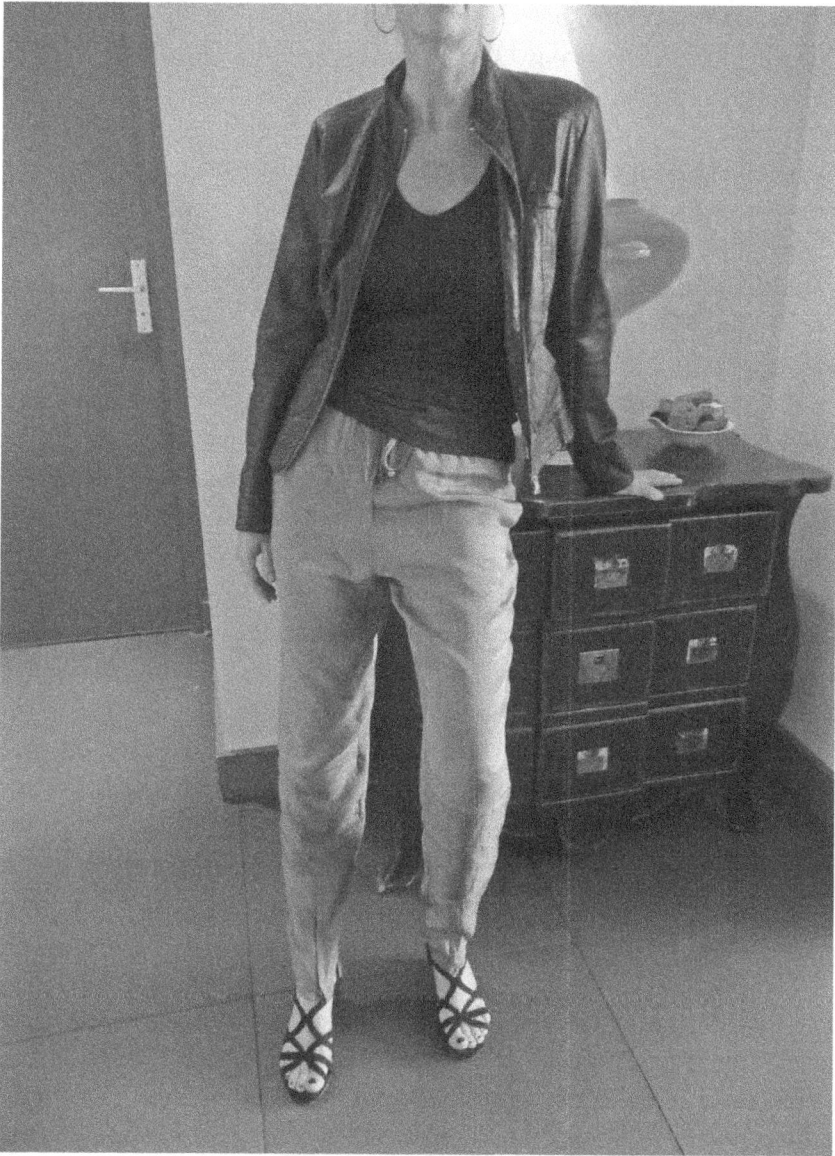

Figure 9.2 Eleanora wearing her 3.1 Phillip Lim pants as a decommodified fashion object. *Photo*: Leyla Belkaïd-Neri.

The physical perceptions of Eleonora unveil an experiential cosmos (Seremetakis 1994, 12) that appears wider than one would expect, seeing her in her pants. The intimate appropriation of the garment in relation to her physical behavior and movements, at different moments of her daily life, shows how the object reincorporates materiality into the social. It reveals how the worn garment does not only implicate "a difference in clothing, but a significant difference in what it means to be a woman" (Seremetakis 1994, 16). In another sequence of the interview, Eleonora associates her fluid trousers with a need for appeasement when she feels bad or when she has what she calls "a bad day." She chooses the metaphor of "comfort food" to describe the reassuring feeling provided by the garment. The sentiment of relief, particularly associated with the sweat issue symptomatic of her menopause, is intertwined with aesthetic observations and practical facts. The object perfectly fits the seated postures of her body, provides ease, and preserves the beauty of her outfit because it does not wrinkle.

The association between the clothing and the city is also highlighted as an ulterior indicator of its deep crystallization in the wearer's personal identity and social life. Eleonora is convinced that the 3.1 Phillip Lim style is adapted to women who live like her in Los Angeles. She knows that the designer grew up and started his career in the fashion industry in California.[5] By talking with a sales person at the 3.1 Phillip Lim store in West Hollywood, she discovered this shared belonging to the city where she has been living for more than forty years. The love she feels for her city overlaps with the strong attachment she has for the pants designed by someone she considers as affiliated to her place. This cultural tie reveals a triangular intimacy between user, designer, and location. The urban environment of Los Angeles is perceived as a shared cultural background that enhances the identification of the wearer with the designer's style through the materiality of the garment and the sensoriality it involves.

Eleonora's experiences demonstrate the gap between the fashion object as a commodity and its social existence as used and lived clothing. They reflect "a process of decommodification and personalization, domestication or incorporation" (Warnier [1999] 2005, 144) with multiple dimensions. The testimony of the wearer expresses a form of fusional consumption that deals primarily with issues of comfort, ergonomics, intimate sensations, identity, and daily action in space and time. It sheds light on the inalienable value of the fashion artifact that follows its alienable condition as a commodity (Miller 1987, 190). It also emphasizes the gendered awareness of the relation between body and dress (Tseëlon 1997, 61). The perception of the movements of the body through space in relation to the 3.1 Phillip Lim pants would probably have been differently described by a man, even if the time spent seated in cars jammed on the streets of Los Angeles involved the same bodily postures and constraints for both genders. It is worth noting that, for the interviewee, the ergonomic qualities of the garment are embedded with the persistence of specific physical reactions that are recurrent in the lives of this generation of women.

Exploring sensuous cartographies

I have a lot of satin kimonos and Asian things like that . . . I don't distinguish Chinese stuff from Japanese, I mix everything together without distinction. I know that the confusion between Asian cultures is a political error that many people make, but this is not my case. For me, it's about physical sensations only, I'm talking about the feel . . . I also like the colors of the kimonos, these kinds of pinks, peach, sometimes with touches of gold . . . I thought that maybe there is something Asian in this Phillip Lim top, even if it obviously doesn't look like a kimono. It is only when I wear it that it looks beautiful because it moves like a kite in the wind . . . When I walk, it dances. I just lift up my arm and the silk spreads . . . Actually, I always wear fine silk kimonos. I have several . . . I wear them at home, but some of them I can also wear outside. Sometimes, I organize dinner parties with friends and I give them kimonos so that they relax . . . I think that the sensation I have in my kimonos is quite similar to the way I feel in my Phillip Lim piece.

Johanna is an African American professor of Caribbean and African dance, based in New York. She lives in Harlem. She was forty when I first met her and interviewed her. She regularly moves from one side of Manhattan to the other to give lessons. She owns a 3.1 Phillip Lim top made of two rectangular pieces of crepe silk, sewn together along the sides with free extremities (Figure 9.3). The front is white. It is narrower than the pastel orange back. The two rectangles are not parallel: the twenty-degree inclined angle of the front piece gives an asymmetrical shape to the object. This construction is however hard to notice on the body because of the continuous movements of the free extremities of the piece. Johanna's top has no sleeves, no pockets, no buttons, no zips, and no lining. It only has two thin straps. This abstract, bidimensional garment comes to life on the body of the woman who wears it as soon as she starts walking. It follows the pace of her body and the direction of the wind. Hence, it perfectly illustrates the theme of the kites that Phillip Lim took as a poetic source of inspiration for his spring 2012 collection.

The interviewee did not specify if she had the opportunity to see on the internet the 3.1 Phillip Lim show to which the piece belongs, but she calls it

Figure 9.3 Johanna wearing her "flying top." *Photo*: Leyla Belkaïd-Neri.

her "flying top." On the day of the interview, she wore it with ripped jeans and blue, high-heeled sandals. This personal association of garments does not match the look created by the designer as shown on the runway. Johanna's grungy, tight-fitting denim pants replaced the fluid pink pants worn by the model. This disjunction corresponds to what Arjun Appadurai defines as "diversities in taste, understanding, and use between producers and consumers" (1986, 47) that create a distance in terms of knowledge, interest, and role among subjects who are involved in the circulation of commodity flows. On the other hand, Johanna's top, like Kee's shorts, draws the outlines of a personal cosmogony that incorporates intimate perceptions associated with the artistic practices of the subject: manipulation of clay in ceramics for Kee and the body in dance for Johanna. "When I walk, it dances": the words used by the interviewee express the mobile perception of movement that she experiences with her daily bodily practices as a professional dancer.

Johanna dreamed of a journey through the air with her "flying top" as soon as she acquired it, and Phillip Lim did too, some months earlier, when he drafted the shapes of the transformed kites for his spring 2012 collection. For both the designer and the consumer, who do not know one another and who have evolved in different social environments, this need for levitation in space is expressed through the sensorial and emotional impact of a specific textile: light silk crepe. Even if the interviewee is not well informed about the designer's biography, she knows about his Asian roots. Did this information encourage the spontaneous association of the feelings caused by the fluid silk with the ones raised by the kimonos she frequently puts on and shares with the friends who visit her? Or is it that the typology of silk selected by the designer, and recurrently used in his production, is a consequence of his own memory of traditional East Asian clothing, made in fabrics with similar qualities, which would in turn inform the user's sensoriality? These mnemonic entanglements contribute to the understanding of style as a dynamic, shared, and collective social production involved in the daily construction of embodied practices (Entwistle 2000, 325).

In the conclusion of their enquiry on the intimate relationship that Indian women have with their saris, Mukulika Banerjee and Daniel Miller have emphasized that "a study of clothing should not be 'cold'; it has to be involved in the tactile, sensual, emotional, intimate world of feelings. The task of an anthropological account is firstly to convey these feelings empathetically: that is, to try to experience the sari from the point of view of the various women who wear them" (Banerjee and Miller 2003, 253). The ethnographic survey conducted with subjects who wear elements of one single Chinese American fashion designer's work brought to the surface a myriad of details, micro-experiences, and intimacies that contradict the anathema of fashion commodities as a tool of alienation and cultural uniformization. The physical perception of the clothing is assimilated to sensations that are intimately interconnected with the wearer's practices of the self (Foucault [1984] 1990).

Heterogeneous logics of practice

The narratives of consumers or wearers who have no relationship of any nature with the designer reveal a huge diversity of practical uses, perceptions, and social behavior. Following Michel de Certeau ([1980] 1984) who describes the proliferation of heterogeneous histories and operations that composes the everyday, the wearers appear as subjects who express their own creative ethos through the personal interpretation and manipulation of the designer's concepts and production. This mechanism reveals the complexity of the silent negotiations between the style of the subject and the style designed and communicated by the brand at an earlier stage of the social process. It also emphasizes the subjective entanglements that take shape at the crossroads of the imaginaries of various anonymous consumers and an established designer who has created some of their fashion artifacts. Indeed, the incorporation of a fashion design product into the personal actions and habits of contemporary subjects conveys singular uses that often go beyond the intentions of the designers and the terms of use that they and their collaborators initially identified and anticipated.

In *The System of Objects* ([1968] 2006), Jean Baudrillard observes the psychological and sociological lived reality of the objects beyond their sensitive materiality and explains how technological systems are continuously disrupted by that reality. We have seen how the lived reality of clothing depends on conscious and unconscious practical and symbolic needs that can transform or jeopardize the initial techniques and functions of the object. The constant interferences between a system of practices and a system of techniques (Baudrillard [1968] 2006, 17) are highlighted by the narratives of the wearers of 3.1 Phillip Lim apparel. From the very first sketch of the designer to the personal and social environment of the wearer, the artifact is permanently transformed and recontextualized. Its materiality, inseparable from its meanings, is not only subject to the morphology and the bodily techniques of the user but also to their personality, emotions, aesthetic, taste, cultural background, professional activity, actions, and gestures.

The observation of the appropriation and reinvention of the object's dynamics brings us back to the anthropological paradigm of *Techniques du Corps* (1936) as Marcel Mauss has first defined the social uses of the body in connection to a specific environment. The paradigm focuses on the cultural expressions in which the body's motor functions are involved, from walking and running to swimming: "The ways in which humans, society by society, in a traditional manner, know how to use their bodies" (Mauss [1950] 2010, 365; my translation). Mauss examines the social nature of what he calls *habitus* in Latin, a notion that better translates the notion of capability than does the word habit. He insists on the existence of skills and habitus, which do not only vary from subject to subject but are influenced by society *and* also influence society. Additionally, he mentions the education principles that overlap with modes of imitation, status, and social codes to determine what he sees as techniques of the body. The bodily techniques and habitus of the users of 3.1 Phillip Lim's products come from the narratives of their practices and perceptions. They are determined by the traditions and individual family backgrounds of each wearer, but they are at the same time embedded with the traditions of the designer. In two interviews, the users spontaneously evoked the ethnic origin of the designer to justify the strong compatibility of their 3.1 Phillip Lim clothing with their own personal habitus, bodily practices, and cultural backgrounds. Once the parallel was emphasized in relation to the common factor of belonging to Los Angeles where the designer grew up. One other wearer establishes a natural connectivity between her tactile perception of the silky piece and the designer's Asian descent.

The issues raised by the wearers' narratives can also be addressed through the dialectic between objectification and embodiment, as analyzed by Pierre Bourdieu (1989) in his theory of practice. Bourdieu examines the notion of habitus to describe how the use of tools and objects is acquired by younger subjects as an extension of their own bodies. The subjective experiences of the users I interviewed reflect the habitus that each individual has incorporated into the practical and ritual uses of specific fashion artifacts. What we can define as 3.1 Phillip Lim style, therefore, arises from the habitus and logics of practices of both the wearer and the designer. As observed in the case of Kee's secondhand shorts, the users can be multiple, as are the designers since design always happens in collective teams and spaces. Thus, the career of the object is never linear. At each stage of the process, "an eventful biography of a thing becomes the story of the various singularizations of it" (Kopytoff 1986, 90).

In this chapter, I have argued that the diversity of the processes of objectification and practices of embodiment observed in the daily life of subjects living in various contexts helps us reconsider contemporary fashion design as a transformative operation, able to shape material culture and to participate in social interactions. The accounts gathered in New York and Los Angeles show how the style developed by Phillip Lim and his studio is integrated into the lifestyles of the wearers. The users' narratives often described 3.1 Phillip Lim clothing as comforting, durable, and timeless. The quality of the fabric, cut, and finish has also been emphasized by most of the informants. As a matter of fact, the observation of the clothing artifacts has highlighted the designer's propensity to use silk crepe, geometric patterns, clean lines, and fluid volumes that free the body and its movements in space. These characteristics could be somehow correlated with his childhood memories of Asia and his Asian heritage, but, first and foremost, they open up avenues for greater expression of the self for a myriad of users from different cultural backgrounds. No longer can we regard designers as makers of ephemeral novelties who maintain and enhance alienating modes of consumption. The experiences of the wearers emphasize the importance of fashion design as the creation of unlimited embodied possibilities in the social space.

Notes

1 The quotations from five different users of 3.1 Phillip Lim clothing correspond to short abstracts of longer semi-structured interviews conducted in 2013.

2 I could retrace the origin of the piece to the fall 2007 collection.

3 In another sequence of the interview, Kee compares her shorts to the clay she manipulates to create ceramic works.

4 An accurate observation of a selection of lookbooks of the company allows me to presume that the interviewee's pants come from the pre-fall 2011 collection.

5 Phillip Lim is an American designer of Chinese descent. He was born in Thailand in 1973 but grew up in Orange County. He cofounded the Los Angeles-based label, Development, in 2002. He then moved to New York City where he cofounded 3.1 Phillip Lim, with Wen Zhou in 2005.

References

Appadurai, Arjun, ed. 1986. *The Social Life of Things: Commodities in Cultural Perspective*. Cambridge: Cambridge University Press.

Banerjee, Mukulika, and Daniel Miller. 2003. *The Sari*. Oxford and New York: Berg.

Baudrillard, Jean. (1968) 2006. *The System of Objects*. Translated by James Benedict. New York: Verso Books.

Bourdieu, Pierre. 1989. *Outline of a Theory Practice*. Cambridge: Cambridge University Press.

de Certeau, Michel. (1980) 1984. *The Practice of Everyday Life*, Vol. 1. Translated by Steven Rendall. Oakland: University of California Press.

Douglas, Mary, and Baron Isherwood. 1979. *The World of Goods: Towards an Anthropology of Consumption*. London: Routledge.

Entwistle, Joanne. 2000. "Fashion and the Fleshy Body: Dress as Embodied Practice." *Fashion Theory* 4(3): 323–48.

Foucault, Michel. (1984) 1990. *The History of Sexuality*, Volume 2: *The Use of Pleasure*. Translated by Robert Hurley. New York: Vintage Books.

Foucault, Michel. 1994. *Dits et écrits, IV. 1980–1988*. Paris: Gallimard.

Kaiser, Susan B. 2001. "Minding Appearances: Style, Truth, and Subjectivity." In *Body Dressing*, edited by Joanne Entwistle and Elizabeth Wilson, 33–58. Oxford and New York: Berg.

Kopytoff, Igor. 1986. "The Cultural Biography of Things: Commoditization as Process." In *The Social Life of Things: Commodities in Cultural Perspective*, edited by Arjun Appadurai, 64–94. Cambridge: Cambridge University Press.

Latour, Bruno. (1991) 1993. *We Have Never Been Modern*. Translated by Catherine Porter. Cambridge: Harvard University Press.

Mauss, Marcel. 1936. "Les Techniques du corps." *Journal de Psychologie* 32(3–4).

Mauss, Marcel. (1950) 2010. *Sociologie et anthropologie*. Paris: Quadrige/ Presses Universitaires de France.

Miller, Daniel. 1987. *Material Culture and Mass Consumption*. Oxford and New York: Basil Blackwell.

Miller, Daniel, ed. 2005. *Materiality*. New York: Duke University Press.

Seremetakis, C. Nadia. 1994. *The Senses Still. Perception and Memory as Material Culture in Modernity*. Chicago and London: The University of Chicago Press.

Tilley, Christopher. 2006. "Objectification." In *Handbook of Material Culture*, edited by Christopher Tilley, Webb Keane, Susanne Küchler, Michael Rowlands, and Patricia Spyer, 60–73. London: Sage.

Tseëlon, Efrat. 1997. *The Masque of Femininity*. London: Sage.

Warnier, Jean-Pierre. (1999) 2005. *Construire la culture matérielle. L'homme qui pensait avec ses doigts*. Paris: Presses Universitaires de France.

10

The left-hand pose: Alchemic realism and the intra-action of music, body, and dress in metal yoga

Otto von Busch

"We don't do sun salutations because we're saluting the darkness." (Metal Yoga Bones teacher Saskia Thode, cited in Brinton 2015)

A "new materialist" perspective on fashion can shift focus on the agency of dress, from language, symbols, and the "system," to how dress and bodies couple into assemblages of what Karen Barad (2001) calls "intra-action." Barad's "agential realism" puts focus on materiality, embodiment, and affects. This chapter aligns with this materialist perspective on how fashion operates on the body of the wearer. By tracing a parallel approach in the histories of alchemy, tantrism, and yoga, and especially the esotericism of what is called the "left-hand path," I examine the practice of "death metal yoga" at the Metal Yoga Bones studio in Brooklyn, where aggressive music and occulture mix with the tantric roots of yoga. Drawing from the opaque and controversial teachings of Western esotericism, which keeps recurring in the darker themes of the metal scene, the death metal-infused yoga helps accentuate three points that are tangential to a materialist approach to fashion-at-large. First, that fashion is an embodied experience and fuses into an assemblage with the body: it is not only a symbolic draping over the skin. Second, the dark, so-called "fetish look" acts not only as a layer of representation but also as a physical passage of affect and change of body states, in the same way that music moves bodies. And, third, that fashion—from the perspective of Barad's "agential realism"—should, at least in the case of metal yoga, also be read as an "alchemic realism." In other words, fashion is not just a matter of materialism: with affects animating human relations to matter, the esoteric perspective aligns bodies with a nihilist and erotic affirmation. The left-hand pose of occult yoga helps reveal how fashion as an assemblage of bodies and dress is a mundane experience of the left-hand path. It is a rebellion against submissive routine, the amoral celebration of the individual over the collective or righteous. It is the embodied feeling of power as growing.

Fashion beyond representation

In middle school, I made an anorak in sewing class, and I attached patches of the metal bands of which I was a fan. After being harassed by the rich, cool kids, something inside me changed whenever I wore the jacket. Not only had my sewing skills been proven, I now wore something I had made myself, distinct from the others. The jacket inverted the status of previous rejection, it had become a badge of honor—a medal indicating that I was now worth something. Not only had the surface changed—my strides and posture were more confident as I moved into a territory beyond the parental income scale—but this difference was perhaps also charged with a new sinister emotion I had been starved of for so long: I had found an arena where I could excel, even if this meant facing a haunting darkness.

In earlier writings, I have used the story above as a starting point for a "hacktivist" approach to fashion, putting focus on the pride taken from the capability of co-creation and agency in the realm of dress (von Busch 2008). It was as if my younger self had managed to remake the status of the "social skin" of dress (Turner [1980] 2012). However, these interpretations did not, perhaps, put enough focus on metal music and the transformation in the depths of the body. As elucidated by fashion scholar Joanne Entwistle in her important work *The Fashioned Body*, fashion produces a certain form of cultural body as "fashion is about bodies: it is produced, promoted and worn by bodies" (2000, 1). Even if fashion is about bodies, there has been a habit of seeing fashion as aimed outward, not inward. Similarly, the intertwined evolutions of youth culture, fashion, and music tend to be seen through symbols and signals rather than through embodied emotional practices (Greil 1989; Muggleton 2000).

As I revisit my anorak memory today, I am interested in what energies I tapped into at that moment that fueled my self-confidence. Not only did my jacket take me away from the judgment of my peers, but it also energized me. In the place of the oppressed little kid, a new person had emerged, fueled by new energies in an assemblage of active forces: craft, clothes, music, and a reinvigorated body with new confidence. As Manuel DeLanda suggests, "assemblage" (Fr. *agencement*) "refers to the action of matching or fitting together a set of components (*agencer*)" and is thus much more a process of continuous "arrangement" than a steady product: it is continuous symbiosis, contagion, epidemic, or functioning (2016, 1).

The affective element of my anorak story came to my mind again when I visited a "death metal yoga" session at Metal Yoga Bones studio in Brooklyn. Started in 2014, Metal Yoga Bones is a weekly yoga session instructed by Saskia Thode at the bar and metal music venue, Saint Vitus, in Greenpoint. The sessions draw a mixed crowd of young(-ish) metalheads, men and women not necessarily with the high-def and slim bodies normative of typical New York studios. Having previously experienced some different traditions of yoga, from the spiritual kind to the more secular exercise types, I was drawn to the class in Brooklyn and to the darker sides of the fleshy body: the human as a carnal and wicked creature, bound to "unleash your inner beast," as the tagline goes at Metal Yoga Bones (see Figure 10.1). Not unlike how the metal patches and camouflage pattern of my old anorak had changed my emotional tuning of the assemblage "me-jacket-music," the setting of the metal yoga session likewise tuned into emotional and affectual energies other than those to which I am accustomed. Participants were not dressed in the latest trendy yoga looks, instead the sessions drew a rather mongrel style of looks, from torn band T-shirts and washed-out sweatpants to more style-conscious black spandex and bandanas. The few colors were mostly at the darker end of the spectrum. Compared to the more "holy" and

Figure 10.1 Metal Yoga Bones logo. *Copyright*: Saskia Thode.

self-conscious sessions I had attended at other studios, the metal yoga shifted my attention to how bodies in dress and in musical tune form assemblages with material and embodied affects and with many heterogeneous processes cofunctioning into a symbiosis: music, ambience, emotions, movement, and dress. For me, such a materialist experience aligned well with the esoteric roots of yoga—its ties to alchemy and occultism—and I realized more clearly how Karen Barad's (2001) ideas of "agential realism" and "intra-action" could put a finger on not only the feminist embodiment of fashion (Parkins 2008) but also the alchemic processes that may lie at the root of all fashion. That is, the references to esoteric alchemy recurrent in metal resonate well with Barad's concept of intra-action. As Barad suggests, intra-action is the mutual constitutions of entangled agencies. That is, parts have no inherent boundaries and properties but blend into each other and do not maintain total independence in the way we think of "inter-action" between autonomous parts. Thus, intra-action is not the "comforting concept of 'interaction' but rather entails the very disruption of the metaphysics of individualism that holds that there are discrete objects with inherent characteristics" (Barad 2007, 422). As with transubstantiation in alchemy, change happens not only on the surface, or in the symbolic realm of identity, but also deep within the affective embodiment of life-energies in the darker depths of Being.

Power in the flesh

In her book *Emotion, Depth, and Flesh* (1993), philosopher Sue Cataldi seeks a carnal grounding, or "emotional depth," to human experiences. Cataldi calls this deepening embodiment of emotion a "sensitive space," as experiences come to utilize the whole body as a resonance board: we profess that we "like" someone or we become "angry," but as emotions grow stronger and deeper, we are *in* love, or *in* a rage (Cataldi 1993, 8ff.). Our emotions mobilize the body, and vice versa, into an entwined sensitive and flat "flesh-ontology" (1993, 57ff.).

Similarly, when we wear something tied to emotions, such as a garment, our mood and affects are also "oriented" toward such directions (Ahmed 2010). We move deeper *into grief* as we dress for the funeral of a dear one, and, similarly, when we dress fashionably, we are *in* fashion—and that garment actually changes us *in the body*. The superiority my peers felt over me as they dressed "right" was something they felt in their bodies. It also felt "right" to them to express this embodied emotion in their judgments and bullying. In his early analysis of embodiment, Merleau-Ponty argues, "when we say that the perceived thing is to be grasped 'in person' or 'in the flesh,' this is to be taken literally" (Merleau-Ponty cited in Cataldi 1993, v). To be *in fashion* must be taken literally.

At Metal Yoga Bones, the dammed up emotions *in my body*, were now finding an outlet. They sought not only transformation on the surface, but *transubstantiation*: the deeper alchemic change of matter and flesh. Yoga, metal music, and dress formed an assemblage animated by such energies. Perhaps the metal scene in general, with its ubiquitous denim and black clothes, studs and patches, alchemic symbols and tattoos, leather and chrome, sometimes also matched with fetish or bondage, discipline, dominance and submission (BDSM) wear, does not only utilize these references to signal antisocial or underground alignments. These material elements of dress also affirm the uncontrolled "beast" in men and women: sinners and fallen angels, werewolves and ghosts, sexual demons like incubi and succubi, all esoteric and shape-shifting creatures.

It may thus not be a coincidence that so many of the clothing references within the metal community are recycled rebel imagery: the leather jackets and denim, the motorcycles and T-shirts, the tattoos and studs—they all emerge out of what were once symbols of nonconformity (Hebdige 1979). Anarchist elements mix with esoteric ones; as also for Mikhail Bakunin, Satan is "the eternal rebel, the first freethinker, and emancipator of worlds" (Bakunin [1882] 1970, 10).

Esoteric traditions, that is, the hidden, perennial, and "inner" traditions of mysticism, which have largely stood in opposition to Judeo-Christian religion and Enlightenment rationalism, often differ between two different paths of practice. The moral trajectory, or the righteous path, is popularly called the "right-hand path" (Flowers 2012). This path encourages equality, mercy, and harmony with nature in order to reach some form of heaven or nirvana: a path striving for the righteous and holy. Yet, by doing so, it also submits to "law and order," even if the regime is oppressive or unjust. The "left-hand path," on the other hand, seeks the empowerment of the individual human, the rebellion against the supreme order, the freedom that comes with agency and will, and ultimately, the rule over one's world. It is the Nietzschean and forcefully nihilist path of rebellion against the slave mentality, where happiness means "the feeling that power is *growing*, that resistance is overcome. Not contentedness but more power, not peace but war, not virtue but fitness" (Nietzsche [1895] 1960, 570).

The left-hand path is the path of the individual who controls and takes command over his or her own destiny. Religious and moralizing institutions claim that such a path is "evil," yet fail to examine power abuse within their own orders. Instead, for the follower of the left-hand path, the claim of the will is the very affirmation of life, the body, and its desires and passions. The history of yoga is connected to the many forms of ancient, Indian religious mysticism: tantrism, alchemy, sexual magic, and occulture, all with historic elements tied to the left-hand path. Thus the "left-hand pose" is not necessarily a sinister form of yoga, as yoga is never about seeking to celebrate the social or team effort, or about submitting to rules from a god above. Rather it is concerned with seeking inner strength and individual power, and with overcoming whatever limits our liberation from collective and individual restraints. As distinguished by Eugene Thacker (2011), this type of darkness should not be confused with "evil"—it is mystical wisdom, which has echoed through the ages and yet stands awkwardly with both state morality and the Enlightenment.

A death metal yoga class may seem far from our everyday experience of fashion, but I would like to argue the opposite. It offers the opportunity to elucidate how fashion can be seen as a mundane experience of the left-hand path: it is a rebellion against cowardly routine, the celebration of the individual over the collective or righteous, the feeling that power is *growing*.

Alchemic realism: Yoga and embodied intra-action

As Karen Barad so eloquently put it: "We do not obtain knowledge by standing outside the world; we know because 'we' are *of* the world. We are part of the world in its differential becoming" (2007, 185). It is the quality of being of the world that makes it impossible to cut apart our functioning into separate and independent parts, and, following Barad, interaction between parts is more accurately a form of "intra-action" (action between parts of an assemblage). In the case of the dressed body and, specifically, the darkly dressed bodies at Metal Bones Yoga, we can trace the actions of an alchemic body: a body that not only transforms but alters the functional couplings of the body-dress-affect assemblage (see Figure 10.2).

The Metal Yoga Bones class I visited took place at Saint Vitus, a heavy metal bar and music venue in Brooklyn, New York. I had visited the venue for concerts many times and, just a few weeks earlier, I had seen the epic Swedish death metal band Entombed play there. The crescendo of the show was the title track from their groundbreaking 1990s album, *Left-Hand Path*. It was the right place to practice yoga—to guttural screaming, distorted guitars, and rapid-fire, blast beats.

Figure 10.2 Warmup for metal yoga. *Photo*: Otto von Busch.

With the lights low and music blaring loudly from the speakers, the class was not as solemnly rigid and dogmatic as the yoga classes I had attended at other studios. Similarly, many of the postures were adjusted to the music. In a standing lunge pose we used the hands to reach down and "start the chainsaw," stretching the arm from the floor and up into a wide arch across the body to then move over to put the balance on the other foot while cutting down our enemies with strong gestures. Later, as we stretched to an extended side-angle pose, we did so to the hand movements of digging the graves of our fallen adversaries, and all to the guttural commands shouted out by our teacher with a tongue-in-cheek wit. As instructor Saskia Thode notes, "I've tried to rename each pose from the feeling it gives you. Warrior 1 is The Destroyer, because you're getting ready to go into battle and destroy" (Thode cited in Brinton 2015).

In a playful rejection of dogma, halfway through the session, other participants in the class were invited to lead the class with a series of improvised moves, punishing the body through an extended triangle pose and then giving praise to the dark energies flowing through our suffering muscles. However, the ludic elements of the class should not distract us from the depth of what the class accomplished; in contrast to the holier-than-thou atmosphere of many yoga studios, at Metal Yoga Bones one's aching body and pools of sweat worked as a passage of intra-action, a release of anger and frustration, or of the darker and creature-like energies of the body.

Indeed, yoga practice is based on ideas of bodily life-energies, chakras, and fusing such energies, not only for well-being but also in the quest for power. According to Mark Singleton's (2010) research on the history of the posture-based *asana* yoga, the most popular form of yoga today, parts of its history go back to "esoteric gymnastics," which formalized the "fakir" elements of spiritual asceticism to promote a more wholesome type of bodybuilding in resonance with the trends of the late nineteenth century. Yoga's evolution in India was informed by the Scandinavian traditions of gymnastics used by the occupying British army, cultivating yoga as a bodily practice of corporeal hygiene and a purifying "physical culture." As Singleton argues, it is the global circuits of the late nineteenth century that merge fakir practices of sexual magic, alchemy, and esotericism with medical gymnastics, physical culture, and bodybuilding, which gives shape to the current forms of yoga. By a century ago, yoga had already become a celebrity-infused practice of athletes, dancers, and performers, all striving for a purification of the body in a quest to become superhuman. However, in the grassroots, indigenous communities in India, individuals also mobilized yoga practice to resist the corrupting "decadence" of British rule (Singleton 2010, 101ff.).

The rebellious element of yoga not only concerned colonial geopolitics. Early promoters of yoga in the West, such as H. P. Blavatsky, at the end of the nineteenth century, and Aleister Crowley, in the early twentieth century, connected it to esoteric practices, tantrism, and sexual magic, elements often neglected in modern teaching (Singleton 2010, 64ff.). The esotericism of yoga also tied into Blavatsky's ideas of Lucifer as the dynamic and light-bringing rebel—set against the reactionary and repressive demiurge (Jehovah)—who, like Prometheus of the Greeks, brought humans the gifts of fire, knowledge, and free will (Blavatsky [1888] 1974; Flowers 2012, 63ff.).

The Promethean promise of yoga practice also resonates through Metal Yoga Bones, and it is the embodied affects that fuel the energy of the session:

> The classes are as intense as possible. Halfway through, I play death metal and grind to push the students further. I put on Death, Suffocation, Sodom, Possessed, Venom, Nile, and Onslaught, and try to piss them off by having them hold standing poses for ages. I'll say: "Are you angry now? I can't hear you! Tell me how angry you are . . ." The emotions and the energy in the music and the endorphins release so much positive energy in the body. (Thode cited in Brinton 2015)

In the traditions of the left-hand path, releasing the power of the body is an act of rebellion against both reason and the supremacy of holy contemplation (in the form of docile submission to power) (Flowers 2012). With esoteric yoga, the rebellion against reified morality is incarnated: it is about releasing the full potential of embodied matter against the predetermination of instated order. As Gordon Djurdjevic argues,

> Unlike classical Yoga, intent on liberation, this other major style of Yoga, often associated with Tantra, is primarily interested in power, which fundamentally and ultimately involves the notion and goal of the divinization of the practitioner. (Djurdjevic 2014, 4)

In his study on medieval tantric alchemy, David Gordon White (1996) highlights the transformation of the body and spirit through alchemic and carnal practices. Here, the body of the yogi and the alchemical processes of magic act in consistent harmony, and the transformation of one is to be accompanied by the other, following the classic Indian aphorism, "as in metal, so in the body" (White 1996, 5). Thus, the metallurgy of the alchemist merges with sexology, shamanism, alchemy, pharmacology, and therapeutics—all occult practices of magic originally striving for the transformation of matter and spirit as a functional assemblage. The ultimate goal is not modest in any sense, as the practitioner, the *siddha*, translates to "realized, perfected one." This term is generally applied to a practitioner with the dual attributions of superhuman powers (*siddhis*, "realizations," "perfections") and bodily immortality (*jivanmukti*), making them demigods and intermediaries between the human and divine (White 1996, 2f).

It is thus of little coincidence that the *ashtanga* tradition is also called "power yoga" as it concerns the purification of the higher elements of the unified spiritual body, which empowers the practitioner to form the world according to his or her will. It is thus no coincidence that Crowley's left-hand path of yoga and the law of "Thelema" (Greek: "will") is the "do what thou wilt." As Crowley suggests in his *Eight Lectures of Yoga* (Crowley [1939] 1985), the word yoga derives from the same Sanskrit root as the word yoke, a unity of elements and powers, carrying body and soul. It is through this unity the magical enforcement of the practitioner's will takes place.

Crowley's attention to the power of the will is also the mark of the "aristocratic spirit," which is naturally in possession of power by virtue of its higher and superhuman purity. With its roots in eugenics and ideals of acquired genetic purity through "medical gymnastics," yoga also offered to change the "germ plasm," reifying the alchemic elements of the genetic body (Singleton 2010,

121ff.). Thus, it is not far-fetched that yoga was embraced by Italian author, esotericist, and fascist mystic, Julius Evola, who suggests "when the left and right hands are in equilibrium we experience samsara [karmic cycles], but when the left hand prevails, we find liberation" (Evola [1949] 1992, 30). By purifying the aristocratic spirit, a practitioner not only acquires power to rule and form the world according to his or her will, but, as Evola highlights, also moves "beyond good and evil, honor and dishonor, merit and sin, and any other value cherished by ordinary people" ([1949] 1992, 55). Even as yoga plays an important role in the struggle for Indian independence, aligning physical culture with anti-imperial liberation, the empowerment through yoga is by no means a matter of some inherent equality or social justice. Instead, the yogi becomes an *Ubermensch*, in Nietzsche's true sense of the word, a being standing beyond the judgment of the docile slave of duty. However, this does not mean yoga carries the seeds of fascism, but rather the opposite: the left-hand path refuses submission to authority since it strives for the power of the will. Perhaps it is this nihilist rebellion that Thode captures in the Metal Yoga Bones class, pushing her peers toward the "Fuck You pose, because it's the pose when you know that you're better than everyone else" (Thode cited in Brinton 2015).

In the blackened room, sweating and swearing to the loud music, bending into painful postures, and screaming with guttural anger, my body shivered with emotional energy. It was as if my flesh was being hammered as I was bending like a sheet of metal, burning my adversaries. As in metal, so in the body. Was this "agential realism" or "alchemic realism"? Whatever! I do not know if I was in a proper Fuck You pose, but after a while, it felt as if I was floating like a wave on top of my everyday small agonies. My mind a raft on a surface of burning oil.

Becoming demon: One and many assemblages of eroticism

As often noticed, the first mythical clothing in the Old Testament, the fig leaf, is not only a symbol of a transformation of human knowledge, but is also the first cover of a transformed body and hierarchy: the human rivalry against God's order. As Efrat Tseëlon observes, "since the Fall is blamed on the woman, the links between sin, body, woman and clothes are easily forged" (1995, 14). The sinful body is a body that has regained control and rebelled against previous submission. It is a liberated body, a body of transgression, a body of rapture and ecstasy, refusing to be controlled by social norms. As Per Faxneld (2012 and 2014) suggests, it is thus no surprise that Blavatsky's esotericism introduced Lucifer as a light-bringer to challenge the Victorian times, and that this move also coincided with the cult of Lilith as a protofeminist, a patron saint of abortion, and a liberator of the woman's body with her refusal to submit to Adam and God's patriarchy.

This type of refusal is also apparent in the nonconformity of black metal dress, in its hardly readable scripts of band names, and its lyrics and imagery that call upon transgressive behavior and left-hand references (not least the previously mentioned Entombed album with the name *Left-Hand Path*, a milestone in the death metal genre). The fact that Metal Bones Yoga plays albums like this is no coincidence, and as yoga instructor Thode argues, "metal acknowledges the darkness we carry" (Thode cited in Brinton 2015). The guttural croaking of black metal is more the organ of corpses, unholy creatures, and feral animals, than the voices of angels. The image of the sinful or fallen angel in the iconography of metal is not a metaphor but points to an affect in the body: the exuberance, destruction, and squandering of eroticism.

However, the flow of such dark desires should not necessarily be seen as a form of accumulation of pleasures, but rather the opposite. From a perspective of black metal, desire is a black hole, an all-consuming passion, an excelling fire (Connole 2015, 364). Or as Georges Bataille would have it: "Our only real pleasure is to squander our resources to no purpose, just as if a wound were bleeding inside us; we always want to be sure of the uselessness or the ruinous of our extravagance" (Bataille 2012, 170f.).

As mentioned in the previous section, the life-energies released through yoga and body alchemy have roots in tantrism and sexual magic. It is a matter of releasing the desires of the body in a way that liberates the will and gains the practitioner pleasure as well as power. It is not a matter of suppressing desire (the right-hand path promotes abstinence), but of celebrating the will-to-life in its many forms and shapes. The aim must thus be to release desire, using the "demonic" sexuality within, becoming animal as a pack of affects, a multiplicity, a population. However, it must not be limited to the worn comparisons of carnal lust and the "animal inside," but rather understood as the liberation from the realm of the codified culture (Beckman 2013). Ultimately, the dark desires of tantrism in black metal must be an escape from Freud's imprisonment of human sexuality in what Rosi Braidotti calls a "Fort Knox of the Libido" (2002, 140).

It is here the "intra-action" of metal yoga comes into play. It is not so much a game of communication, or of impressing peers with poses and looks of holy purity, as much as an alchemic transformation of the body itself. The black dressed body of leather and spandex, occult runes and skulls, studs, and ripped denim, is as much alchemic as a demonic body: an affirmation of bodily affect, refusing to be imprisoned by righteous morality or the strict regimen of corporate yoga studios. In the dim lights and to the deafening sound of screaming guitars, I take part in a ritual unifying annihilation, fury, and despair as much as affirmation, seduction, and creation. The central path is the release of emotion and the venting of anger and rage—rage that is *in* as much as *of* the body. Moreover, all the occult references in the dress do not signal outward as much as act in a functional coupling with *the inner change* of the body. In this way, the esotericism of Metal Yoga Bones is an alchemic practice of the body, perfectly in tune with Blavatsky's and Crowley's heritage. It is about releasing the *kundalini*, one's coiled up primal energy, and purifying the alchemical elements of the body: "power dressing" the left-hand path.

It is an affirmation of those bodily states and affects that arouse, move, and heighten the pleasures of the body—even if those may be painful. Pain is an ancient tool used in body practices, and many rites of passage include painful challenges. The erotic use of pain is also essential to what Stephen Flowers and Crystal Dawn Flowers call *carnal alchemy*, or the "sado-shamanist" techniques of using sexuality, pleasure, and pain to release the great "Unknown" from within the body on the path of self-transformation (Flowers and Flowers 2013). In carnal alchemy, BDSM and fetish elements are thus not mere symbols but tools that facilitate certain *doings* of the alchemic body. Thus, the demonic and tantric sexuality of dress in black metal stands in opposition to the Freudian heritage of seeing the fetish elements in dress as Flügel's erogenous zones of dress (1950), König's sexual "exhibitionism" (1973), Laver's "seduction principle" (1969), or even Steele's reworkings of fetishism in fashion (1996), because it is never a matter of symbolism or of having/not having the phallus. Fetish elements in dress are alchemic tools. They change the affects and functions of bodies, change skin sensibilities, and hide or give access to parts of the body for manipulation. The body is open for power but also open to release its power (see Figure 10.3).

The practitioners at Metal Yoga Bones are not geared up for the BDSM scene, yet even in black spandex and cut-up band T-shirts, the dark and emotionally charged yoga practice embraces the alchemic assemblage of intra-action: dress, body, and emotions in a ritualist transubstantiation—one and many bodies fused by a nihilist-yet-elitist Fuck You attitude. As the darkly dressed, vinyl- and leather-clad participants in the BDSM scene reveal, or as the angered postures and practices at Metal Bones Yoga show, fashion is *in* the flesh, it is happening *in our bodies*. Yet it is also a fashion *of* the flesh: the body as a passage of affects—of

Figure 10.3 Group session of metal yoga. *Photo*: Otto von Busch.

anger, arousal, rage, and hatred—and demonic emotions affirmed throughout the body. This is the Fuck You pose—the left-hand pose. And it feels good.

The fashion of dark intra-actions

We may usually think of yoga and fashion as two entirely different practices, the first being about exercise and the second about identity and communication. However, I would like to suggest that both are very similar, not only in the sense of their popularity but also in how they are assemblages of affects and material functions, or of esoteric alchemical processes in the body. Both fashion and fetish share the same Latin root: *facticium* and *facere*, which means "to do" or "to make" (Barnard 2014, 199). Thus, both fashion and fetish are imbued with agency; they grant the wearer access to refigurations and to manipulations of the alchemic assemblage of the body, and with this comes power. The dark fetish does not represent: it *does things*. Fashion, as well as fetish, will thus fall outside the dominant paradigm of representation and text-referenced forms of "meaning," to instead be a form of acting and agency, much in tune with the "affective turn" (Clough and Halley 2007).

In the dim lights at Metal Yoga Bones, fashion does not so much signal, but operates in the body of the wearer as an alchemic form of Baradian intra-action. My muscles burn with the music ripping through my body. It then becomes apparent fashion is an embodied experience fusing music, clothes, and emotions into a full assemblage with an unknown body, a body that is truly a "dark continent" of affects. To put it in Brian Massumi's terms in his translator's foreword to Deleuze and Guattari's *A Thousand Plateaus* ([1980] 2004):

> The question is not: is it true? But: does it work? What new thoughts does it make it possible to think? What new emotions does it make it possible to feel? What new sensations and perceptions does it open in the body? (Massumi in Deleuze and Guattari [1980] 2004, xv)

The yoga wear of the black metal yogi may help us expose how fashion is intrinsically a matter of magic, but beyond mere ritual or superstition, as Wilson suggests (2004). This practice of alchemic fashion is always about transgressive intra-actions between human and beast, between sin and virtue. Perhaps even more so, because fashion in this space becomes a true form of magic, an alchemic use of sorcery to feel power is *growing*, resistance is overcome. Fashion, like alchemy, is part of the "dark arts," the darkness of affirming the power of body, not submission to higher abstract ideas, but a full embrace of eroticism, sensuality, and squandering destruction. As Flowers suggests, this is the essence of the left-hand path:

> The common trait of all left-hand-path practitioners is that they focus on their own selves as their first source of power and they seek to cultivate, develop, and enhance that separate and unique source as the surest path to happiness. That turning inward to the dark depths of one's own self to find the light is as old as mankind. (Flowers 2012, xxi).

The left-hand pose at Metal Yoga Bones would align well with that. As Thode says, "You need to be really grounded and in my classes, I will always try to push over my students to test how strong they are. Metal yoga is also an attitude" (Thode cited in Brinton 2015).

References

Ahmed, Sara. 2010. "Orientations Matter." In *New Materialisms: Ontology, Agency, and Politics*, edited by Diana Coole and Samantha Frost, 234–57. Durham: Duke University Press.

Bakunin, Michael. (1882) 1970. *God and the State*. New York: Dover.

Barad, Karen. 2001. "Re(con)figuring Space, Time, and Matter." In *Feminist Locations: Global and Local, Theory and Practice*, edited by Marianne DeKoven, 75–109. New Brunswick: Rutgers University Press.

Barad, Karen. 2007. *Meeting the Universe Halfway*. Durham: Duke University Press.

Barnard, Malcolm. 2014. *Fashion Theory: An Introduction*. New York: Routledge.

Bataille, Georges. 2012. *Eroticism*. London: Penguin.

Beckman, Frida. 2013. *Between Desire and Pleasure: A Deleuzian Theory of Sexuality*. Edinburgh: Edinburg University Press.

Blavatsky, Helena. (1888) 1974. *The Secret Doctrine*. Pasadena: Theosophical University Press.

Braidotti, Rosi. 2002. *Metamorphoses: Towards a Materialist Theory of Becoming*. Cambridge: Polity Press.

Brinton, Jessica. 2015. "Death Metal Yoga: Some of Us Need a Little Bad to be Good." *Amuse*, September 21, 2015. Available at: https://amuse-i-d.vice.com/death-metal-y oga-some-of-us-need-a-little-bad-to-be-good/

Cataldi, Sue. 1993. *Emotion, Depth, and Flesh: A Study of Sensitive Space, Reflections on Merleau-Ponty's Philosophy of Embodiment*. Albany: State University of New York Press.

Clough, Patricia Ticineto, and Jean O'Malley Halley, eds. 2007. *The Affective Turn: Theorizing the Social*. Durham: Duke University Press.

Connole, Edia. 2015. "Seven Propositions on the Secret Kissing of Black Metal: OSKVLVM." In *Mors Mystica: Black Metal Theory Symposium*, edited by Edia Connole and Nicola Masciandaro, 333–66. New York: Schism Press.

Crowley, Aleister. (1939) 1985. *Eight Lectures of Yoga*. Phoenix: Falcon Press.

DeLanda, Manuel. 2016. *Assemblage Theory*. Edinburgh: Edinburgh University Press.

Deleuze, Gilles, and Felix Guattari. (1980) 2004. *A Thousand Plateaus: Capitalism and Schizophrenia*. Minneapolis: University of Minnesota Press.

Djurdjevic, Gordan. 2014. *India and the Occult: The Influence of South Asian Spirituality on Modern Western Occultism*. New York: Palgrave.

Entwistle, Joanne. 2000. *The Fashioned Body: Fashion, Dress and Modern Social Theory*. Cambridge: Polity Press.

Evola, Julius. (1949) 1992. *The Yoga of Power: Tantra, Shakti, and the Secret Way*. Rochester: Inner Traditions.

Faxneld, Per. 2012. "Lilith as Patron Saint of Abortion in Satanist and New Age Discourse: A Comparison." Paper for The Second Annual INASWE Conference, Haifa, March 2012.

Faxneld, Per. 2014. *Satanic Feminism: Lucifer as the Liberator of Woman in Nineteenth-Century Culture*. Stockholm: Molin & Sorgenfrei.

Flowers, Stephen. 2012. *Lords of the Left-Hand Path: Forbidden Practices and Spiritual Heresies*. Rochester: Inner Traditions.

Flowers, Stephen, and Crystal Dawn Flowers. 2013. *Carnal Alchemy: Sado-Magical Techniques for Pleasure, Pain, and Self-Transformation.* Rochester: Inner Traditions.

Flügel, John. 1950. *The Psychology of Clothes.* London: Hogarth.

Greil, Marcus. 1989. *Lipstick Traces.* London: Secker & Warburg.

Hebdige, Dick. 1979. *Subculture: The Meaning of Style.* London: Methuen.

König, Rene. 1973. *The Restless Image: A Sociology of Fashion.* London: Allen & Unwind.

Laver, James. 1969. *Modesty in Dress: An Inquiry into the Fundamentals of Fashion.* Boston: Houghton Mifflin.

Metal Yoga Bones. "Metal Yoga Bones: Unleash Your Inner Beast." Website, available at: https://metalyogabones.com.

Muggleton, David. 2000. *Inside Subculture: The Postmodern Meaning of Style.* Oxford: Berg.

Nietzsche, Friedrich. (1895) 1960. "The Antichrist." In *The Portable Nietzsche*, 565–656. New York: Viking.

Parkins, Ilya. 2008. "Building a Feminist Theory of Fashion: Karen Barad's Agential Realism." *Australian Feminist Studies* 23(58): 501–15.

Singleton, Mark. 2010. *Yoga Body: The Origins of Modern Posture Practice.* Oxford: Oxford University Press.

Steele, Valerie. 1996. *Fetish: Fashion, Sex and Power.* New York: Oxford University Press.

Thacker, Eugene. 2011. *In the Dust of this Planet: Horror of Philosophy*, Vol. 1. Winchester: Zero Books.

Tseëlon, Efrat. 1995. *The Masque of Femininity: The Presentation of Women in Everyday Life.* London: Sage.

Turner, Terence. (1980) 2012. "The Social Skin." *HAQ: Journal of Ethnographic Theory* 2(2): 486–504.

von Busch, Otto. 2008. *Fashion-able: Hacktivism and Engaged Fashion Design.* Gothenburg: ArtMonitor.

White, David Gordon. 1996. *The Alchemical Body: Siddha Traditions in Medieval India.* Chicago: University of Chicago Press.

Wilson, Elizabeth. 2004. "Magic Fashion." *Fashion Theory* 8(4): 375–85.

11

"Feeling premium": Athleisure and the material transformation of sportswear

Jennifer Craik

It could be argued that, increasingly, the individual performance of a person resides in a body that is encased in, and propelled by, the uniformed outside or clothed "shell." Despite the overpowering individualist nature of consumer culture or its thriving on the belief in individuality, individual choice, and mercurial tastes in selecting clothes and putting them together, there has been a massive proliferation of uniforms in diverse contexts, including official regalia, educational organizations, occupations and workplaces, clubs and societies, and sport and leisure contexts. While extensive research has been undertaken to develop highly specialized and customized uniforms for different sports at competitive and professional levels, there has also been a rapid crossover and uptake of these innovations in everyday clothing. Sportswear has been adopted by the general community, as clothing for, first, various forms of exercise (running, walking, yoga, amateur sport, etc.), and, second, for everyday and fashionable wear. One prominent example of this is the fashion for so-called "activewear" and "athleisure"—a type of clothing that is not just functional for sports, but also conveys the appearance of "sportiness" and "fitness" (Figure 11.1). Worn at cafes, school drop-offs, lecture rooms, shopping centers, markets and festivals, airplanes, and tourist venues, activewear has become a dominant fashion genre shaping all dress codes. Athleisure has different price points, from premium fashion to bargain basement, reflecting ideas of status as well as values and qualities inscribed in the body-hugging garments themselves. This chapter argues that the uptake and materiality of sports-derived clothing is changing perceptions of the fashionable human body in Western societies and globally impacting the relationship between bodies and clothes.

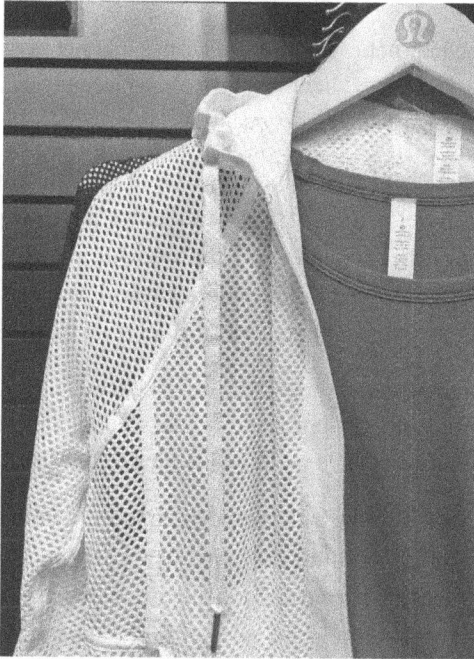

Figure 11.1 Detail of activewear by Lululemon. "Classic" sportswear pieces with technological features (flat seams, smooth, stretchable materials, lightweight, permeable/absorbent). *Photo*: Julie Macindoe.

Athleisure and the active body

The phenomenon of athleisure and activewear has transformed the "fashion-scape" of the twenty-first century, with people wearing sports-derived casual clothing in diverse places around the world. The term "athleisure" was coined in 1976, in an advertisement for sneakers, but it was not until 2015 that the term was defined in the *Merriam-Webster Dictionary* as "casual clothing—such as yoga pants, sweat pants, and hoodies—that are designed to be worn both for exercising and for doing (almost) everything else" (Armstrong 2016). Similarly, the term "active wear," or "activewear," was coined in the 1980s (Horton, Ferrero-Regis, and Payne 2016). This marked the adoption of "performance wear as everyday wear for women" (Marlowe 2016). As 3D knitwear designer, Lindsay Mann, observes:

> If I were to describe an Athleisure outfit, it might look like a lightweight shirt made from the latest technology, jogger pants, and a pair of Nike FlyKnits. In many cases, this look has become completely acceptable in the workplace. No

more poking fun at the business woman rushing to work in her power suit and sneakers. She may not even decide to change into her heels when she gets into the office. Athleisure is about comfort. Designs are lighter, simpler, more functional, well designed and higher quality. (Mann 2015)

Athleisure is an example of a clothing genre (sportswear), which was designed for a particular material context (sports and active physical pursuits) but has been repurposed for other activities and contexts. On the one hand, the design of garments has been modified to look more streamlined and fashion-forward; while, on the other, new smart fibers and fabrics create garments that are:

sweat wicking, temperature controlling, skin clearing, stain resistant, anti-microbial, UV protectant, etc. Imagine that your clothing can work for you just by wearing it . . . Lucky for all of us, it's a blooming reality. (Mann 2015)

Indeed, athleisure has become a default contemporary clothing phenomenon, surpassing sales of other clothing styles in such a way that its materiality has become ubiquitous in mainstream fashion and dress in the global market. While sales of athleisure continue to grow, sales of other apparel types are declining (Mintel Press Team 2016). To compete within the market, the stretchy fibers and fabrics used in athleisure are now incorporated in many other clothing types, such as jeans, to create a more comfortable and body-hugging feel (Moskowitz 2016). How has this material transformation of a clothing genre, initially crafted for performing in highly codified and regulated contexts, come to dominate clothing behavior on a global scale?

Training body and mind: The legacy of uniforms and sportswear

The origin of athleisure clothing resides in the nexus between uniformity, materiality, and identity and how that became inscribed in the genre of sportswear (Bielefeldt Bruun and Langkjaer 2016). The history of sports clothing derives from the history of uniforms, especially those associated with military and educational institutions, where training and performance of the body was part and parcel of creating the material bodies of these institutions (Craik 2005). While the uniforms of these institutions were central to constructing a distinctive collective identity, they also constructed individual personae, underpinning appropriate codes of conduct and deportment. The philosophy of individual identity constructed by bodily discipline flowed into the arena of sport and exercise. Central to both philosophies was the disciplining of mind and body, with the underlying idea that the shell of the body was trained to perform in certain ways that would affect the body or that the qualities and values of psychological, emotional, and philosophical nature could be actualized. A strong sporting body was understood as the physical representation of a strong inner self. Codified uniforms and outfits maximized this articulation of strength and discipline and demarcated members of the same group, side, or team, and, in competition, marked the opponents or enemy. In addition, sportswear was based on traditional men's clothing and on the uniforms at all-male institutions. While subsequent adaptations of sportswear for women modified male garments (and sometimes added skirts), they were still based on male garments that neither fitted nor suited the female body shape.

Early sportswear codified how particular garments and looks should be worn and styled. These in turn created different forms of sportswear: namely, sportswear for different sports (e.g., swimming costumes, football shirts and shorts, fencing suits); sports uniforms for team sports and competition; and sportswear that was worn for leisure, informal, or casual activities (Craik 2005, 139–59). The key driver of sportswear has been sports uniforms. Yet, although uniforms are often considered to be anti-fashion, uniforms derive from fashion as well as drive it. Moreover, the history of the development of uniforms reveals a close dependence on available fibers and fabrics, sewing techniques, and changes in embellishments and accessories, as well as developments in fiber technology and design innovation.

Taken together, the evolution of uniforms in different contexts and cultures demonstrates the finessing of specialist clothing that enhances bodily techniques and the performance of the (active) body. However, uniforms also appear in other contexts outside those spaces, via material changes and uses of uniforms in "in-between places" and "non-places." The assumption here is that uniforms have shaped the material development of sportswear and sporting uniforms, which have catalyzed the emergence of the athleisure genre. At the heart of this new genre is the tension between performing bodies as individual and unique manifestations versus bodies that are part of a corpus (a collective and coordinated performance).

The performance of bodies can be understood as choreographed by the garments that clothe bodies and animate its routines. The uniformity of these clothes conveys the appearance of "sportiness" and "fitness," and creates a new relationship between the body, space, and place. In other words, uniforms have become a material adjunct to—or the lived-in *habitus* of—the active body in designated roles.

Materials, fitness, and comfort

While extensive research has been undertaken to develop highly specialized and customized uniforms for different sports at various competitive and professional levels, there has been a rapid crossover and uptake of these innovations in non-sporting contexts (Salazar 2008). In 2016, the *Uniformity* exhibit, held at the Museum at the Fashion Institute of Technology, New York, traced the power of different kinds of uniforms on social attitudes, fashion, and cultures. With regard to sportswear, the exhibit's curator Emma McClendon declared:

> Right now, the biggest impact of sports uniforms on fashion is in the "athleisure" trend. Consumers want to be comfortable, so the material, construction, and aesthetic of functional athletic attire is having an increasing impact on fashion and everyday clothing. (McClendon quoted in Radin 2016)

Athleisure is the result of the desire of "fashion designers [to] deconstruct the iconography of sportswear mainly for visual impact and also, possibly, to imply participation in sport" (Angus 2013b, 528).

Developments in fiber and fabric technology, especially synthetic and stretch materials, have had the greatest impact on sports uniforms. The invention of nylon in 1938, followed by the inventions of acrylic, polyester, polyurethane, synthetic rubber, and spandex, revolutionized the qualities of both fabric fit and stretch-and-recovery (Craik 2005, 139–59; Goodrum 2016; Handley 1999; O'Mahony and Braddock 2002). As most of these inventions were originally products of research for military, space travel, or medical purposes, the applications for clothing, fashion, and sports were only belatedly recognized. For example, spandex (used in Lycra) was developed in the late 1950s, but was not introduced to fashion apparel until the early 1980s, coinciding with "disco fever" and aerobics, and marketed to the general public through popular films such as *Flashdance* (1983). Subsequent developments in "fast suits" for competitive swimming in 2000 and onward revolutionized the sport by creating high performance, seamless compression garments that contributed to and could be modified for active apparel (Angus 2013b, 529–30).

Lycra is now used in many forms of apparel—from denim jeans to men's suiting—due to its ability to soften the fit, feel, and look of garments. Even newer fabrics embody moisture-wicking properties that take sweat away from the skin and regulate temperature, reducing rashes and abrasion (Bielefeldt Bruun and Langkjaer 2016, 185–86; Goodrum 2016, 185). Synthetic fabrics are almost exclusively used in athleisure, sometimes in combination with natural fibers such as bamboo and merino wool. Along with Lycra, new generations of smart fabrics—such as Supplex (stretch and wicking jersey), Tactel (lightweight, soft, and fast drying), Dri-Fit (perforated wicking polyester, trademarked by Nike), and Meryl (nylon microfiber, with high stretch-and-recovery, and wicking and odor control)—are being supplied to the at-home sewer as well as the apparel manufacturers (Fehr 2015). As these fabrics become commonly available, at-home sewers and designers can create their own customized and unique athleisure garments that emphasize better fit and comfort, and are cheaper than commercial apparel (Mann 2015; Fehr 2015). Innovations in digital printing, such as surface printing, have also created infinite possibilities in fabric design.

Apparel for active pursuits has been embraced in a range of contexts, including aerobics, yoga, jogging, cycling, and Pilates. In a relatively short space of time, sports-type wear has been adopted as exercise-wear for the general community (running, walking, amateur sports, etc.) and subsequently for everyday and casual wear. In the past decade, athleisure wear has straddled sporting, exercise, casual, and traveling activities. But it has also become a feature of "high" fashion, in designer and luxury fashion collections, collaborations, and eyewear. Popular outfits incorporate many elements of athleisure wear including T-shirts, track pants, leggings/jeggings/cropped pants, knitted jackets/sweatshirts, compression garments, athletic shoes/runners, sweatbands, caps, and backpacks.

Today, athleisure can be seen in a wide range of social contexts around the world, including cafes, school drop-offs, lecture rooms, shopping centers, markets, festivals, concerts, airplanes, public transport, entertainment complexes, and tourist venues, among others. As the baby boomers have aged and started to reach retirement age, versions of activewear and athleisure have become a standard form of clothing—casual, loose-fitting, easy-care, and all-purpose. In short, activewear based on sporting uniforms has become universal. Given the mainstream debates over the appropriateness of athleisure in the workplace, for shopping, on the street, and in other contexts, its ubiquity does not mean that it is not controversial (Green 2017; Marlowe 2016). Some brands and buyers are observing a trend toward design that blurs the lines between sportswear and everyday clothing by creating garments that are designed to better match with shirts, coats, skirts, and boots (Marlowe 2016). The use of more subtle colors and patterns blends in with other garments better than the previously ubiquitous white, black, or fluorescent hues and combines two trends—"durability and comfort—in a versatile way" (Green 2017). *Business Insider* reporter, Dennis

Green, cites fashion historian, Deirdre Clemente, who declared that athleisure is a "weird hybrid" of "business casual and athletic wear":

> Athleisure is the new casual . . . [that] perfectly fits with a variety of trends that have been culminating for a century . . . Styling is evolving to merge business casual and sportswear into one. (Clemente quoted in Green 2017)

Alison Goodrum quotes Ted Polhemus in describing how the hierarchical structure of the athleisure industry creates "the athleisure style tribe" who endorses particular brands and looks (see Figure 11.2). The tribe also invests in the "careful curation" and hard (physical) work required to maintain this "never to be fully completed" project (Goodrum 2016, 155). These tastemakers set a high bar for becoming part of the athleisure style tribe via membership exclusivity and snobbishness toward lesser sportswear-clad people. On the other hand, athleisure wear has become mainstream in the office and other professional contexts as the emphasis on being comfortable has become allied to the idea of "fitness" as a marker of the contemporary workplace. The emphasis on lifestyle straddles the home, exercise/sporting, and work arenas with work practices adapting to suit a competitive 24/7 labor market that thrives on individualism. In this context, the notion of comfort can be extended with the link between "fitness" and "fitting in" (Miller and Woodward 2012). Even denim—that ubiquitous global clothing genre—has incorporated stretch fabrics and fibers into its iconic designs, for example, its 501 jeans (Steele 2017, 27). As Levi's chief executive Chip Bergh has recognized: "The market has moved to super-stretchy, supersoft fabric, and

Figure 11.2 Street image of athleisure. *Photo:* Getty Images.

we're out there with more rigid fabric" (quoted in Steele 2017, 27). Similarly, Old Navy's Alison Partridge has reflected that "athleisure's focus on comfort has pushed the denim industry to evolve and innovate" (quoted in Steele 2017, 27).

Luxury athleisure and the labor of self-improvement

Of course, not everyone in athleisure wear is sporty, yet the clothing suggests qualities of sportiness, fitness, bodily care, and the hard work of maintaining a trim body:

> Women's activewear . . . is a highly ambiguous form of contemporary fashionable dress that signals a healthy body and a leisured lifestyle devoted to the improvement of the self. Therefore, while time spent in the gym or exercising is characteristically classified as leisure, the fashionable body in the twenty-first century is also the site of hard work. (Horton, Ferrero-Regis, and Payne 2016, 181)

Gender—or specifically the female body—has been the preeminent focus of the design of and debate about athleisure. Although this is changing, the promotion and marketing of athleisure in advertisements via sports star and celebrity endorsements and popular culture features invariably model thin and fit bodies, and leading athleisure brands only produce in sizes up to Australian size 16 (UK 14, US 12, Japan 15, Europe 42), although a minority are now offering 18 to 26 size ranges (Castle 2015). A classic example of this process is the Australian brand, Lorna Jane, which is now globally marketed but maintains a tight grip on the forms of its promotion, marketing, and curation (Allen 2015; Horton, Ferrero-Regis, and Payne 2016). This extends to precise body types selected to work in Lorna Jane stores, namely blonde, thin, fit, and sassy "gym-bunnies." In 2015, a former employee sued the company for AUD 550,000 for discriminatory bullying and harassment about her weight—a case that is still before the court (Butler 2015; Staff Writers and AFP 2017). While the case created a social media backlash, it does not appear to have changed the recruitment policies of the retailer. Rather, Lorna Jane encourages devotees to post inspirational "selfies" on its online platforms as "fitspiration" for other consumers, thus creating an elite club of Lorna Jane look-alikes who reinforce the body and lifestyle ideals promoted by the brand. Occupations like modeling have become entrenched symbols of "glamour labor" (see Wissinger 2015), stoked by social media posts that set beauty and lifestyle standards for "ordinary" people who consume high profile athleisure brands and buy memberships at "fashionable gyms." However, the reality is, that larger bodies are a majority and likely a growing side effect of contemporary lifestyles, which are mostly sedentary and screen-dependent. This growing demographic is not being served by the mainstream market (Amour 2016). Moreover, consumer research by activewear brand, Female for Life, suggested that 50% of Australian women stop or avoid exercise when clothes do not fit or are uncomfortable, while 63% "found it difficult to simply find gear that suited their body shape." On the contrary, 87% "found that wearing flattering and comfortable workout gear made them more motivated to exercise" (Amour 2016). These results confirm those of an earlier study on attributes sought in sporting apparel, which found that

> Females ranked fit as being more important in selecting apparel than men which may be explained by the lack of availability of sports apparel designed for the feminine silhouette and the overall importance females place on fit of apparel. (Fowler 1999, 84–85)

Fowler also analyzed retailers and merchandising practices and discovered that there was an overall lack of attention to three distinct types of female sporting apparel consumers: "the serious athlete, the weekend athlete, and the woman seeking comfortable apparel." Moreover, the market gap for these consumers affected their psychological well-being because they had to wear ill-fitting gear (Fowler 1999, 86).

Inevitably, athleisure wear is appearing at all market levels from designer luxury brands, to fashion brands and retailers, to department stores, chain stores, and discount stores. While 81% of sales occur in the mass market, 13% are premium, 3% are luxury, and 3% are value chains (Milnes 2016). Price points serve to moderate the number of sales at each level by the volume of sales. As a result, new labels are created for individual niches by lifestyle designers and brands that trade on scarcity and exclusivity. Athleisure's main brands are the main sports apparel brands. However, the advent of athleisure has encouraged the emergence of successful niche brands, some of which have become global players. These include Lululemon in Canada (often regarded as the original athleisure brand), Adidas in Germany, Reebok in the United States, Sweaty Betty in the United Kingdom, Lorna Jane in Australia, Under Armour and Lily Lotus in the United States, and Canterbury in New Zealand (Allen 2015; Horton, Ferrero-Regis, and Payne 2016; Routh 1993; Schlossberg and Lutz 2016; Wolfe 2001).

Despite this active market, there is little research comparing value for money in purchases of athleisure clothing. One of the few published studies was conducted by the Australian consumer magazine, *Choice*, which compared seven brands of gym tights (leggings) ranging in price from AUD 7.50 to AUD 109—Lululemon AUD 109, Lorna Jane AUD 99.99, Nike AUD 69.95, Adidas AUD 60, Big W's Michelle Bridges AUD 35, Cotton On AUD 29.95, and Kmart AUD 7.50 (Castle 2015). The study noted that there were much higher price points, such as AUD 454 for neoprene leggings and AUD 380 for stretch jersey leggings from Net-a-Sporter, the athletic gear offshoot from high-end online retailer Net-a-Porter, neither of which were machine washable. *Choice* compared quality of fabric (stretch-and-recovery), colorfastness to washing, pilling, moisture-wicking, seam strength and stitching, stitch type, and care instructions. The results suggested "that quality doesn't necessarily increase with price" (Castle 2015). Adidas and Nike performed best for quality, stitch count, and colorfastness:

> The two most expensive pairs of tights—Lorna Jane ($99) and Lululemon ($109)—certainly didn't fare badly in the fabric tests, but they didn't come out on top either, suggesting you don't necessarily have to fork out big dollars to get quality sportswear.
>
> In terms of value for money, . . . the Michelle Bridges were [considered] the best at $35, with good construction and nice detailing. However, . . . the Lorna Jane and Lululemon were [considered] the best in terms of construction . . . The Adidas and Nike were well made, but rated . . . just after the Lorna Jane and Lululemon tights, mostly because the waistband didn't feel as firm. (Castle 2015)

Overall, *Choice* concluded that, "given the trend toward sportswear as fashion, it's likely that the extra dollars you fork out may well be for style or brand rather than quality" (Castle 2015). It recommended that consumers look out for fabric with twelve to fourteen stitches per inch, a flat or overlocked seam, smooth stitch tension, good stretch-and-recovery, good sweat-wicking properties (how quickly water soaks in), and comfortable fit when moving, bending, etc. (Castle 2015). Of greatest importance is that athleisure makes the wearer "feel premium" irrespective of the brand: "It's about creating product that's desirable, product that resonates with consumers. The luxury isn't in the garment, it's in the lifestyle, and the concept" (Reece Crisp, buyer for Farfetch, quoted in Milnes 2016). The emphasis on the premium feel encapsulates the material connection between mind and body. By equipping the wearer to perform in his/her choice of clothes and knowledge of premium brands, athleisure wearers can promote their social values through their clothing. Customizing designs has been a consequence of the digital marketing and retailing age in a genuinely global marketplace, where designers are competing with all levels of players and seeking to be more business savvy in order to add something that can convert a browser or window-shopper into a loyal, repeat consumer. Both Fowler (1999) and Chang et al. (2015) have emphasized two important factors for a positive activewear retail experience: the store's design and ambience should articulate the brand DNA and lifestyle connotations, and the sales staff should be actively engaged with customers, demonstrating detailed knowledge that informs and guides the shopper to suitable apparel types. Whereas customers do not like to be confronted in other fashion stores, they seek "personal interaction and store atmosphere" in activewear stores that train "knowledgeable, friendly sale associates and [offer] a fun shopping environment" (Chang et al. 2015, 146 and 148).

A recent study of activewear trends and drivers showed that when women "put on activewear it helps motivate them, get in that zone to do a physical activity" (Fox Koob 2017, 3; ASGA 2016). Women are prompted by a combination of value, style, fit, and function, and want to know "is this functionable, good quality, is it breathable?" (Fox Koob 2017, 3). The relatively wide price range makes athleisure wear attractive at different price points, while the promotion of athleisure consistently portrays high-end values and qualities that are visibly inscribed in the body-hugging garments and appeal to millennial consumers. These are distinct from the athletic wear of sports teams with logos. Often worn directly from the gym to class or office, and later to the yoga studio, the body-hugging athleisure clothes—and the "premium feeling" they may entail—is enhanced by marketing and advertising that link brands and products with "sporting giants or brand ambassadors, and [are] made glamorous by association with leading designer names" such as Stella McCartney (Adidas), Raf Simons (Adidas), Kanye West (Adidas), Yohji Yamamoto (Adidas), Giorgio Armani (Reebok), Hussein Chalayan (Puma), Rihanna (Puma), Kylie Jenner (Puma), Alexander Wang (H&M), and Beyoncé (Topshop) (Angus 2013a and b, 531; Team 2016; Milnes 2016). Athleisure also features prominently in seasonal collections by iconic designers, thus cementing the association of athleisure with high fashion (Gallagher 2017, 16).

Branding athleisure in the global marketplace

Athleisure has become a global phenomenon across all market levels and marketplaces, and is the largest growth apparel sector, growing at 8.5% in 2016 and estimated to continue to grow apace (Emler 2017; Team 2016). In the United Kingdom, athleisure sales grew by 42% between 2010 and 2016 (Armstrong 2016) and have been estimated to grow by 30% by 2020. In the United States, activewear sales increased by 16% in 2015 compared with all apparel sales growing by only 2%. Athleisure sales in the United States has been estimated to grow to USD 83 billion by 2020, with global sales of the emerging major apparel type projected at USD 350 billion by 2020 (Team 2016). Globally, the industry is estimated to be worth AUD 270 billion and expected to grow by 20% between 2016 and 2020 (Fox Koob 2017, 3; ASGA 2016).

While sales of athleisure have been fanned by the fad for healthy lifestyles, wellness, and fitness, Mintel (2016) estimated that 50% of UK consumers bought sports apparel for non-sport use, favoring fashion-forward brands and celebrity athleisure collections. While consumers of all ages buy athleisure, 75% of people in the United Kingdom aged 16–24 years purchased sports apparel in 2016, reflecting the importance of millennials to this market and to the adoption of new casual clothing codes. Of consumers who bought athleisure for active pursuits, 45% did so for running or jogging, 28% for going to the gym, 23% for cycling, 7% for yoga or Pilates, and 7% for rugby (Mintel Press Team 2016). Outside sporting activities, athleisure is becoming part of streetwear and workwear, with 86% of women wearing athleisure while running errands, 61% while sleeping, 59% while shopping, 20% while dining out, and 29% casually wearing yoga pants (AGSA 2016, 5).

Of all types of athleisure, sports shoes or sneakers dominate sales as athletic footwear becomes "a mainstream fashion trend" (Elmer 2017; Angus 2013b, 530–31). Brands such as Nike, Adidas, Puma, Reebok, North Face, Ellesse, Kappa, and Ivy Park have the major share of the market, and are stocked by athletic shoe specialist retailers such as JD Sports, reflecting JD Sports' transformation "into an amazing lifestyle business that was really sport-related" (Traill-Nash 2017, 27). Sales of sports footwear increased by 34% in 2016 (Mintel Press Team 2016), while 25% of new collections or ranges in 2015 were designed by luxury designers or brands (Milnes 2016). Footwear is becoming the most lucrative and desired garment in sports apparel:

> Whilst clothing continues to be the dominant category, footwear is an increasingly crucial part of any sports retailer's assortment. The substantial growth we're seeing in the footwear segment is likely driven by the increased acceptance of sports clothing in society. In particular, athletic footwear has become a big mainstream fashion trend. (Mintel Press Team 2016)

The new CEO of Adidas, Kasper Rorsted, has committed to expanding "lifestyle products" to reflect a "shift in consumer taste away from performance wear toward casual, fashion-forward looks" as "the division between performance and fashion products is blurring" (Germano and Divac 2017, 25). In order to cater

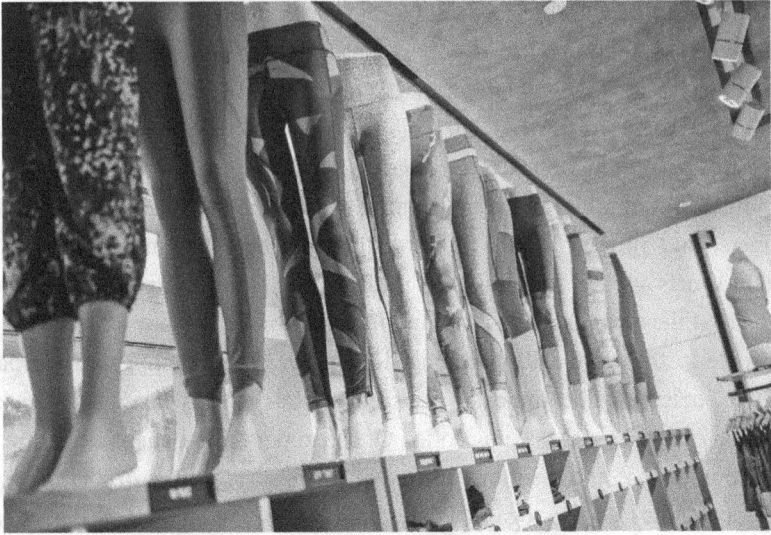

Figure 11.3 Store display of leggings. *Photo:* Getty Images.

for "time-poor" millennials, retailers such as JD Sports are aiming to seamlessly blend online, virtual, and physical exposure and shopping experiences. To this end, online retailer, Farfetch, launched a design-your-own sneaker site in 2016:

> Fashion brands and retailers also are starting to catch onto the myriad of ways that consumers want to shop. It varies considerably by age and life stage, and also by their interests and the "channels and retailers that each generation grew up with," reported NPD Group and Wharton. Yet all generations want one-stop or convenient shopping, value and leisure and entertainment as they shop. (Elmer 2017)

Recent studies emphasize that the ways in which athleisure is being designed and marketed are based on "old patronising gender stereotypes" that do not reflect contemporary women's lives or the specific qualities they seek in making purchases (ASGA 2016; O'Sullivan et al. 2017) (Figure 11.3). Athleisure is a global phenomenon most visible in the ubiquitous availability of the major sportswear brands, yet complemented by niche brands that proliferate in local markets and are promoted by local celebrities.

Conclusion: The future of athleisure

This chapter has argued that the uptake and materiality of athleisure is changing perceptions of the fashionable human body in Western culture. While major international brands have driven athleisure fashion, local and niche brands have actively entered the market by offering customized athleisure wear for particular contexts and customers as the sportswear category has widely expanded and become normative as everyday dress in a global marketplace. The wide appeal of sportswear at the symbolic level, is also seen in licensing specific trademarks, such as Adidas's three stripes, or in the way athleisure has spawned a major industry in counterfeits and "inspiration" copies and adaptations of popular apparel.

There are parallels between athleisure and surfwear, as Jon Anderson has argued, observing that surfing apparel and equipment is increasingly driven by marketing aspects of the lifestyle associated with surfing. He concludes that four cultural ideals structure the surfing dress code, namely performance, cultural authenticity, transient engagement, and cyborgian skin (organic and mechanical) (Anderson 2016, 212). These characteristics can be seen as relevant to athleisure wear in general, but to which we might add the pursuit of pleasure and enjoyment, or "calculated hedonism" (Crocket 2016), and new experiences (Team 2016), and where feeling and looking good, or "premium," arguably aid the sports and exercise endeavor (Fowler 1999; Catsoulis 2016).

In short, wearing athleisure has become "entirely inspirational," as well as aspirational, and has been called "the new black" (Armstrong 2016). Although the fad for athleisure will probably slow down and be replaced—or modified—by another trend, it nonetheless reflects "a big change in the way women dress" (Simon Hill-Norton, owner of Sweaty Betty, quoted in Armstrong 2016). Although a number of athletically inclined brands and retailers have failed or been bought out (e.g., City Sports, Sports Authority, Pacific Sunwear, American Apparel, Juicy Couture, Quiksilver, and Billabong), there are plenty to replace them as the market grows. Thus:

> Since athleisure reflects a lifestyle shift, it is unlikely it will disappear soon, despite the market being over-stretched. The retailers will have to keep adapting, and this will mean using different materials, new features such as odourless fabrics, and keeping up to pace with the changing fashion trends. (Team 2016)

Athleisure epitomizes fashion that is casual, customized, and personalized, embraces futuristic inventions, denotes identification with status and role model celebrity, and reproduces ideal body shapes and sizes. These have become the new coordinates of the materiality of fashion in the "body-con era" of the twenty-first century (Angus 21013b, 531).

But, can it last? Retail investment consultant, Jan Rogers Kniffen (2016), believes that the trend is "rolling over" as consumers tire of wearing their gym gear on the streets and for everyday use and are trending toward denim and footwear that incorporate smart fibers. While Rogers Kniffen predicts that athleisure is "entering the death throes of the uncool," he acknowledges that smart technologies such as sensors, Wi-Fi connectors, augmented reality, and other performance enhancing measures, are increasingly driving the emerging fashion scene. The challenge is to maintain profitability in an increasingly competitive marketplace by more strategic pricing, reducing stock levels, developing quicker design-to-market systems, and reviewing supply chain logistics (Germano and Divac 2017, 25). With developments in 3D printing, there will be abundant opportunities for consumers to create customized or personalized garments and accessories that fuse functionality with fashion and occasion (Elmer 2017). Athleisure may transition into new forms as it enters a new phase of the materiality of fashion and dress: "Wearables are just lathering up for a bigger change. [This trend] is soon all going to be about smart fabrics that will help us live better lifestyles we want to show on Instagram" (Milnes 2016).

In short, athleisure epitomizes the relationship between the clothing that exhibits a fit body, or makes a body want to be fit, and the Western social mandate toward continuous self-improvement. This ties to the concept of individuality and the sense of self that is linked to the dialectical relationship between production and consumption, both of things and of experiences. Achievement of these qualities depends on working on the body continuously as well as working on the self to be fit for the market in the widest sense.

References

Allen, Lisa. 2015. "How Lorna Jane Took on the Activewear World." *The Australian*, June 19, 2015. Accessed February 22, 2017. http://www.theaustralian.com.au/bus iness/the-deal-magazine/how-lorna-jane-clarkson-took-on-the-activewear-world/ news-story/96c8592f0ceb3bf0c7fb0b7abe1bcd40

Amour, Anastasia. 2016. "How the Right Activewear Can Help Motivate Your Healthy Lifestyle." *Female for Life*, January 17, 2016. Accessed March 3, 2017. https://ww w.femaleforlife.com.au/Exercise-and-Fitness/activewear-motivates-healthy-lifesty le.htm

Anderson, Jon. 2016. "On Trend and on the Wave: Carving Cultural Identity through Active Surf Dress." *Annals of Leisure Research* 19(2): 212–34.

Angus, John. 2013a. "All-purpose Sportswear 2004." In *Fashion: The Whole Story*, edited by Marnie Fogg, 532–33. London: Thames and Hudson.

Angus, John. 2013b. "Sportswear and Fashion." In *Fashion: The Whole Story*, edited by Marnie Fogg, 528–31. London: Thames and Hudson.

Armstrong, Ashley. 2016. "The Rise of Athleisure: How the High Street is Cashing in on Office-to-Gym Wear." *The Telegraph*, September 17, 2016. Accessed March 3, 2017. http://www.telegraph.co.uk/business/2016/09/17/the-rise-of-athleisure-how-the-high-street-is-cashing-in-on-offi/

Australian Sporting Goods Association (ASGA). 2016. *Active Wear: Forecasting Future Trends in Female Consumer Behaviour*. Melbourne: Victoria University. Accessed March 10, 2017. http://www.asga.com.au/wp-content/uploads/2016/02/ASGA-Active-Wear-Literature-Review-Infographic-REVISED-May-2016.pdf

Bielefeldt Bruun, Mette, and Michael Langkjaer. 2016. "Sportswear: Between Fashion, Innovation and Sustainability." *Fashion Practice* 8(2): 181–88.

Butler, Nicole. "Jane Lawsuit: Former Fitness Label Employee Became 'Suicidal' After Alleged Bullying Over Weight." *ABC News*, September 10, 2015. Accessed March 9, 2017. http://www.abc.net.au/news/2015-09-10/lorna-jane-lawsuit-former-employee-became-suicidal-over-size/6764132

Castle, Jemma. 2015. "Fashion or Gym Wear?" *Choice*, February 16, 2015. Accessed February 22, 2017. https://www.choice.com.au/health-and-body/diet-and-fitness/sportswearsportswear-and-shoes/articles/sportswearsportswear-why-is-it-so-expensive

Catsoulis, Sophie. 2016. "Activewear Edit: Looks to Inspire Your Exercise." *Style Magazines*, December 7, 2016. Accessed February 22, 2017. http://stylemagazines.com.au/fashion/activewear-edit-looks-inspire-exercise/

Chang, Hyo Jung, Hyeon Jeong Cho, Thomas Turner, Megha Gupta, and Kittichai Watchravesringkan. 2015. "Effects of Store Attributes on Retail Patronage Behaviors." *Journal of Fashion Marketing and Management* 19(2): 136–53.

Craik, Jennifer. 2005. *Uniforms Exposed: From Conformity to Transgression*. Oxford: Berg.

Crocket, Hamish. 2016. "Tie-dye Shirts and Compression Leggings: An Examination of Cultural Tensions within Ultimate Frisbee via Dress." *Annals of Leisure Research* 19(2): 194–211.

Emler, Vickie. 2017. "Fashion Industry," *Sage Business Researcher*, January 16, 2017. Accessed February 22, 2017. http://businessresearcher.sagepub.com/sbr-1863-101702-2766972/20170116/fashion-industry

Fehr, Melissa. 2015. "A Guide to Activewear Fabrics." *Seamwork Magazine*, January 2015. Accessed February 22, 2017. https://www.seamwork.com/issues/2015/01/a-guide-to-activewear-fabrics

Fowler, Deborah. 1999. "The Attributes Sought in Sports Apparel: A Ranking." *Journal of Marketing Theory and Practice* 7(4): 81–88.

Fox Koob, Simone. 2017. "Active Where Activewear Goes." *The Weekend Australian*, March 11–12, 2017.

Gallagher, Jacob. "Sportswear off Field and on Runway." *The Australian*, February 21, 2017.

Germano, Sara, and Natascha Divac. 2017. "New Adidas Boss Hits the Ground Running." *The Australian*, March 10, 2017.

Goodrum, Alison. 2016. "The Dress Issue: Introduction." *Annals of Leisure Research* 19(2): 145–61.

Green, Dennis. "Athleisure is Not Just a Trend—It's a Fundamental Shift in How People Dress." *Business Insider Australia*, February 5, 2017. Accessed February 22, 2017. http://www.businessinsider.com.au/athleisure-is-more-than-a-trend-2017-2?r= US&IR=T

Handley, Susannah. 1999. *Nylon: The Manmade Fashion Revolution*. London: Bloomsbury.

Horton, Kathleen, Tiziana Ferrero-Regis, and Alice Payne. 2016. "The Hard Work of Leisure: Healthy Life, Activewear and Lorna Jane." *Annals of Leisure Research* 19(2): 180–93.

Mann, Lindsay. 2015. "Athleisure and the Future of Fashion." *Knitting Industry*, August 3, 2015. Accessed March 5, 2017. http://www.knittingindustry.com/athleisure-an d-the-future-of-fashion/

Marlowe, Rachel. 2016. "The 5 Golden Rules of Athleisure: Is It Really Acceptable to Wear Yoga Pants All Day Long?" *Vogue*, January 7, 2016. Accessed February 22, 2017. http://www.vogue.com/article/rules-for-wearing-workoutwear

Miller, Daniel, and Sophie Woodward. 2012. *Blue Jeans: The Art of the Ordinary*. Berkeley: University of California Press.

Milnes, Hillary. 2016. "Designer Sneakers and $200 Leggings: How Luxury Stepped into the Rise of Athleisure." *Digiday*, March 22, 2016. Accessed March 5, 2017. http://dig iday.com/marketing/designer-sneakers-200-leggings-luxury-stepped-rise-athleisure/

Mintel Press Team. 2016. "Fashionistas Cause Sales of Sportswear to Sprint: UK Sports Goods Sales Estimated to Surpass £7 Billion in 2016." *Mintel*, August 8, 2016. Accessed March 3, 2017. http://www.mintel.com/press-centre/retail-press-centre/ fashionistas-cause-sales-of-sportswear-to-sprint-uk-sports-goods-sales-estimated -to-surpass-7-billion-in-2016

Moskowitz, Samford. 2016. *Advanced Materials Innovation: Managing Global Technology in the 21st Century*. Hoboken: Wiley.

O'Mahony, Marie, and Sarah Braddock. 2002. *Sportstech: Revolutionary Fabrics, Fashion and Design*. London: Thames & Hudson.

O'Sullivan, Grant, Clare Hanlon, Ramon Spaaij, and Hans Westerbeek. 2017. "Women's Activewear Trends and Drivers: A Systematic Review." *Journal of Fashion Management and Marketing* 21(1): 2–15.

Radin, Sara. 2016. "Uniformity: A New Exhibit Shows How Uniforms Hold Power Over Us." *WGSN*, August 5, 2016. Accessed August 12, 2016. https://www.wgsn.com/blog s/uniformity-a-new-exhibit-fit-museum/#bulletin

Rogers Kniffen, Jan. 2016. "The Demise of Athleisure." *The Robin Report*, August 10, 2016. Accessed March 5, 2017. http://www.therobinreport.com/the-demise-of-athlei sure/

Routh, Caroline. 1993. *In Style: 100 Years of Canadian Women's Fashion*. Toronto: Stoddart.

Salazar, Ligaya. 2008. *Fashion V Sport*. London: V&A Publishing.

Schlossberg, Mallory, and Ashley Lutz. "19 Up-and-Coming Athleisure Brands That Aren't Lululemon." *Business Insider*, February 3, 2016. Accessed March 9, 2017. http://www.businessinsider.com/brands-that-could-be-next-lululemon-2013-11/?r=AU&IR=T

Staff Writers and AFP. 2017. "Bullied Former Lorna Jane Manager 'Suicidal' and too Scared to Go to Work, Court Hears." *News.com*, February 15, 2017. Accessed March 9, 2017. http://www.news.com.au/finance/business/retail/bullied-former-lorna-jane-manager-suicidal-and-too-scared-to-go-to-work-court-hears/news-story/bc30c732f2833732d32294701ff7a3ee

Steele, Anne. 2017. "Jeans Brand Makes the Stretch to Greater Comfort to Take on Sports Apparel." *The Australian*, June 13, 2017.

Team, Trefis. 2016. "The Athleisure Trend is Here to Stay." *Forbes*, October 6, 2016. Accessed February 22, 2017. https://www.forbes.com/sites/greatspeculations/2016/10/06/the-athleisure-trend-is-here-to-stay/#1e792e0128bd

Traill-Nash, Glynis. 2017. "Sport's New Cause Walking the Talk." *The Weekend Australian*, March 4–5, 2017.

Wissinger, Elizabeth. 2015. *This Year's Model: Fashion, Media and the Making of Glamour*. New York: New York University Press.

Wolfe, Richard. 2001. *The Way We Wore: The Clothes New Zealanders Have Loved*. Auckland: Penguin.

Material exchanges: Fashion and migration

Introduction

Reconnecting to the previous sections in this book on the entanglements between fashion, humanity, and materiality, this last section, with chapters by Andrea Hauser and Elke Gaugele, extends the perspective on how fashion intersects with the personal and the political, with a focus on the recent refugee and migration movements in Europe and how they are dealt with at various local and international levels.

As a substantial component of socialization, fashion and clothing act forcefully in the production of social categorizations and the construction of difference along the lines of gender, class, race, ethnicity, and place. Moreover, there is an ongoing historical relationship between the global production and circulation of fashion, and the production of social asymmetries that emerge between those who make clothes—often at the expense of their well-being and health—for the benefit of those who want to consume fashion. Sometimes, in one of the bitter ironies of the fashion business, these are even the same people.

As an object of labor, fashion employs millions of workers worldwide in its factories. Most of them are migrant workers pouring from remote areas into the big fashion-producing regions and cities. Christina Moon gives in her chapter on fast-fashion cities in China (Chapter 8) a stark example of the scale, as she describes the biggest "urban village" in Shenzhen, Baishizhou, "where 150,000 migrant worker residents per 0,23 square miles of mixed-use residential space," have formed the densest populated neighborhood in the world. The worldwide free-trade zone factories are able to sustain themselves only by the labor of people who, in many cases, have substantial routes of migration behind them. In 1995, for example, a human rights group discovered three dozen illegally employed workers, who came from as far as Bangladesh, put to work in a factory in Honduras (Howard

2007, 37). In Italy, *pronto moda* (fast fashion) has formed its own production and economic activity. Here, many Chinese immigrants, sometimes entire families, work at the cheapest wages in the local textile and footwear industries. It can be assumed that, in addition to the several thousand legal workers in Prato, a city with 190,000 inhabitants, a large number of workers are non-registered migrants, with far-reaching negative consequences for their labor and human rights as well as remuneration. For these people, and across these various places, work and everyday life—both usually under inhumane conditions—become an inseparable entity, coupled with the dreams of a better life.

The superficial "democratization" associated with consumption and the availability of (fast) fashion evokes equally old and new forms of social stratification. Historically, the expansion of fashion to its current state as a widely accessible low-cost and rapidly disposable commodity, has only been made possible through the ongoing exploitation of human labor at a global scale. In an ongoing race to the bottom, the fashion industry continues to locate and relocate its production sites via subcontractors to places with the lowest cost, from China, to Vietnam, and then to Bangladesh, where the lack of safety regulations in 2013 led to the collapse of the Rana Plaza factory building, and the fatal deaths of 1,135 garment workers, with an additional 2,438 people injured. As Robert Ross notes in his book *Slaves to Fashion*, the "apparel industry is among the world's largest manufacturing industries and among those very few industries where extreme exploitation of vulnerable labor is central to the labor process and to the chain of profit making" (2004, 12). Extreme exploitation is not, and was not, confined to the garment-producing industries, but includes the production of fashion's raw materials. For example, the historic growth of the cotton industry in Great Britain and the United States (accelerated by Eli Whitney's invention of the cotton gin that mechanized the separation of cotton from its seeds), was a large-scale driver of the forceful importation and enslavement of people from the African continent, which was only formally abolished in America in 1865, roughly 250 years after the first slave ship landed in Jamestown, Virginia. Further into the nineteenth century, the rise of fashion capitals such as Paris and New York relied largely on the mobility and "flexibility" of work and workers. Between 1880 and 1900, more than three million immigrants poured into American cities, Jews fled pogroms, and people from across Europe faced economic hardship and emigrated to the United States to advance their lives, thereby forming a large workforce for the sweatshops of the fashion and textile-producing industries. Ross cites an observation the New York state license superintendent Daniel O'Leary made in 1900 about the living and working conditions in New York's Lower East Side: "Workers toiling in dark, humid, stuffy basements on Division Street, children of eight years and women, many of them far from well, sweating their lives away in these hellholes" (*The Jewish Daily Forward* 1900, 21, cited in Ross 2004, 19). In his study of sweatshop labor in 1990s America, Ross adamantly reminds us that such working and living conditions are not located in the past or elsewhere, but still occur today among the most affluent countries in the world.

Most recently, Europe's fashion industry has witnessed and been the subject of crucial political upheaval. Since 2015, Europe, a region of relatively high prosperity, has been confronted with a large-scale refugee movement that has posed an unprecedented political and humanistic challenge for countries in the European Union. In one fell swoop, the ethnoscapes of European states changed with the incoming, wandering streams of people from African and Middle Eastern countries, with many aiming toward northern Europe as their most hoped-for destination. Old problems and their effects on Europe—including, for example, the legacy of colonization (especially in France, Belgium, and the United Kingdom); the conception of migrants as temporary "guest workers" since the 1950s, as, for example, in Germany; or the migration of people as a result of the Kosovo War—were far from resolved, but rather lay fomenting and unattended beneath the surface until there was a sudden rupture. The most recent large-scale migration of people from Syria to Europe caused a wave of anxiety, such as the fear of "foreign infiltration," or *Überfremdung*, which seemed to be confirmed by the fact that the arrivals looked "different." Many of the Syrian refugees wore scuffed clothes and shoes from weeks-long travel by foot, with only as many items as they could carry themselves.

Clothing, as both a materially essential and sociocultural good, played a significant role in the way society, affected local communities, as well as the fashion industry responded to the crisis. Levi Strauss & Co., for example, donated Levi's and Dockers brand clothing at an estimated value of 800 million euros to a local aid organization in Berlin. And with the mediatization of the refugee crisis, especially in Germany, aid organizations received overwhelming masses of used clothing donations. In collective memory, especially within Europe, it still seems firmly rooted that clothing can be scarce in times of need and is an important material asset. Donating clothing has a long tradition in charity, and confronting others' material losses touched and urged many people to sort through their wardrobes for things they no longer needed, donating them to the cause. Yet, it was not recognized that most of the refugees did not want to be (further) marked and identified as needy, by wearing secondhand goods, but they rather preferred to spend their own money to buy new clothes according to their own taste. This raises important questions, including, most significantly, how best to support refugees in their precarious state of transience. How do you enable self-empowerment and active engagement and integration in a new environment?

As the two chapters in this section show, the issue of migration results in material exchanges on multiple levels through a variety of different strategies, internationally and locally. In her chapter, Andrea Hauser explores the organization of a fashion show in a predominately migrant neighborhood in the German city of Bremen, arguing that differences in clothing and fashion can be used productively as a source of attention. In an attempt to foster intercultural communication and exchange, and as a way to dismantle cultural prejudices, fashion has been incorporated into a task force that materially merges aesthetics, education, and politics. Hauser describes how clothing is used as a tool in integration policies as the city of Bremen and local NGOs have organized DIY fashion initiatives to counteract growing social pressures occurring through migration. She describes how women from various countries work together in the staging of "international fashion shows," in which they present their self-made clothing and alterations, drawing inspiration from clothing styles worn in their previous home countries. In this case, the material exchange, through the collective making and presenting of clothing in various local or cultural styles, is intended to promote social and cultural exchange to enhance community-building among the participants.

As migration has become a core issue in the twenty-first century, and such an exceptionally divisive one, various cultural institutions have come to approach it with their own underlying agendas. One could perhaps draw parallels between the display of cultural-sartorial difference in the staging of the DIY international fashion show to the increasing "museumization of migration." Joachim Baur (2009) describes the trend to establish immigration museums, in various countries, as an extension of the historical development of the national museum and, as such, as a representative new iteration of the promotion of national identity: "in the service of portraying host nations as multicultural and tolerant. As a consequence, they tend to idealize and simplify the immigration experience for ideological purposes" (Jenkins 2016). Seen from this lens, the act of staging cultural diversity in the DIY international fashion show glosses over the more complex reality of migrants and refugees in the same way that some museum displays "overlook the more troubling and difficult problems [migrants] encounter as they travel and upon arriving; as well as the feelings and actions of those in the host nation who are uncomfortable or hostile toward immigrants" (Jenkins 2016). However, as Hauser argues, the attention potential that lies in staging fashion on a runway is understood by the organizers to generate positive attention and even a reciprocal social gain for the performers *and* the audience. Fashion and clothing, understood as having a general common or shared relevance, formed the pivotal material point for the experiment. The medium of the fashion show charismatized the presented styles and—compared to the everyday situation—enabled and increased the visibility and aesthetic recognition of the presenting women. At the same time, this local DIY fashion event represented a symbolic invitation for the audience and presenters to recognize and meet one another in the actual core zones of everyday life.

Moving from the local community level to the broader international scope of the connection between fashion and migration, Elke Gaugele, in her chapter, turns to international fashion designers who broached the issue of the refugee crisis in a related way: they incorporated the theme and look of refugees in their runway shows. Although, in this case, the runway shows were ultimately centered on the promotion of the latest designer collections, they nonetheless drew attention to migration in an aesthetic way. Featuring fashion with multivalent layers of meaning, the 2016 menswear shows highlighted the disturbing ambivalence of a refugee aesthetic that wavered between charismatization and stigmatization. As Gaugele further discusses in her chapter, this appropriation of the theme of migration and the fashion designer's urge to draw attention to the humanistic issue occurred at the same time as many Europe-bound Syrian refugees were being recruited as cheap laborers for the large fashion-producing industry in Turkey. As Gaugele shows in her chapter as well, not only did the fashion industry set out to address the issue of migration with efforts ranging from "aesthetic politics" and "refugee" styling of designer collections to actual donations of clothing, but political and cultural institutions also recognized the potency of fashion in their work as they dealt with diversity and processes of cultural heterogeneity in terms of nation branding. Elke Gaugele highlights in her chapter the Ethical Fashion Initiative (EFI), a joint agency of the United Nations and the World Trade Organization, founded in 2006 to promote the work of African designers. The EFI recently extended its reach as a global governance tool for the "refugee regime complex," which included the Generation Africa show during Florence Menswear Fashion Week, featuring Walé Oyéjidé's (founder and creative director of Ikiré Jones) "After Migration" collection, which had three asylum seekers as models. In approaching the entanglements of fashion and migration through a multisited approach—from runway shows, to the capitalization of migrant workers in the Turkish fashion industry, to clothing donations in an aid facility in Germany—Elke Gaugele illustrates the global and cultural complexities of the current nexus between fashion and migration.

Fashion and dress have a unique capacity in their materiality: it envelops and comes to blend with the body of the wearer, and that functionality is assumed to visualize or reveal at the exterior something about the interior. In their materiality, as Gabriele Mentges puts it, "dress practices can provide a sensual memory and bond shared by different people" (2017, 12). As such, it offers a unique tool in the processes of social and cultural change and exchange to foster respect for diversity and the formation of new communities. However, as the two chapters in the final section of this book show, the links between fashion, materiality, and migration processes are highly sensitive ones, both personally and politically. Fashion can clearly be an effective tool in drawing attention to current social issues, yet it requires consideration and an evaluation of who gains from this attention, and how. Together the two chapters highlight the asymmetries, ambivalences, and possibilities that come to materialize in and through fashion as a cultural practice and a global field of labor that, as Elke Gaugele argues, confronts future fashion scholarship with the task of making a deeper connection with global and migration studies.

To end this last section's introduction with a further outlook, and hope: rather than reinforce in complicity, fashion and fashion scholarship need to actively work against the way we have become conditioned by the logics of capitalism and consumer culture, not least in the way it has come to organize time. As Russell West-Pavlov writes in his book *Temporalities*, "[t]ime today, in its most commonsense meaning, is the most everyday but also the most ubiquitous practical codification of contemporary capitalism" (2013, 5). He says that this version of time is so "insidious because it has managed to persuade us that it is the very fabric of existence itself" (2013, 5). The rise of enlightenment and industrialization has brought a "progressive narrowing of the spectrum of temporal modes . . . The gradual streamlining of temporality down to universal linear time as the self-evident calibration of human existence, has repressed and elided other possible temporal forms or structures of individual and global existence" (2013, 6). Fashion in its association with modernity has been a key actor in this calibration of human life according to industrial, capitalist time. In an article on fashion's politics of time, Aurelie van de Peer (2014) unpacks how the fashion industry and fashion media, by aligning fashion with natural seasons, have institutionalized fashion change as something that is perceived to occur so "naturally" that it has habitualized the expectation that one ought to buy new clothes every season. The seasonal rhythm has sped up in such a way that clothes shopping is now for many people literally an *everyday* practice, leading to a diminishing value of clothing as material goods. Since the 2000s, global clothing production has more than doubled to nearly a hundred billion garments produced in 2014, yet only 40 percent of these mass-produced clothes are actually ever worn. Kate Fletcher has described this type of clothing as "value-free" fashion, in the sense that it is entirely out of sync with people and soil (2014, 141), where the promotion of ephemerality works against forging lasting relationships to clothing. However, the rise of fashion activism and various initiatives such as the Fashion Revolution movement over the recent years exemplify an increasing campaigning by the public to hold the fashion industry more accountable for its actions and to move toward more sustainable, circular models (see Fashion Revolution 2015).

Considering that the linearity and speed of fashion is nothing natural, but something to which we have been socialized, as we learn to consume and learn how to relate to things, there is not only the possibility but, in fact, the urgency to *un*learn such time strategies and to rethink and use fashion again as valuable *materials* to have meaningful relationships with. The way fashion materiality affects humanity is so deep and vast in scale that we cannot afford not to think or rethink fashion in material terms as meaningful matter.

References

Baur, Joachim. 2009. *Die Musealisierung der Migration: Einwanderungsmuseen und die Inszenierung der multikulturellen Nation.* Bielefeld: transcript Verlag.

Fashion Revolution. 2015. "Its Time for a Fashion Revolution." *White Paper*, December 2015. Written by Sarah Ditty. Accessed June 1, 2017. https://www.fashionrevolution.org/wp-content/uploads/2015/11/FashRev_Whitepaper_Dec2015_screen.pdf

Fletcher, Kate. 2014. *Sustainable Fashion and Textiles: Design Journeys.* London and New York: Routledge.

Howard, Alan. 2007. "Labor, History, and Sweatshops in the New Global." In *The Object of Labor: Art, Cloth and Cultural Production*, edited by Joan Livingstone and John Ploof, 31–50. Chicago: School of the Art Institute of Chicago Press, and Cambridge: MIT Press.

Jenkins, Tiffany. 2016. "Politics are on Exhibit in Migration Museum, not History." *Foreign Policy*, October 19, 2016. Accessed March 31, 2017. http://foreignpolicy.com/2016/10/19/can-curators-stop-marine-le-pen-migration-museums-europe/

Mentges, Gabriele. 2017. "Introductory Remarks." In *Textiles as National Heritage: Identities, Politics and Material Culture*, edited by Gabriele Mentges and Lola Shamukhitdinova, 9–28. Münster: Waxmann.

Ross, Robert J. S. 2004. *Slaves to Fashion: Poverty and Abuse in the New Sweatshops*. Ann Arbor: University of Michigan Press.

van de Peer, Aurelie. 2014. "So last Season: The Production of the Fashion Present in the Politics of Time." *Fashion Theory* 18(3): 317–39.

West-Pavlov, Russel. 2013. *Temporalities*. London: Routledge.

12

International fashion shows: Creating transcultural relationships through clothing

Andrea Hauser

Thinking of international fashion shows, the ones that typically come to mind are those in well-known capitals or "fashion cities," such as Paris, London, or New York (see Breward and Gilbert 2006). During their bi-annual fashion weeks, designers present their latest collections, which, today, are rapidly circulated in images across social media, setting trends for the upcoming season. As Pamela Scorzin notes, since the 1960s, fashion shows have become increasingly mediatized. They have evolved from elaborate scenographic performances enacted in a specific location with an exclusive front-row audience into far-reaching multimedia events (Scorzin 2016, 21). Due to digitalization, the fashion show as a localized, temporary, multisensory *Gesamtkunstwerk* expands instantly into the space of social media immersing audiences around the world (Scorzin 2016, 56). Alongside the increasing globalization of the fashion industry, fashion design and its presentation have become highly adaptive to the current concerns of contemporary culture, while also drawing on influences from the past, such as historical styles or cultural and regional forms of dress (Keller-Drescher 2015), which can be translated into the latest fashion. As recent fashion weeks have demonstrated, fashion shows are also frequently used as sites to address and aesthetically process current politics. In an article on the interplay between fashion and migration, Elke Gaugele (2016) discusses how a number of designers' presentations at the Paris haute couture shows, in January 2016, responded to the Paris terrorist attacks of November 2015. During the menswear shows, presented at that time, Walter van Beirendonck, for example, made a very concrete political statement with his collection "WOEST," meaning wild, furious, and irate, with the explicit demand to "stop terrorizing our world." According to Gaugele, such outspoken political positions became even more frequent following the terrorist attacks in Brussels in March 2016 (Gaugele 2016). Similarly, in the light of the latest escalation of migration throughout Europe, the largest in recent history, with some 65 million refugees, migration has become increasingly topical in the world of fashion (see Chapter 13, by Gaugele, in this volume).

Moving beyond the realm of designer shows in fashion cities, however, in this chapter I focus on the interests that drive the production of a different form of international fashion show (*Internationale Modenschauen*), as they are organized in Bremen. The city of Bremen is located in North Germany, and has a population of 557,000, including about 180,000 people with a migrant background. Emerging as community events in Bremen's city district, Tenever, these *Internationale Modenschauen* are events in which women (with and without migrant backgrounds), present themselves in self-made fashions and in elaborately choreographed performances in both semi-public and public spaces. Tenever is a very multicultural city district that is home to a population of roughly 6,000 people from about ninety different nations. For the members of the Tenever community, these self-organized international fashion shows are events designed to foster social and cultural exchange, and to present and engage with the diversity of their national and ethnic backgrounds alongside the vibrancy of and pride in their local district. Independently organized, these low-budget shows are not driven by the economic interests of the fashion industry, as they do not provide a stage for the dissemination of commercial fashion. Rather, the *Internationale Modenschauen* in Bremen appropriate the established, yet continuously changing, format of the fashion show for community-based interests. As alternative fashion shows, they are organized to offer opportunities especially for the empowerment of migrant women who are positioned at the social margins and to create a space to initiate processes of intercultural learning and exchange.

After observing these fashion shows on several occasions and speaking with various participants, they raise for me several questions I seek to address in this chapter: How do these international events materialize connections between fashion, migration, and cultural identity? In what way do these fashion shows serve as a medium to deal with questions of *Herkunft* or "origin," the migrant experience, and cultural identity? What is the role of clothing and its materiality in this context: where is it derived from, how is it made, what is chosen for display, and why? And how do these international fashion shows resemble and/ or differ from commercial fashion shows? In order to approach these questions, I will first provide some local background on how these fashion events began to emerge.

International fashion shows in Bremen

The so-called *Internationale Modenschauen* in Bremen are organized by the *Mütterzentrum* (Center for Mothers) Osterholz-Tenever: a community center that was set up to provide special support for women. Tenever is a former satellite town built in the 1970s on a greenfield site on the periphery of Bremen. Over the past few years, the district has been strategically downsized to improve the living conditions of its multiethnic population (Reuß 2005; Seebacher 2013). The *Mütterzentrum* was founded in 1989 as a nonprofit organization, providing job opportunities for disadvantaged women, often single mothers and migrants. It is financed through membership fees, donations, and sponsors as well as contributions from public municipal, federal, and European funds. The nonprofit organization supports the district through career counseling, employment opportunities, intercultural training for adults, cultural events, various neighborhood cafés, and children's facilities as well as a sewing and creative making center, and a place to swap secondhand goods (Mütterzentrum 2016). The *Mütterzentrum* works in conjunction with the district's cultural department (*Kulturbüro*), founded in the 1980s to facilitate community access to arts and culture, and to support collaborative projects with artists and other cultural industry professionals. From early on, in order to increase public awareness for this peripheral district, the mission was to bring greater attention to everything created or happening in Tenever—within and beyond the local community.

The international fashion show was one of the earliest cultural projects launched by the district, utilizing clothing as a medium of social and cultural exchange. In 2005, as part of the initiative "Made in Tenever—Recycling Design," the *Mütterzentrum*'s secondhand shop started to showcase a fashion line made from repurposed, used clothes. Since 2013, the city's cultural department (*Kulturbüro*) has also cooperated with the *Mütterzentrum* in organizing Tenever's various fashion art projects including Chain Stitch [*Luftmasche*] in 2013; Cloaks Galore [*In Hülle & Fülle*] in 2011/2012; and Textile Metabolism— Le Dernier Cri from the Recycling Bin [*Stoff Wechsel—Le Dernier Cri aus der Wertstoffsammlung*] in 2014. This last was a collection of innovative clothing and accessory designs made from upcycled materials, such as bottle caps, garbage bags, and paper. Using the medium of the fashion show, these cultural initiatives brought awareness to social issues such as considerate consumption and managing resources, questioning beauty standards, and recycling precious materials (Quartier e.V. n.d.).

The first *Internationale Modenschau*, held in the *Mütterzentrum* on International Women's Day, March 2012, was organized by and for women from different cultural backgrounds, hailing from a variety of nationalities. The theme of the show centered on questions of migration, origin, and identity as experienced through fashion practices. Perceptions of "self" and "other" are historically understood to be at the core of Western or Euro-American fashion, which has been infused by the cultural and material exchange with "foreign" clothing traditions from as long ago as the Crusades (Lehnert and Mentges 2013). However, as Gertrud Lehnert notes, at least since the eighteenth century, such material or sartorial exchanges between Western and non-Western fashion have become mutual: initially occurring in the context of colonialism, with the mandatory introduction of European clothes and customs, they have led to a dynamic of their own in subsequent centuries (Lehnert 2014, 152).

As Susan B. Kaiser puts it, there "is not merely one model for fashion subjectivity. Rather, there are multiple subjectivities, shaped in part by the interplay among diverse subject positions, for example, nationality, race, ethnicity, class, gender, sexuality" (Kaiser 2012, 28). The human diversity that results from migration movements and cross- or intercultural relationships visibly shapes the cultures of Western countries. In the globalized present, this also leads to new practices in the fashion business. Following Homi K. Bhabha's concept of hybridization, or, in more general terms, the notion of "fusion," regional and global trends emerge as apparently independent styles (Lehnert 2014, 154). Yet, in the global or "transnational outfits" and hybrid fashion styles that manifest themselves in everyday life (Kaiser 2012), social attributions, subject positions, and cultural discourses around nationality, ethnicity, and/or race, still play a dominant role: they are not "outside of the fashion process in terms of cultural representations, appropriations, and hegemonies" (Kaiser 2012, 81).

What is interesting to observe in the international fashion shows in Tenever, Bremen, is a rather playful attitude toward such attributions. If and how this may lead to an inquiry into cultural systems of order is one of the questions I want to focus on, based on the observation of two fashion shows: one in Bremen's central station and another in the city's market square. In addition, I am drawing on local newspaper coverage and interviews with the initiators and organizers of the project, including the current director of the sewing workshop and organizer of the current fashion shows, Ludmilla Schulz—herself a migrant from Russia—and with the culture and theatre educator, Gabi-Grete Kellerhof, who choreographed the first fashion shows and acted as the "runway coach."

As a participant observer at a rehearsal, I also had the opportunity to interview some of the women who modeled in the show.

The presentation—hybrid fashion

Since 2012, the Tenever *Internationale Modenschauen* have been presented in a variety of public spaces including community and shopping centers. On International Women's Day in March 2016, the *Mütterzentrum* Osterholz-Tenever staged its first fashion show in a public transit space, the Bremen train station. As part of the "One Billion Rising" initiative, a global campaign to end violence against women and girls, Bremen central station was declared a "Welcoming Train Station," an event celebrated on February 14, 2016, with a dance in resistance to gender-based violence. In Germany, the concept of a "culture of welcome" (*Willkommenskultur*) emerged in 2015, when more than half a million people migrated to the country, receiving a warm welcome from the many German people who went to the train stations to greet the refugees and who volunteered in support work (Otto 2016). As such, the train station became a symbolic site. The fashion show, choreographed by Gabi-Grete Kellerhoff, utilized the prominent staircase in the public entrance area of the station. Accompanied by music, women from seven different countries or regions (Ghana, Kosovo, Philippines, Poland, Siberia, Syria, and Russia) emerged, one after the other, from the train station lounge area onto the stair landing and then descended the staircase, each individually presenting her clothes. The moderator, Gabi Kellerhoff, presented the name of each model, her country of origin, and the individual stories of each woman's arrival in Germany, including their current living conditions and hopes for the future. Each model, in her mother tongue, greeted the growing audience assembled below, saying "Hello" and "Welcome" before descending the stairs and joining her companions. After the women had assembled in a line, they re-ascended the stairs, stopping at the top to wave and say "Goodbye" (*auf Wiedersehen* in German, which translates as "see you again") (Figure 12.1).

In contrast to professional models, for example, at international fashion weeks, whose bodies are usually employed to serve the designer and therefore notions of fashion within a less individual, standardized display, the *Internationale Modenschauen* allowed these women to perform and present their own personal histories. Their backgrounds and reasons for migration became identifiable, as did their hopes for new lives in Germany. In this way, experiences of alienation

Figure 12.1 International Fashion Show, Bremen central station. *Photo:* Sabine Prioletti.

and estrangement, often kept anonymous in the migration process, were not only addressed but also translated into a new context to make it intelligible to others. The existing cultural ambivalences surrounding the often unknown experiences of migration were transformed "into a knowable opposite," through what Kaiser refers to as a necessary process of individualization (2012, 43). What fascinated the audience in this case was less the design of the women's clothing and more the embodied image of cultural diversity, showing the courage of these women in organizing a public fashion show that, self-consciously, pointed to their precarious intercultural situation and history of migration. As Ansgar Schnurr argues, all those who participate in contemporary iconography are confronted with increased complexity and ambiguous affiliations (2014, 69). These felt ambiguities were also visibly expressed in the women's outfits. In contrast to conventional fashion shows, with stylistically coherent designer collections, these women presented individualized fashion that manifested itself in culturally heterogeneous styles. Next to a little black dress worn with a hat and scarf, was a skirt and blazer, a ball gown, and pants with a long jacket, a dress from Ghana, or another hybrid mix of clothes, such as a band of fabric arrayed over pants and a T-shirt, worn by a woman from the Philippines. Global and regional trends mixed liberally without becoming a coherent, uniform style. Thus, the *Internationale Modenschauen* displayed new sartorial tendencies for a globalized world where, increasingly, "bodies, materials and images flow through time and space" (Kaiser 2012, 32). Despite the notoriety of "melting-pot" ideals of assimilation, globalization does not necessarily lead to cultural homogenization but, on the contrary, can also lead to ever more cultural heterogeneity. The fashion show articulated this process "through the (re)invention of local cultural heritage and vestimentary traditions as powerful means of distinction" (Jansen and Craik 2016, 4).

The Bremen *Internationale Modenschau* presented a remix of existing visual perceptions, working against ingrained expectations associated with professional fashion shows, for example, the expectation to see a specific new fashion design style. Instead, current and "handed down cultural clichés" were reassembled in a new way and transferred to the current context (Lutz-Sterzenbacher and Schnurr 2014, 21). Similar to the formation of new images, these performances can enact transcultural experiences that can reach or become accessible to a broader audience.

Owing to the great success of the event in Bremen's train station, these public fashion shows are now put on with an increased frequency. In just a short period of time following the *Modenschau* described above, further shows were organized in a large shopping center as part of the Bremen Ecumenical Day. After the initial success of the shows and the audience's clear enthusiasm, the presentations have become increasingly professional. Whereas hybridization, or "fusion fashion," was originally a product of the open, somewhat haphazard format, questions of what exactly should be presented have now become part of the strategic planning of the show. These changes were particularly noticeable in the fall, 2016, performance held in one of Bremen's largest shopping centers, as part of the GO 16 trade show (*Gewerbeschau Osterholz*). Ludmilla Schulz, who studied art and design in Russia for a few semesters, oversaw the clothing production and performed in the fashion show. Schulz recalls that the planning and preparation of the first presentations did not offer enough time to produce new clothes. Thus, for the Bremen train station show, existing looks were repurposed. European Union subsidies, however, now permitted the production of clothes specifically for the *Modenschau*. This had important consequences as the collection was now divided into one section featuring existing and self-sewn fashion and another section with self-sewn, "traditional" clothes or regional *Tracht* (or folk dress) (see Figure 12.2).

The definition of *Tracht* has become increasingly disputed in German cultural anthropology since the 1980s. In the course of the social science turn in fashion and dress studies, it was found that "the old habit of dividing clothing into

Figure 12.2 Women at the International Fashion Show, Bremen, presenting clothing from or inspired by their home countries. *Photo:* Sabine Prioletti.

fashion-based clothing and 'Tracht' has often enough prevented a deeper insight into the complexity of the phenomenon" (Deneke 2000, 85). Conceived in the strict binary opposition of *Mode* (fashion) versus *Tracht*, the "volatile, short-lived fashion" relegated to the dress historian, was contrasted with the "historical continuity and tradition-bound quality of the *Tracht*" (Mentges 1989, 27f.). The function of the *Tracht* was narrowly reduced to the notion of the *Gemeinschaft* (Mentges 1989, 27f.). In research on traditional clothing, *Tracht* was then, in a way, made synonymous with the continuity and durability of peasant culture or, in a negative definition, stood for an absence of social dynamism (Mentges 1989, 27f.).

Liberation from such dichotomies, especially that of "fashion" versus *Tracht*, but also that of urban versus rural, and, in an international context, "ethnic dress" and "world fashion" became unavoidable within cultural studies' larger critiques of Eurocentrism and ethnocentrism. As early as 1980, Mary Ellen Roach and Kathleen Ehle Musa in their *New Perspectives on the History of Western Dress* pointed to the problematic division between clothing of the West and the "rest," which was commonly referred to as ethnic, non-Western, rustic, "folkloristic, primitive, tribal, exotic, regional, national, pre-industrial and traditional" (Roach and Ehle 1980, 5). In English-language cultural anthropology, "ethnic dress" was long contrasted with "Western dress" or "world dress," and thought to exist in "societies within and beyond Europe but still relatively isolated from the developing global economy, and peoples with distinctive cultures who were nonetheless impacted by European expansion" (Cerny, Baizerman, and Eicher 1993, 2; for discussion see also Jansen and Craik 2016, 1–3). Like language, architectural styles, and lifestyles, clothing was considered to be an expression of ethnic boundaries. Catherine Cerny, Suzanne Baizerman, and Joanne Eicher dissented from this view in 1993 by defining "ethnic dress" as being non-static:

> ETHNIC DRESS may include borrowed items from other cultures; the new item is culturally authenticated. It is not usually static (unchanging over time), variety can be found within a group at any point in time. Creativity and individuality are common to all, may not always be worn daily; may be for special occasions or a special location. An individual's wardrobe may contain both ethnic and world fashion, to be worn in appropriate times and places. (Cerny, Baizerman and Eicher 1993, 2)

Today, we must undertake both local and global investigations of the long-standing interrelationships and dependencies between non-Western fashion and Western fashion, between tradition and modernism, between clothing and fashion, and avoid the misleading boundaries and binary hierarchies of the past. A cross-cultural perspective, thus, needs to consider multiple systems of fashion (see Jansen and Craik 2016, 1ff.).

Is it counterproductive for their own project, then, that the Tenever women explicitly differentiate between *Tracht* and their "own fashion"? Yes and no. Their modified "traditional" or regional clothes do evoke and risk reviving certain cultural stereotypes. Thus, cultural identity or "origin" in these performances risks being interpreted as an act of "Othering." In fact, as Barbara Lutz-Sterzenbach and Ansgar Schnurr claim, cultural differences always entail a danger of producing new stereotypes (see Lutz-Sterzenbach and Schnurr 2014, 18). Possibly this opposition of *Tracht* and fashion was never intended in the first place, with traditional clothing providing a source of inspiration for the participants. It is quite possible that the very example of the *Internationale Modenschau* demonstrates the function of modernism and its desire for authenticity as a catalyst for the reinvigoration of tradition (Jansen and Craik 2016). Or, perhaps, the shows are simply a reflection of the women's own hybrid identities? Fashion studies emphasize that "styling, dressing, adorning, or fashioning the body is a fundamental part of subject formation (shaping, sustaining, and shifting): an ongoing sense of self and identity in a changing world" (Kaiser 2012, 30).

Possibly, the participants of the *Internationale Modenschauen* are part of a process of subjectivization, "in an ongoing, changing way—'who I am' and 'who I am becoming'" (Kaiser 2012, 30).

The new choreography of the *Internationale Modenschauen* subverted standard mechanisms that lead to cultural homogenization. While each performer welcomed the audience in their native language, unlike the previous *Modenschauen* held at the Bremen train station, this time there was no reference to an individual's biography. The first section of the show presented "Folk dress from around the world," inviting the audience to guess the origin of each presented outfit. A correct guess was rewarded with a prize. In the second phase of the performance, the women transformed into fashion models, presenting their, usually, self-designed outfits. Whereas the salutatory opening dealt with the women's cultural background or country of "origin," the second could be read as a representation of their unique "arrival" into German culture. The choice of dress in the "fashionable" second section of the show, suggests the issues involved in the arrival process. Rather than dressing in Western-style fashion, some women presented themselves in their regional-style everyday clothing such as the Shalwar Kameez, the pants and long shirt more widely worn by men and women in or from Southern Asian countries. In another example, the women from Ghana and Nigeria complemented their dress with local accessories, characteristic of their cultures, including special print fabrics. Such styles can be viewed as material displays of the women's narratives around personal origin and arrival, highlighting how experiences of identity or difference are produced in the course of migration and globalization (cf. Hall 1999). Demonstrating agency and creativity in the face of the "disturbance" wreaked by colonial conditions, and their migration and immigration experiences, these women use clothes to deal with the new cultural situation in which they live, without simple assimilation (see Hall 1999, 435). In this way, "origin" is playfully transcended through an "ethnomasquerade" (Konuk 2004) that enables reflection on arrival in a foreign culture. By accentuating particular aspects of cultural identity or by mixing various "components of identity formation," a familiarity with the foreign culture can emerge (Konuk 2004, 1). Whether the message is received in this way by the audience, however, requires investigation. Fortunately, no xenophobic attacks against the *Modenschauen* have been registered, as of yet, in spite of an increasingly hostile climate toward migrants in Germany in recent years. The reaction of the audiences to the *Modenschauen* seemed mostly full of enthusiasm and excitement. However, the *Modenschauen* participants were also clearly aware of the danger of creating new stereotypes. For their next performance, they are again planning to suspend the division between "traditional" and "modern" clothing. The idea is for women to also swap their clothing or combine fashionable dress with traditional or regional accessories that may not come from their own cultural backgrounds, for example, a woman from Ghana who might choose to wear a Polish hat. Such types of "fusion fashion" exemplify the dynamic material manifestations of transcultural networking on the body.

The models—fashion shows as empowerment

The models of the *Modenschauen* are mainly migrant women from approximately ten European and non-European countries, including women from Ghana, Poland, Turkey, Kosovo, and Russia. Just as the locations of the Bremen *Modenschauen* are continuously in flux, the roster of participants is likewise changing, with new participants always welcome.

During the rehearsal for the *Modenschau* on International Women's Day, I asked each participant what these shows meant to them. One German-born woman with a Kosovan family background told me that the show allowed her to reflect on her cultural heritage through clothing. A woman from Poland, who is part of the sewing workshop for the *Modenschau*, told me, with visible pride, that the events provided wonderful opportunities for the *Mütterzentrum* to present its work and community to the wider public. For another, the friendship provided by the group of women, culminating in the performance, was a sign of the possibility of living together peacefully and in solidarity. The women have formed a German-speaking group on the internet with the self-ironical name *Modepüppchen* (fashion dolls). On this shared platform, they have created a network through which they also support each other in everyday life. Their strong attachment to each other was apparent in the group rehearsal. Although the nervousness among some members was noticeable, they radiated great self-confidence as a group, an impression confirmed by one performer who reported overcoming the psychological hang-ups of her past as a result of working with the *Modenschau*. "Chest out and head up," confirmed Ludmilla Schulz, the rehearsal director, reminding the players: "Always present yourself and the clothes to the audience with self-confidence." Indeed, the *Modenschau* provides a space for these women to present themselves as who they are or how they see themselves (Figure 12.3).

The rehearsal also indicated what the women have learned with each new show. And they have come to know exactly what the audience wants. The women

Figure 12.3 International Fashion Show, at the community center (*Mütterzentrum*) in Osterholz-Tenever, Bremen. *Photo:* ©Mediengruppe Kreiszeitung/ Martin Kowalewski.

find that it is important to welcome the audience in German as well as in their native languages, ensuring they are understood as well as demonstrating their command of both languages. The *Modenschau* also raises questions of autonomy and agency. In contrast for instance to the Miss World contest, where models are also "invited" to present clothes in their "national" style, the focus in Tenever is not on presenting regional or "exotic" dress styles as a sexy vision of a diverse global community but on fashion and clothing as means of self-empowerment. Although conventional fashion shows are also now starting to break with long-standing norms of beauty—young, white, and thin—a conventional show does not typically present such diversity in national or cultural identity, personality, and age. In Tenever, the participants' ages ranged from two to seventy years old, and was inclusive and representative of the wide spectrum of body shapes and sizes found in everyday life.

Fashion shows and material culture

The *Mütterzentrum* projects are developed in collaboration with the women working at the center. Clothing and fashion-themed projects emerged naturally as the sewing and creativity sector of the center represents a relatively broad area of activity and education. In sewing courses, women learn to read sewing patterns, do mending work, and sew the most recently learned designs for themselves and their children. The secondhand clothing exchange managed by the workshop accepts orders for alterations or repair work, and provides expert guidance for the design, sewing, or alteration of the clothing owned by the women, including, for example, the altering of African clothing. Moreover, the in-house sewing studio, *Mosaik,* turns "old into new" by creating its very own fashion designs. The center not only provides extra income, but also permits those migrant women who already possess a strong skill in or affinity to textile handicrafts, to apply their techniques creatively. Other training programs in artistic and cultural areas are also utilizing these craft techniques, a trend that is currently experiencing a veritable boom in the fashion industry (see Dorner 2014, esp. 151).

In the sewing studio, *Mosaik,* participants also design clothing for the show, often modifying and reworking extant pieces of clothing. Another important difference in comparison to professional fashion shows is that new clothes are designed without guidelines or any directive from a prominent designer. Instead, designs are created autonomously or collaboratively in exchange among the participating women. The fashion designs may be developed with a view toward current commercial looks and/or in reference to the clothing practices and traditions associated with the women's own cultural backgrounds. This decision enables the women to "experience their own subjectivity and to obtain an autonomous mode of expression and agency" (Lutz-Sterzenbach and Schnurr 2014, 20). The individual clothing practices, manifesting themselves in the selection and assemblage of a specific clothing repertoire and, in more-or-less strategic consumer decisions, contribute to a "collection of one's self" (Clifford 1990)—as part of the process of identity formation. The manager of *Mosaik* describes how clothing becomes a medium to both negotiate cultural affiliations and disrupt them:

> Here in the Mosaik studio, we have sewn with five women. What was interesting was that they come from different countries, from Ghana, Poland, Turkey, from Kosovo, and I am from Russia. . . . We got along really well. We consulted with one another which fabric to use. Sometimes, we just tried out this and that and then decided: this looks great. (Schulz 2016)

Thus, the process of designing oneself is more important than the product. The collaborative process of making clothes, the interpersonal exchange, and the sampling and trying out of new images is fundamentally a social and transcultural experience. This becomes particularly apparent in the production of the regional or traditional-style clothing presented in the show. The intercultural sewing group reconstructs such clothes cooperatively, cutting the fabric into shape and sewing it using the available materials and decorations. Memories and photographs recovered from the home country and found on the internet serve as patterns. As the budget of the *Mütterzentrum* is limited, fabric remnants or clothing from the secondhand shop is used for resources. The goal is not so much to produce "authentic" clothes with respect to fabric and techniques, but to provide an impression of traditional or regional clothing. Ludmilla Schulz explains:

> If a piece of clothing would normally have been ornamented with hand embroidery, we might for example imitate this with industrial embroidery. More expensive fabrics might be imitated using more reasonably priced materials. (Schulz 2016)

On the one hand, this concession reveals something of the makers' objective distance to their culture of origin, including the agency to decide which dress or dress elements from a specific culture are appropriate. The resulting products are wide-ranging, including, for example, an eighteenth-century Russian dress made from golden brocade, the clothing of a simple Russian farmer woman, an imitation of folk dress from Ukraine, or clothes made from West African wax print.

We might think of the way these women simulate the clothing of their cultures in terms of Homi K. Bhabha's concept of mimicry (Bhabha 2012). For Bhaba, in the process of colonial contact, the hegemonic culture of the colonist is imitated by the colonized, albeit with significant differences, representing a form of resistance. In the case of the *Mosaik* sewing shop, the women's making or modification of clothing associated with their cultural backgrounds produces a difference that could be reflective of the complex process of finding a place in German culture as independent subjects. The collective sewing of clothing with the individual selection of material expresses a sense of cultural identity, belonging, or in-between-ness (perhaps in a manner similar to the wearing and creation of folk dress in the context of modernization and industrialization at the end of the nineteenth century) and can aid in the process of individual and social positioning, helping actors to access networks and find a place in the community (see Hauser and Engelbracht 2015, 109). In this way, the women have adopted a cross-cultural perspective on clothing practices, cultural change, and the dynamic processes around identity or identification. Due to the close connection between clothing and the body, the textile artifact becomes central to the "cultural and social construction of identity, of social representation and of constructions of subjectivities" (Mentges 2005, 22).

Fashion shows—alternative appropriations

The Bremen *Modenschauen* deviate from the underlying ideas of conventional fashion shows, fashion weeks, and fashion contests. They do not present the trendiest new collections or designer lines, nor is the clothing presented by professional models with ideal measurements, nor is their primary goal to market or sell any of the showcased clothing. Rather, the shows aim to facilitate communication, public performance, and visibility for women who have to engage with the complex negotiations of identity within and across cultures. In this way, the Bremen *Modenschauen* are primarily understood as a community-building educational venture. The function of clothing, as a central part of material culture, is not only pragmatic but it also serves as a significant basis for negotiation of the creation and shaping of social relationships (Mentges 2005, 14). As Gabriele Mentges notes, the materiality of clothing and textiles makes this most evident: their quality cannot only be rationally explained but, in their immediate contact with the human body, it also affects us emotionally, and makes us present (2005, 32).

In its materiality and design, clothing is a technology of the body and serves as a complex form of personal and social representation. The processes of production, perception, and visualization operate on these meanings in equal ways. The Bremen *Modenschauen* commandeer this complexity as an educational medium. In the images produced through these shows, the women skillfully subvert society's habitual patterns of perception (Lutz-Sterzenbach and Schnurr 2014). This is accomplished using the basic elements of a classical fashion show including, for example, role reversal between actors and audience (see König 1999, 127). The audience is meant to represent something akin to public opinion. The "spectators who previously had applauded for the actors" are now placing themselves in the position of the applauded, becoming "actors through imitation" (Kühl 2015, 39).

What is new in Tenever, then, is the "remix of images" displayed through strategic performances in their specially designed choreography: "When images and affiliations are reshuffled and overlayed [sic], origin, culture, and ethnic and national identities continue to play a role, but they are reinterpreted, relativized and assume new perspectives" (Lutz-Sterzenbach and Schnurr 2014, 20). In this sense, the appropriation of the medium of the fashion show by the Bremen *Modenschauen* is a form of intercultural education through aesthetic work. The resulting images are extremely powerful as they attenuate prejudices through role reversal and thus "re-organize, change and mix existing orders" (Lutz-Sterzenbach and Schnurr 2014, 13). After all, "seeing but also creating images has . . . a special significance for the identification of affiliations or for symbolically marking them" (Lutz-Sterzenbach and Schnurr 2014, 13). The images presented or embodied by the *Modenschauen* can be interpreted with a nod to Judith Butler (1991) as "fashion trouble," an evocation of transculturality. They present diversity as semiotic wealth and potentially support openness toward the "Other." By mixing and overlaying cultural stereotypes—in this case, traditional or regional styles or ethnic dress—open and contradictory affinities and identities come to emerge. With Beate Schmuck, we may speak of the *Modenschauen*'s oscillating and tilting effects initiated through fashion, that is, "the process of irritation and experience of complex emotional moments of disconcertment" that acts as a catalyst for deeper social reflection (Schmuck 2014, 353).

Interestingly, a return to non-Western fashion trends, as observed in Tenever, also exists in some of the women's own countries of origin. The heritage trend, which relates explicitly to clothing and textile techniques, seems to be an important "hinge between the generation and times" (Mentges 2015, 349; also Jansen and Craik 2016). Thus, fashion, in these international *Modenschauen*, proves to be a significant medium for the performance of cross-cultural images, possessing the potential to reflect back to both the performers and the audience. In the process of the shared production of clothes, and in rehearsing and presenting the fashion shows, the subjects interact with other subjects whereby "[i]ndividual processes of subjectivity become collective processes of intersubjectivity when individuals engage, influence, and perceive one another" (Kaiser 2012, 30). The women in Tenever demonstrate in this sense, at a small-scale, local level, what it can look like to wear "globalization on our bodies" (Kaiser 2012, 33).

In this rendering of globalization, the historically marginalized populations—that is, women and migrants—have found a way to formulate their agency, in the "in-between-space" (Kaiser 2012, 37). These women articulate and represent the intersectionalities of their identities through the imitated and hybridized fashions of their culture of origin and Western modern fashion. In this way, they open up a creative space beyond the binary way of thinking between the "Self" and the "Other." At the same time, the actors playfully perform the necessary entanglement of these binaries. We will see whether the Bremen *Modenschauen* can preserve their counterhegemonic potential, or whether they will run the risk of turning into yet another mere performance of the exotic.

References

Bhabha, Homi K. 2012. *Über kulturelle Hybridität: Tradition und Übersetzung.* Wien and Berlin: Turia + Kant.

Breward, Christopher, and David Gilbert. 2006. *Fashion's World Cities.* Oxford and New York: Berg.

Butler, Judith. 1991. *Das Unbehagen der Geschlechter.* Frankfurt am Main: Suhrkamp.

Cerny, Catherine, Suzanne Baizerman, and Joanne B. Eicher, eds. 1993. *Bibliography of Theses and Dissertations on Ethnic Textiles and Dress.* ITAA Special Publication 6. Monument: International Textile and Apparel Association.

Clifford, James. 1990. "Sich selbst sammeln." In *Das historische Museum: Labor, Schaubühne, Identitätsfabrik,* edited by Gottfried Korff, 87–106. Frankfurt am Main and New York: Campus.

Deneke, Bernward. 2000. "Kleidung und Historismus." In *Dinge und Menschen: Geschichte, Sachkultur, Museologie: Beiträge des Kolloquiums zum 65 Geburtstag von Helmut Ottenjann,* edited by Uwe Meiners, 85–94. Cloppenburg: Museumsdorf.

Dorner, Birgit. 2014. "Interkultur neu verhäkelt. Transkulturelle Perspektiven der Multicultural Art Education." In *Bildwelten remixed: Transkultur, Globalität, Diversity in kunstpädagogischen Feldern,* edited by Barbara Lutz-Sterzenbach, Ansgar Schnurr, and Ernst Wagner, 147–64. Bielefeld: transcript.

Gaugele, Elke. 2016. "Geteilte Geschichten? Mode, Flucht und Migration." *Pop. Kultur und Kritik* 8: 10–17.

Hall, Stuart. 1999. "Kulturelle Identität und Globalisierung." In *Widerspenstige Kulturen. Cultural Studies als Herausforderung,* edited by Karl H. Hörning, 391–441. Frankfurt am Main: Suhrkamp.

Hauser, Andrea, and Gerda Engelbracht. 2015. "Vestimentäre Formen der Lüneburger Heide und des Wendlandes—Objekte, Bilder, Texte." In *Trachten in der Lüneburger Heide und im Wendland,* edited by Karen Ellwanger and Andrea Hauser, 23–156. Münster: Waxmann.

Jansen, M. Angela, and Jennifer Craik. 2016. *Modern Fashion Traditions: Negotiating Tradition and Modernity through Fashion.* London [et al.]: Bloomsbury Academic.

Kaiser, Susan B. 2012. *Fashion and Cultural Studies.* London: Berg.

Keller-Drescher, Lioba. 2015. "Aus der Ornamental Farm in die 'Chanel Scheune'— Inszenierungen und Transformationen ländlicher Mode." In *Trachten in der Lüneburger Heide und im Wendland,* edited by Karen Ellwanger and Andrea Hauser, 355–62. Münster: Waxmann.

König, René. 1999. *Menschheit auf dem Laufsteg: Die Mode im Zivilisationsprozeß.* Wiesbaden: VS Verlag für Sozialwissenschaften.

Konuk, Kader. 2004. "Ethnomasquerade in Ottoman-European Encounters: Re-enacting Lady Mary Wortley Montagu." *Criticism* 46(3): 393–414.

Kühl, Alicia. 2015. *Modenschauen: Die Behauptung des Neuen in der Mode.* Bielefeld: transcript.

Lehnert, Gertrud. 2014. *Mode: Theorie, Geschichte und Ästhetik einer kulturellen Praxis.* Bielefeld: transcript.

Lehnert, Gertrud, and Gabriele Mentges, eds. 2013. *Fusion Fashion: Culture beyond Orientalism and Occidentalism.* Frankfurt am Main [et al.]: Peter Lang.

Lutz-Sterzenbach, Barbara, and Ansgar Schnurr. 2014. *Bildwelten remixed: Transkultur, Globalität, Diversity in kunstpädagogischen Feldern.* Bielefeld: transcript.

Mentges, Gabriele. 1989. *Erziehung, Dressur und Anstand in der Sprache der Kinderkleidung: Eine kulturgeschichtlich-empirische Untersuchung am Beispiel der Schwälmer Kindertracht.* Frankfurt am Main, Bern, New York, and Paris: Peter Lang.

Mentges, Gabriele. 2005. "Einleitung: Für eine Kulturanthropologie des Textilen. Einige Überlegungen." In *Kulturanthropologie des Textilen,* edited by Gabriele Mentges, 11–56. Berlin: edition ebersbach.

Mentges, Gabriele. 2015. "Zwischen Design und 'Nationaltracht': Die Bedeutung traditioneller Kleidungspraktiken im Prozess usbekischer Nationsbildung." In *Trachten in der Lüneburger Heide und im Wendland,* edited by Karen Ellwanger and Andrea Hauser, 341–54. Münster: Waxmann.

Mütterzentrum. 2016. "Herzlich willkommen im Mütterzentrum Osterholz-Tenever." Accessed March 31, 2017. http://www.mütterzentrum-tenever.com/index.php

Otto, Ferdinand. 2016. "Illusionslos glücklich." *Zeit,* September 5, 2016. Accessed January 30, 2017. http://www.zeit.de/gesellschaft/zeitgeschehen/2016-09/willko mmenskultur-fluechtlinge-rueckblick-muenchen-ehrenamtliche

Reuß, Brigitte. 2005. *Tenever ist irgendwie—30 Jahre Osterholz-Tenever. Eine Dokumentation mit Fotos und Interviews.* Bremen: Zelin-Verlag.

Roach, Mary Ellen, and Kathleen Ehle Musa. 1980. *New Perspectives on the History of Western Dress: A Handbook.* New York: NutriGuides.

Schmuck, Beate. 2014. "Transdifferente Schleier: Blickwechsel—Wechselspiele." In *Bildwelten Remixed: Transkultur, Globalität, Diversity in kunstpädagogischen Feldern,* edited by Barbara Lutz-Sterzenbach and Ansgar Schnurr, 353–58. Bielefeld: transcript.

Schnurr, Ansgar. 2014. "Fremdheit loswerden—das Fremde wieder erzeugen. Zur Gestaltung von Zugehörigkeiten im Remix jugendlicher Lebenswelten." In *Bildwelten remixed: Transkultur, Globalität, Diversity in kunstpädagogischen Feldern,* edited by Barbara Lutz-Sterzenbach and Ansgar Schnurr, 69–89. Bielefeld: transcript.

Schulz, Ludmilla. 2016. Interview by Andrea Hauser. February 13, 2016.

Scorzin, Pamela C. 2016. *Scenographic Fashion Design. Zur Inszenierung von Mode und Marken*. Bielefeld: transcript.

Seebacher, Wendelin. 2013. *... das tun wir nicht wieder: Bremen Osterholz-Tenever— Geschichte eines Demonstrativbauvorhabens*. Bremen: Donat.

13

Entangled histories: Fashion and the politics of migration

Elke Gaugele

In the light of the large-scale refugee movements in 2015, when more than one million people migrated to Europe, and the Office of the United Nations High Commissioner for Refugees reported a record high of 65.3 million forced migrants worldwide (UNHCR 2016, 2), the topic of flight and migration began to shake the epicenter of the European fashion industry. In January 2016, Miuccia Prada presented her fall/winter 2016 menswear collection on a runway that was styled like an *auto-da-fé*, recalling the religious tribunals of the Spanish, Portuguese, and Mexican inquisitions. As a secular ceremony, the fashion show evoked cultural memories of executions, assassinations, shootings, wars, and forced displacement that were historically legitimized by the Catholic church. The show's theatrical display blurred the boundaries of observers and judges, past and present, spectators and executioners. Visually alluding to the one million migrants arriving in Europe by boat in 2015 and to the 3,770 people who died or were reported missing in the Mediterranean Sea (UNHCR 2016, 32), the fashion models were styled as seafarers, looking sad and ghostly. Sailor hats and collars as well as striped fisherman shirts, knapsacks, and "flood-length pants" (Fury 2016) underscored the theme of voyage, mixing memories of historic and contemporary migration to and from Italy (see Figure 13.1). In modern history, the immigration of the Italian population to the Americas, as well as to countries in Europe, has been stated as a major mass migration. Immigration to Italy did not occur until the mid-1970s, when mostly men from Tunisia, Senegal, and Morocco arrived as cheap laborers for the agricultural and fishing industries (bpb 2012). In 2015, Italy recorded the highest number ever of asylum applications: 83,200 (UNHCR 2016, 39). Considering this context, Prada's display of an *auto-da-fé* could even be extended to asylum tribunals, bureaucratically performed

Figure 13.1 Backstage at Prada fall/winter, 2016, Milan Fashion Week, Italy. *Photo*: Virgina Arcaro.

under the gaze of the public at the immigration officers who determine the "threshold" of inclusion and exclusion to the country (Sigona 2014, 370).

This chapter will investigate how the large-scale refugee movement from 2015 to 2016 influenced the work of fashion designers as well as the material cultures of fashion. Aiming for a multisited knowledge production, it methodologically connects the "global turns" of material culture (Appadurai 1996) and fashion and design studies (Adamson, Riello, and Teasley 2011), bridging fashion studies with global and forced migration studies (Fiddian-Qasmiyeh, Katy Long, and Sigona 2014). Thus, it recognizes "the multiplicities and fragmented condition in which we experience and enact design" (Adamson, Riello, and Teasley 2011, 3), considering global asymmetrical power and exchange structures, and highlighting "the importance of writing histories that introduce the multisited and various nature of design practices" (Adamson, Riello, and Teasley 2011, 3). Shedding light on the capitalization of the precarious state of refugees, this chapter brings together three different sites of fashion: fashion design, fashion production, and the social interaction with clothes as part of donation campaigns. First, it examines the aesthetic representation of the theme of forced displacement and migration during fashion weeks in Florence, Italy, and Paris, France, in January 2016. Following a postcolonial view on global migration, it mainly focuses on Walé Oyéjidé's work for Ikiré Jones and, subsequently, briefly sketches the influence of the Parisian terror attacks on designer collections. Second, the chapter considers the situation of refugees working, mostly illegally, in the Turkish textile and fashion industry, and how this situation has been taken up as a discourse of national economy. And, third, it draws on a field study in a clothing distribution depot for local refugee camps in Frankfurt, Germany. This chapter seeks to draw connections across these three sites of fashion to explore various layers of the entanglements between fashion and forced migration, and how each of these sites or layers deals with the precarious state of refugees. To this end, it unpacks the cultural, global, and political layers that are embedded in the relations between the recent mass migration of people, fashion practices, and fashion materialities.

Fashioning ethnoscapes: Vulnerability and the celebration of sub-Saharan African immigrants

The recent influx of asylum seekers in Italy (UNHCR 2016, 39) has influenced not only the fashion capital of Milan, as exemplified in the 2016 Prada show, but also fashion shows in Florence. Arriving in Italy via the Mediterranean Sea in 2015, asylum seekers Gitteh, Abdoulay, and Madi from Mali and Gambia were invited directly from the refugee reception center as runway models in the Generation Africa show at Florence Menswear Fashion Week, Pitti Immagine Uomo 89. Organized by the UN Ethical Fashion Initiative (EFI), a flagship program of the International Trade Center in cooperation with Lai-momo, an Italian NGO social cooperative society, the Generation Africa fashion show could be described as part of a "refugee regime complex," acting across different institutions and various levels of governance, to "shape and define how states and other actors can and do respond to forced displacement" (Betts 2014, 68).

The decision to feature three asylum seekers on the runway attracted significant international attention to the issues of "class" and "othering" in fashion: the decision being understood to give "them [the asylum seekers] an opportunity to earn a wage," to "raise awareness on migration," and to "demonstrate fashion's capacity to support the betterment of society" (EFI website 2016 on Pitti Immagine Uomo 89). Nigerian American fashion designer for the label Ikiré Jones and licensed attorney, Walé Oyéjidé, emphasized that asylum seekers on the catwalk would represent his philosophy of fashion perfectly, namely that fashion could foster ideas of equality and promote discussions on migration and borders. According to fashion critic, Suzy Menkes, in her January 2016 blog post for *Vogue*, not even professionals recognized which of the models walking the runway at the Generation Africa show were asylum seekers.

The idea itself is credited to Simone Cipriani, head of the EFI. In times of global forced displacement, the EFI, a joint agency of the United Nations and the WTO, intended to demonstrate that migrants are "resources." After the show, Simone Cipriani and Lai-momo announced a joint pilot training program for asylum seekers to work and learn in Italy's fashion industry, contingent on their future return to their country of birth. Founded in 2006, EFI was established as a global governance strategy to utilize fashion and textiles as a means of developmental and economic politics by creating platforms for African designers, as well as new manufacturing facilities for luxury fashion brands in African countries. The showcasing of the fall/winter 2016–2017 collections by Generation Africa designers and labels—AKJP, Ikiré Jones, Lukhanyo Mdinigi, Nicholas Coutts, and U.Mi-1—marks an extension in the work of the EFI from developmental political website presentations to the performance of ethics of fashion within the global governance of the "refugee regime complex" (Betts 2014, 68). This corresponds with the political situation where Africa had been the main continent of origin for asylum seekers in Italy, with Nigeria the primary country of origin in 2015 with 17,800 applicants (UNHCR 2016, 40).

Designed by Walé Oyéjidé, the Ikiré Jones collection gained the most attention of the Generation Africa labels due to its title "After Migration." Oyéjidé claimed to shift perceptions of African migrants in Italy and Europe through his fashion performance of men's suits and his lookbook dedicated to "[a] meditation on the uncelebrated roles of Sub-Saharan immigrants in Western society" (Ikiré Jones 2016). The lookbook features Gitteh, Abdoulay, and Madi, the three immigrant models, who at first sight resemble contemporary "dandies" in the style of the Sapeur movement. Staged in picturesque alleys in Florence, the models are photographed by Neil Watson using both the lens of a tourist gaze and the recurring motif of the threshold, an oriental-style doorstep. The stylish lookbook images are contrasted with text blocks in the layout of a poem that narrates the precarious routes and status of the asylum seekers. While storytelling is the fashion designer's firm aspiration, Oyéjidé's poem aestheticizes the precarious status, the danger of life, poverty, and heartfelt hopes of asylum seekers. In the picturesque alleys of Florence, the figure of the sub-Saharan African immigrant becomes an aesthetic fusion of tourist, pilgrim, and migrant. This is reminiscent of Arjun Appadurai's concept of "ethnoscape," defined as a landscape of persons who constitute the contemporary shifting world: "tourists, immigrants, refugees, exiles, guest workers and other moving groups and individuals. They constitute an essential feature of the works and appear to affect the politics of (and between) nations to a hitherto unprecedented degree" (1996, 33).

Performing an Africanness represented by the Sapeur-like flâneurs, Ikiré Jones' dandyish suits in wax prints and monochrome tribal textures in stylish black-and-white graphics form a new public persona and globalizing voice of resistance, characterized by James Clifford as "indigènitude," a "vision of liberation and cultural difference" (2013, 16). At the same time, they encompass the "myriad routes and connections, flows and tensions" of the African diasporic styles shaped by those on the continent and the groups that followed the Atlantic slave trade, colonialism, and imperialism (Tulloch 2016, 5).

Celebrating the "perspectives of unheralded people of color," Oyéjidé's lookbook displays five silk prints, which are montages of eighteenth-century tapestries, to "illustrate stories of far-flung myths and undiscovered histories" (Ikiré Jones 2016). These silk cloth collector pieces consist of various montages, replacing white faces of aristocrats on eighteenth-century European silk tapestries with black faces (see Figure 13.2). This creates new portraits of an imaginative black history of noble elegance as well as alternative histories of entangled

Figure 13.2 Foulard *Untold Renaissance* designed by Walé Oyéjidé, After Migration collection fall/winter, 2016. *Photo*: Ikeré Jones Design Archive.

European and African royalties: *The Courtship, The Nobleman, The Nobleman I–II*, and *The Creator Has a Master Plan* (Ikiré Jones 2016). As decolonizing histories and shared narratives of an "aesthetic of the cool" (Thompson 1973; Tulloch 2016), the lookbook challenges "Eurocentric" constructions of histories as well as the "colonial global": "There is no longer a place from which to tell the whole story (there never was)" (Clifford 2013, 23).

Oyéjidé's design ties three narratives together that according to James Clifford have been active in the last half-century: decolonization, globalization, and indigenous becoming. Each of them represents distinct historical energies, scales of action, and politics of the possible that construct, reinforce, and trouble each other (Clifford 2013, 8). Oyéjidé draws upon the decolonizing textile and image practices of Nigerian indigo-dyed *adire* cotton textiles to disrupt and trouble a colonized history (Rice 2015, 174). In the 1920s, *adire* became part of a critical moment of juncture between British colonial power and Nigeria's Yoruba people through the transformation of the symbol of the Silver Jubilee into *oloba*, an ornament meaning "the one with a King" (Rice 2015, 172). In 1935, after the twenty-fifth anniversary of the coronation of King George V and Queen Mary, southwest Nigerian Yoruba women began to alter the Silver Jubilee ornament on the *adire* cotton textiles by using resist-dye painting or stenciling techniques. On many *adire* textiles, the British royal couple lost their European facial and sartorial style characteristics, becoming less recognizable through reproductions over time and often transforming into a black African royal couple. English words were replaced with the Yoruba language alongside symbols suggestive of Yoruba royalty, including bird motifs, cowrie shells, and "Oyo" referring to the great Oyo Empire of the Yoruba (Rice 2015, 174). Consequently, the *adire's oloba* pattern came to represent royalty or power in general. Used as an expression of anti-colonialism, changes in the *adire* pattern's appearances were called "devolution," meaning the delegation of power to the regional level. As catalysts for political action, which played a small part in bringing about independence, *adire* patterns became very popular in the 1960s and since then have been adopted by Nigerian artists (Rice 2015, 174)

Oyéjidé draws on the transformative power of *adire oloba* designs in the "After Migration" campaign, suggesting ways to create alternative histories, to represent black royalty in history, and to invoke shifts in colonial power relations. As people are on the move, as Arjun Appadurai states, realities and fantasies now take their effects on larger scales, building "imagined worlds" constituted by the historically situated imaginations of people and groups spread around the globe (1996, 33f.). For Walter Benjamin, "the eternal, in any case, is far more the ruffle on a dress than some idea" ([1935] 1999, 463), an idea expressed by Oyéjidé with postcolonial histories appearing in the form of a silk shoulder scarf. But for Benjamin, fashion illustrates a historical model, where the bourgeoisie quotes its own prehistory and the revolutionary and emancipatory fashion aesthetics are captured within the economies of the ruling class: "Fashion has a flair for the topical, no matter where it stirs in the thickets of long ago; it is a tiger's leap into the past. This jump, however, takes place in an arena where the ruling class gives the commands. The same leap in the open air of history is the dialectical one, which is how Marx understood the revolution" (Benjamin [1940] 2006, XIV, 395). In 2013, Ikiré Jones' suits were described by *OkayAfrica* as fashion for "global style dandies" and for "Western African and international dandies," revealing the status "after migration" as a postcolonial style within the luxury segment for global middle and upper classes (Poundo 2013). In this way, Oyéjidé's design of "African fashion" commodifies the narratives of decolonization, globalization, and indigenous becoming, which as James Clifford says, often occur as "a lumpy verisimilitude in which political, economic, social, and cultural forces intersect but do not form a whole" (2013, 8). Leslie Rabine describes how African fashion is born of both the postcolonial political pressures and the transnational market. As forms of globalization—both postcolonial politics and transnational economies—intensify demands for ethnic identity as well as the use of fashion as a projection surface: "canvasses upon which designers and consumers project dreams, a fragmented text that weaves 'wish images'" (Rabine 2000, 13).

At the same time in Paris, Riccardo Tisci transported heavy metal styles from Botswana to the Givenchy catwalk, representing how African subcultural styles and their wearers migrate across the continents. Suede boots and jackets, leather, fur, animal patterns, and cobras on knitted pullovers, were performed as material signs of "indigenousness" by models styled as multiethnic members of the same subcultural community. While many fashion shows in Paris avoided explicit connection with the themes of migration and forced displacement, there was some acknowledgment of the terror attacks in November, 2015. The shows of Comme des Garçons and Walter van Beirendonck both referred to the experiences of vulnerability, terror, death, violation, dislocation, and deracination. "Stop terrorizing our world!" was the statement of van Beirendonck's show in January 2016, entitled "Woest" in Dutch, which means "furious, irate, and rude." He further orchestrated his reactions to the November, 2015, terror attacks through make-up designs that shimmered between bullet wounds, Arabic ornaments, and masks. The logo of his fashion collection turned chainsaws into soft textile accessories and appliqués. Comme des Garçons shifted anxious creative expression into ambassadors of peace and grief, transforming black rivet stud leather into wreaths of flowers on the heads of models. The fashion label's performative strategies of reenacting iconic photographs were strongly based on "mainstream recognition, wide media circulation and emotional impact" (Zborowska 2014, 234). The finale of the show even culminated in the performance of a funeral, with models appearing in black dresses, carrying opulent bouquets of flowers. Comme des Garçons' staging ostentatiously recalls the images and gestures of mourning, of people laying down flowers, transmitted by the media after the massacre in November, 2015.

From a global design history perspective, Glenn Adamson, Giorgio Riello, and Sarah Teasley point out that "global scares as terrorism . . . remind us precisely how interconnected we have become" (2011, 3). Connecting the latter to forced migration studies and summarizing this first site of investigation, interconnectedness is a central theme here as well. Fashion designers dealt with the precarious state of refugees and forced migration in 2016 by emphasizing the shared histories of Western and non-Western migration. These had been enacted and commodified in fashion shows and lookbooks by blurring historical and contemporary layers of persecution and immigration (Prada), by reenacting iconic images that stir deep emotions of grief and being wounded (Comme des Garçons), and by generating postcolonial histories for shared decolonial presents and futures (Ikiré Jones). Fashion creates an "imagined world" (Apparadurai 1996, 33) as well as "aesthetic politics" (Gaugele 2014) and ethical norms and values. Given its aesthetic-political capacity, fashion has thus been taken up by the EFI as a global governance tool within the current "refugee regime complex" (Betts 2014, 68).

The Turkish apparel industry: Forced migration and new sources of cheap labor

Global fashion production is an industry that relies heavily on undocumented immigrants (Bonacich and Appelbaum 2000, 108). Together with China, the EU, Bangladesh, Vietnam, and the United States, the Turkish textiles and apparel industry is the world's sixth largest production site, growing steadily throughout the last twenty-five years into a global textile-producing giant. Simultaneously, Turkey has become the primary host of refugees, because of the war in Syria, accommodating more than 2.7 million refugees and people in refugee-like situations (UNHCR 2016, 60). A 2014 report of the Clean Clothes Campaign revealed that Syrian refugees were mostly working without legal authorization in the Turkish textile and fashion industry, including for global brands such as Zara and H&M, and were being paid below the legal minimum wage (CCC 2014, 43). The gap between the legal minimum monthly wage of 252 euros and the estimated minimum monthly living wage of 1,002 euros in Turkey tended to be larger than the wage gaps in Asian countries, such as Malaysia or China, and more akin to those in Cambodia, Bangladesh, Moldavia, and Romania (CCC 2014, 31, 35, and 37). As a major supplier to both Europe and the Middle East, the Turkish garment industry is largely unregulated, offering both legal and illegal working options for Syrians with poor wages and conditions. In 2014, the Turkish garment industry employed 508,000 registered workers and about 1.5 million estimated informal laborers (CCC 2014, 18). Among them, approximately 250,000 Syrian refugees, including many children, were working illegally in the agricultural and garment industries, with an estimated 60 percent of textile laborers in the Turkish garment industry working in illegal conditions

(Johannisson 2016). The immigration negotiations between the European Union and Turkey allowed Syrians who had been in the country for more than six months to apply for a work permit, allowing them to receive the minimum wage and protection from discrimination. But this promise was mainly in name only, with just 5,500 refugees receiving work permits by the end of 2016. Emre Eren Korkmaz, a representative of the Ethical Trading Initiative, spoke of an "ethnicization" of Turkey's informal garment sector as evident in the hiring of immigrants from Eastern European and Caucasian states alongside Syrian and Afghan refugees (Korkmaz 2016).

After the EU-Turkey deal in 2016, Turkish debates about the legalization of refugee labor focused on the strengthening of Turkey's economic power, especially in labor-intensive sectors such as the garment industry. Like a rearview mirror to the American sweatshop model that emerged with the rise of mass production of garments and the increase of immigrant workers at the end of the nineteenth century, in May 2016 the chair of the Turkish Foreign Economic Relations Board (DEIK) proposed a trade agreement for a bonded zone, where Syrian refugees were expected to produce raw textile materials as cheap free goods for the United States (Anadolu Agency 2016; Bonacich and Appelbaum 2000, 3). However, after the BBC broadcasted an investigative documentary titled *Undercover: The Refugees Who Make Our Clothes* in October 2016, fast-fashion companies such as H&M used their websites as platforms to espouse support for the legalization of migrant workers in Turkey, condemning discrimination toward such workers. In neoliberal alliances with other companies, trade unions, NGOs, and the EFI, H&M formulated a common code published on its website that suppliers should guarantee the same wages and working conditions for migrant and refugee workers as they do for domestic laborers. But under the current political situation, appeals for wage and working condition codes can also be understood as calls for the legalization and moralizing foundation of cheap labor for the fast-fashion industry.

Forced displacement gave rise not only to a new source of inexpensive labor for the global fashion industry in Turkey but also to the "ethnicization" of its garment sector. The capitalization of the precarious state of refugees by the Turkish garment sector is confronted with the "ethical foundation of markets" (Aspers 2006, 289) through codes of conduct based on a neoliberal agenda, which drives national legal minimum wages down. More than other producer countries within the global fashion industry, at the present time, Turkey capitalizes on refugees and undocumented immigrants who entered the country due to the war in Syria and conflicts in the Middle East.

Narratives of a second life: Enacting
humanitarian values of fashion

In 2015, Germany experienced an immense increase in the number of people seeking protection, welcoming 441,900 new asylum seekers to the country (UNHCR 2016, 38) and causing the donation of clothing to skyrocket. Clothing distribution depots, often run in cooperation with social welfare organizations, such as church-operated Diakonie and Caritas, initiated calls for donations and volunteers to coordinate the care for clothes and everyday objects in the reception camps. This section draws on observations from a field study in a clothing distribution center in Frankfurt, Germany, and comparative interviews conducted in Vienna, Austria, tracing the donation of clothing for refugees from an ethnographic perspective as the juncture of different value creation stages. As Frederic Larsen has shown, the value of an object, whether it is economical, ethical, or otherwise, is "something that is created in the act of exchange and the act of exchange becomes performative" (Larsen 2015, 123).

According to one of the full-time workers in the Frankfurt distribution facility, before Christmas, 2015, the depot was literally swamped with clothes. She noted that most of the donations did not correspond to the needs and tastes of the newly arrived refugees. Also, in Vienna, both volunteers and asylum seekers stood perplexed in front of the clothing donations that neither matched nor fitted the latter's specific body sizes, forms, and styles. Only after the volunteers started to call upon their friends to separate the higher quality, more slim-fitting, and more stylish pieces, did the situation change. Gradually, volunteers learned what to look for: men's clothing in small and medium sizes. Menswear donations in bigger sizes were passed on to the local thrift shop for welfare recipients.

People involved in gift economies treat objects as if they had person-like qualities (see Mauss [1950] 1990; Larsen 2015, 174). The passing on of clothes and the refugees' arrival in the country can be tied together by the connecting metaphor of the "second life." While the donors imagine each piece of clothing as an object that imparts their life as their material involvement in the shelter and humanitarian aid for the refugees in their arrival and settlement in the country, only a small portion of donated clothing is in a condition that would enable the items to have a "second life." In fact, only 15–25 percent of the gifts can be passed on to other people, while about 80 percent are converted into waste, picked up by textile recycling companies. Reflecting the junctures of different value creation stages, the model of charitable clothing distribution mirrors Western material cultures. Fast fashion is not produced for a "second life" at all. As an amalgam formed by stiff, washed-out, and faded tees as well as by cheap synthetic knitwear, fast fashion quickly ends up in the recycling bin. New items are mostly given as donations for companies to claim tax benefits (Larsen 2015, 33). Yet, the "used look" of many fast-fashion and streetwear styles anticipate the status of old clothes even if they are new goods. Therefore, despite their actual material condition, distressed-looking jeans are thrown away as quickly as possible. Other garments witness the care and diligence former wearers have given to them. Freshly laundered, ironed, and neatly folded, they retain the domestic arts of their former owners in the material. These garments arise from the mountain of clothing in such perfect condition and strength that one almost feels intimidated. The donation of kitchen aprons and carnival costumes is frowned upon, yet at the same time such garments may offer a sense of domestic comfort to the immigrants, as well as encourage their participation in local customs. All remaining objects are logistically and efficiently processed, transforming these organizations' mission to aid humans into a rationalized and dehumanized working process. Sorting and evaluation is a commodification process based on a set of practices arranged around transforming donations and gifts into commodities where the economic, social, ethical, and emotional values and interests of the various actors must be well balanced (Larsen 2015, 224).

Global enterprises, such as Procter and Gamble or Lufthansa Cargo Group, release their staff to work in the clothing distribution depot for social service days. While employees help to drag away huge batches of old clothing, they also work for the ethical value of their companies. At various packing tables, they screen the garments alongside the laborers of a second, social employment market comprised of volunteers, "one-euro-fifty-workers," and temporary staff working away hours of their community service. The Frankfurt depot is a medium-sized social business for secondhand clothing and household objects. It is operated by a full-time team manager, thirty regular part-time volunteers, and five skilled full-time employees, who train and supervise fifty-five laborers, who work off the main job market and are subsidized with public money. The categories in which to sort the clothes on the trolleys, before stapling, storing, and delivering them in moving boxes, are taped with labels on beer tables. The categories of women's clothing include blouses, tees, pullovers/jumpers, trousers/jeans, skirts, dresses, coats, jackets, blazers, costumes, Islamic clothing, trouser suits, nightwear, underwear, sportswear, socks, shoes, and boots, as well as caps/shawls/gloves in the sizes S 34–38, M 40–42, L 44–46, XL 48–50, and XXL 52–54. These categories comply with the request forms submitted by the various Frankfurt sports halls and the volunteers who are situated on railway track 24 in Frankfurt's main station and order clothes for arriving refugees. Besides blankets, bags are much needed, as there are no wardrobes in the refugee reception centers or in the converted sports halls. Most of the asylum seekers store their few personal belongings under their beds. Therefore, bags offer storage space as well as the possibility to quickly grab individual possessions if one must leave, even if there is not much to accumulate in one's bag or on one's body.

At the same time, many individuals and families who arrived in Germany decided to reject the alms from the clothing distribution centers, and instead bought new clothes on their own. Fieldwork research on the sartorial identities of young refugees in Germany (Kurt and Kneijnsberg 2016) has shown how essential it is, after the flight, for each youth to build upon his/her own style, developing it further. For their materialization of identity, most young refugees deny the choice and the "taste of necessity" (Bourdieu 1984, 372) that sticks to clothing donations. The shopping for and possession of new clothes is very important for their self-esteem and their sense of well-being in the arrival country (Kurt and Kneijnsberg 2016, 155).

Looking at the material culture and evaluation practices of clothing donations for refugees in Germany, there is a substantial gap between the ways young refugees in Germany complement their styles and personalize the outfits they brought with them and the ways in which the donors and the gift economy create narratives of a "second life." While based on Mauss's theory of the gift ([1950] 1990), donations always imply identification with their receiver; the youths carry on their sartorial lives beyond the idea of a "second life." What remains is a site of abundant material culture and a social contract based on its humanitarian value, created in a performative act of exchange.

During 2016, Frankfurt's clothing distribution center was eventually thinned out due to the building of border fences on the Balkan route and the closures of the European external borders in March 2016, while EU politicians attempted to finalize a deal that could return refugees to Turkey. In summer 2016, with refugees stuck in squalid conditions at the European external borders, most of the moving boxes were transported from the Frankfurt storage to aid agencies at the southeast Schengen borders. After the EU-Turkey deal in 2016, which effectively shut down refugee routes to Europe, those displaced in Turkey remained there. At this point, working in the Turkish garment sector, as specified in the section before, remains one of the only options for refugees.

Conclusion

The large-scale refugee movement with 65.3 million forced migrants worldwide in 2015 to 2016 (UNHCR 2016, 2) requires fashion research and fashion theory to make a deeper connection with global and forced migration studies. Highlighting forced migration as one of the defining characteristics of the current globalization phase, this chapter supports the global change in the study of fashion, design, and material culture through a multisited approach (Stepputat and Nyberg Sørensen 2014, 95). It brings together three sites of investigation—fashion design, fashion production, and the exchange of fashion as clothing donation—to study their entanglements with migration and refugees. While each specific section has shown different views on how fashion is enacted, produced, and experienced in relation to the large-scale refugee movement, taken altogether, this chapter unpacks the entanglements of the different sites and reveals the underlying political divisions and asymmetrical economic exchange structures. Breaches and divisions within the current globalization process are made clearer through a multisited methodology, as Glenn Adamson, Giorgio Riello, and Sarah Teasley point out, emphasizing how "flows of people, information, capital and goods across national and geographical borders accelerate" and at the same time movements are blocked "through immigration controls, tariffs and other trade barriers" (2011, 3). While fashion designers in Italy encounter forced migration and the large-scale refugee movement by the creation of narratives of entangled migration histories and shared decolonial futures, in Turkey the number of refugees and people in refugee-like situations increased the "resources" for the global fashion industry, exposing their vulnerability to exploitation as part of the workforce. This has even been reinforced by the EU-Turkey agreement in March 2016, producing involuntary immobility by the closure of refugee routes to Europe. While demanding work permits for refugees and codes of conducts for fashion companies, based on a neoliberal agenda, the European Union calls at the same time upon the moralization of markets. As David Graeber (2001) has argued, value as a cultural, relational phenomenon, is utterly social in both market and gift economies (Larsen 2015, 119). These ethical mores bridge fashion designers' use of the figure of the refugee and histories of mass migration with the gift economies of clothing donation for refugees. While sartorial identities are not mainly built on the "choice of necessity" (Bourdieu 1984, 372), clothing donations enact a social contract based on the humanitarian value of abundant garments. This connects clothing donations as part of the work of aid organizations with the role of the EFI. Both regulate the behavior of national and transnational actors in terms of migration governance, translating global norms into practices and values at local and national levels (Betts 2014, 69). During the current phase of globalization, which is on a large scale, shaped by global and forced migration, fashion has been taken up by global governance organizations as a tool to demonstrate ethical norms and values. Nevertheless, shows of pan-African fashion designers from the global middle classes, and the deployment of three asylum seekers on the runway, as orchestrated by the EFI, perpetuate the "colonial idea of Africa as a source of inspiration for fashion and textile design" (Rovine 2009, 46) in a doubtful, aesthetic way, passing it on to the figure of the refugee.

References

Adamson, Glenn, Giorgio Riello, and Sarah Teasley. 2011. *Global Design History*. Abingdon: Routledge.

Anadolu Agency. 2016. "Turkish Business Plan to Hire Syrian Refugees in Labor-intensive Sectors, Eyeing US Market." *Hurriet Daily News*, May 18, 2016. Accessed March 22, 2017. http://www.hurriyetdailynews.com/turkish-businesses-plan-to-hire-syrian-refugees-in-labor-intensive-sectors-eyeing-us-market.aspx?pageID=238&nID=99335&NewsCatID=345

Appadurai, Arjun. 1996. *Modernity At Large: Cultural Dimensions of Globalization*. Minneapolis: University of Minnesota Press.

Aspers, Patrik. 2006. "Ethics in Global Garment Market Chains." In *The Moralization of Markets*, edited by Nico Stehr, Christoph Henning, and Bernd Weiler, 287–307. London: Transaction Press.

Benjamin, Walter. (1935) 1999. *The Arcade Project*. Translated by Howard Eiland and Kevin McLaughlin. Cambridge: Harvard University Press.

Benjamin, Walter. (1940) 2006. "On the Concept of History." In *Walter Benjamin: Selected Writings, 4: 1938–1940*, edited by Howard Eiland and Michael W. Jennings, 388–411. Cambridge: Harvard University Press.

Betts, Alexander. 2014. "International Relations and Forced Migration." In *The Oxford Handbook of Refugee and Forced Migration Studies*, edited by Elena Fiddian-Qasmiyeh, Gil Loescher, Katy Long, and Nando Sigona, 60–73. Oxford: Oxford University Press.

Bonacich, Edna, and Richard P. Appelbaum. 2000. *Behind the Label: Inequality in the Los Angeles Apparel Industry*. Berkeley: University of California Press.

Bourdieu, Pierre. 1984. *Distinction: A Social Critique of the Judgment of Taste*. Cambridge: Harvard University Press.

Bundeszentrale für Politische Bildung 2012. "Historische Entwicklung der Migration." Accessed March 22, 2017. http://www.bpb.de/gesellschaft/migration/laenderprofile/145669/historische-entwicklung-der-migration

Clean Clothes Campaign, CCC. 2014. Stitched Up. Poverty Wages for Garment Workers in Eastern Europe. Report written by Christa Luginbühl and Bettina Musiolek. Accessed 24 April 2019. https://cleanclothes.org/resources/publications/stitched-up-1

Clifford, James. 2013. *Returns: Becoming Indigenous in the Twenty-First Century.* Cambridge and London: Harvard University Press.

Ethical Fashion Initative, EFI. 2016. Pitti Uomo 89. Accessed March 22, 2017. https://ethicalfashioninitiative.org/events/pitti-uomo-89/

Fiddian-Qasmiyeh, Elena, Gil Loescher, Katy Long, and Nando Sigona, eds. 2014. *The Oxford Handbook of Refugee and Forced Migration Studies.* Oxford: Oxford University Press.

Fury, Alexander. 2016. "Prada. Fall 2016 Menswear." *Vogue Online,* January 17, 2016. Accessed March 22, 2017. http://www.vogue.com/fashion-shows/fall-2016-menswear/prada

Gaugele, Elke. 2014. "Aesthetic Politics in Fashion: An Introduction." In *Aesthetic Politics in Fashion,* edited by Elke Gaugele, 10–18. Berlin: Sternberg Press.

Graeber, David. 2001. *Toward an Anthropological Theory of Value: The False Coin of Our Dreams.* New York: Palgrave.

Johannisson, Frederik. 2016. "Hidden Child Labour: How Syrian Refugees in Turkey are Supplying Europe with Fast Fashion." *The Guardian,* January 29, 2016. Accessed March 22, 2017. https://www.theguardian.com/sustainable-business/2016/jan/29/hidden-child-labour-syrian-refugees-turkey-supplying-europe-fast-fashion

Jones, Ikiré. 2016. "After Migration" (lookbook). Accessed March 22, 2017. https://ikirejones.com/fw16-after-migration-editorial/

Korkmaz, Emre Eren. 2016. "Syrian Refugees and the Ethnicization of Turkey's Informal Garment Sector." *Ethical Trading Initiative,* October 21, 2016. Accessed March 22, 2017. http://www.ethicaltrade.org/blog/syrian-refugees-and-ethnicization-turkeys-informal-garment-sector

Kurt, Ebru, and Kira Kneijnsberg. 2016. "Vestimentäre Identitätsarbeit von jugendlichen Flüchtlingen—Die Herausforderung, den eigenen Stil zu finden." Master's Thesis, TU Dortmund University, Seminar für Kulturanthropologie des Textilen.

Larsen, Frederic. 2015. "Objects and Social Actions: On Second-Hand Valuation Practices." PhD Dissertation, Frederiksberg: Copenhagen Business School.

Mauss, Marcel. (1950) 1990. *The Gift: The Form and Reason for Exchange in Archaic Societies.* London and New York: Routledge.

Menkes, Suzy. 2016. "Generation Africa: Models Included." *Vogue* (blog), January 18, 2016. Accessed March 22, 2017. http://www.vogue.de/blogs/suzy-menkes/generation-africa-models-included

Office of the United Nations High Commissioner for Refugees (UNHCR). 2016. *Global Trends: Forced Displacement in 2015.* Geneva: UNHCR.

Poundo. 2013. "Prêt-À-Poundo: Ikiré Jones for The Western African & International Dandy." *Okayafrica*, October 2, 2013. Accessed March 22, 2017. http://www.okay africa.com/photos/ikire-jones-fashion-trends-menswear-west-african-prints/

Rabine, Leslie W. 2000. *The Global Circulation of African Dress*. Oxford: Berg.

Rice, Erin. 2015. "Patterned Identity: Textiles and Traces of Modernity in Contemporary Nigerian Art." In *Identitäten / Identities. Interdisziplinäre Perspektiven*, edited by Marlene Bainczyk-Crescentini, Kathleen Ess, Michael Pleyer, and MonikaPleyer, 169–90. Heidelberg: Univeristitätsbibliothek Heidelberg.

Rovine, Victoria. 2009. "Colonialism's Clothing: Africa, France, and the Deployment of Fashion." *Design Issues* 25(3): 44–61.

Sigona, Nando. 2014. "The Politics of Refugee Voices: Representations, Narratives, and Memories" In *The Oxford Handbook of Refugee and Forced Migration Studies*, edited by Elena Fiddian-Qasmiyeh, Gil Loescher, Katy Long, and Nando Sigona, 369–80. Oxford: Oxford University Press.

Stepputat, Finn, and Ninna Nyberg Sørensen. 2014. "Sociology and Forced Migration." In *The Oxford Handbook of Refugee and Forced Migration Studies*, edited by Elena Fiddian-Qasmiyeh, Gil Loescher, Katy Long, and Nando Sigona, 89–95. Oxford: Oxford University Press.

Thompson, Robert Farris. 1973. "An Aesthetic of the Cool." *African Arts* 7(1): 40–93.

Tulloch, Carol. 2016. *The Birth of Cool: Style Narratives of the African Diaspora*. London: Bloomsbury.

Zborowska, Agnès. 2014. "Uses and Abuses of History: A Case of a Comme des Garçons Fashion Show." *Critical Studies in Fashion & Beauty* 5(2): 233–52.

Contributors

Leyla Belkaïd-Neri is Director of the Fashion Design program at Parsons Paris, The New School, France. She received her Master of Fine Arts in Fashion Design from Accademia di Arte in Florence, Italy, and her PhD in Cultural Anthropology from Université Lumière in Lyon, France. She was founding director of the Master in Luxury Management at the Geneva School of Business Administration. She was previously Head of the Fashion Department at the Geneva School of Art and Design, Switzerland. In 2012, she ran the project that led to the registration of the first dress ever acknowledged as an element of the UNESCO Representative List of Cultural Heritage of Humanity. She is author of the first postcolonial study published on the history and ethnography of Algerian dress, *Costumes d'Algérie* (2003). Recent publications in English include "Investigating the *Blusa*: The Cultural and Sartorial Biography of an Algerian Dress," in *Costume* (2014, Vol. 48:1).

Jennifer Craik is Professor of Fashion in the School of Design, Faculty of Creative Industries, at Queensland University of Technology, Brisbane, Australia. Her research interests include interdisciplinary approaches to the study of fashion and dress. She has also researched aspects of cultural studies, cultural policy, and arts funding. Her publications include *The Face of Fashion* (Routledge 1993), *Uniforms Exposed: From Conformity to Transgression* (Berg 2005), *Fashion: The Key Concepts* (Berg 2009), and *Modern Fashion Traditions* (co-edited with Angela Jansen, Bloomsbury 2016).

Daniel Devoucoux received his PhD in History/German studies and Scandinavian studies from Sorbonne University in Paris (Professor Joseph Rovan, Alain Corbin, and Gilbert Krebs). He has worked previously in the tourism and luxury industries in Paris. Since 1990, he has taught cultural studies at various universities in Germany, including in Stuttgart, Freiburg, Mainz, Cologne, Münster and at the Institute of Art and Material Culture, Technical University of Dortmund, Germany. He is author of *Mode im Film: Zur Kulturanthropologie von Film und Mode* (Transcript 2007). Recent articles include "Medien in Medien. Zur Kulturanthropologie von Film und Mode," in Christa Gürtler and Eva Hausbacher (eds.), *Kleiderfragen. Mode und Kulturwissenschaft* (Transcript

2015), "Travail au corps: La chevelure dans le cinéma actuel (1985–2012)," in *Apparence(s). Le poil.* Special issue, Lille, January, 2014 (http://apparences. revues.org/1246, 2014); "Historizität und Modernität. Die Strategien Bollywoods seit den 1990er Jahren," in Susanne Marschall (eds.), *Indiens Kinokulturen. Geschichte—Dramaturgie—Ästhetik* (Schueren-Verlag 2014).

Elke Gaugele is a scholar of empirical cultural studies and Professor at the Academy of Fine Arts in Vienna, Austria, where she developed and directs the concentration on "fashion and styles" at the Institute for Arts and Education, that combines design practice, pedagogy, critical theory, and cultural analysis of fashion/styles. She has previously worked as a curator, researcher, and teacher at the University of Cologne, Germany, Goldsmith College, London, and the University of Vienna, Austria. Her scholarship spans the fields of fashion as well as visual and material cultures, including topics such as epistemologies of fashion and style, fashion and migration, postcolonial and queer-feminist perspectives for fashion studies, biopolitics and aesthetic politics of fashion, and open cultures/DIY. Her recent publications include *Fashion and Postcolonial Critique* (with Monica Titton, Sternberg 2019), *Critical Studies: Kultur- und Sozialtheorien im Kunstfeld* (with Jens Kastner, VS 2016); *Aesthetic Politics in Fashion* (Sternberg 2014); *Craftista! Handarbeit als Aktivismus* (with Sonja Eismann, Verena Kuni, and Elke Zobl, Ventil 2011); "Geteilte Geschichten? Mode und Migration," in *POP. Kultur und Kritik* (No. 8, 2016).

Viola Hofmann is a full-time faculty member at the Institute of Arts and Material Culture at Technical University of Dortmund, Germany. She received her MA and PhD in cultural anthropology of textiles from Technical University of Dortmund, Germany. She is author of *Das Kostüm der Macht: Das Erscheinungsbild von Politikerinnen und Politikern* (Edition Ebersbach 2014), an in-depth study, based on the magazine *Der Spiegel*, that examines the sartorial practices and media representation of politicians in Germany from 1949 to 2013. Her recent research focuses on the interrelationships between technology, materiality, sustainability and fashion.

Karen Tranberg Hansen is Professor Emerita, Department of Anthropology at Northwestern University, Illinois, United States. She is an urban and economic anthropologist, focusing on Africa. Her research concerns the material, social, and cultural dimensions of urban livelihoods in the context of historical, regional, and global dynamics. Her books include *Distant Companions: Servants and Employers in Zambia 1900–1985* (Cornell 1989), *Keeping House in Lusaka* (Columbia 1997), *Salaula: The World of Secondhand Clothing and Zambia* (University of

Chicago Press 2000), and the edited edition, *African Encounters with Domesticity* (Rutgers University Press 1992). She co-edited, with Mariken Vaa, *Reconsidering Informality: Perspectives from Urban Africa* (Nordic Africa Institute 2004) and is lead author of *Youth and the City in the Global South* (Indiana University Press 2008). She edited, with D. Soyini Madison, *African Dress: Agency, Power, Performance* (Bloomsbury 2013), and with Walter E. Little and B. Lynne Milgram, *Street Economies in the Urban Global South* (SAR Press 2013).

Andrea Hauser studied empirical cultural studies/European ethnology, German studies and pedagogy. She received her doctoral degree from Ludwig Uhland Institute at the University of Tübingen, Germany. As a curator, she has worked for numerous museums and exhibition projects (including the new conceptions of the city museums in Ludwigsburg, Esslingen, and Bremerhaven in Germany). Since 2007, she has been an independent curator, author, and editor (www.kultur-und-transfer.de), and a lecturer in material culture and museology, including, among others, at the Martin Luther University of Halle-Wittenberg, Germany, and Carl von Ossietzky University of Oldenburg, Germany. Her research interests include relationships between clothing and place, with a focus on histories of regional and rural clothing and dress practices, and their representation and mediation, including through museum practices.

Heike Jenss is Associate Professor of Fashion Studies at Parsons School of Design, The New School, New York, where she served as founding director of the MA Fashion Studies program. Jenss received her MA and PhD in cultural anthropology of textiles from Technical University of Dortmund, Germany. She is author of *Fashioning Memory: Vintage Style and Youth Culture* (Bloomsbury 2016) and *Sixties Dress Only: Mode und Konsum in der Retro-Szene der Mods* (Campus 2007), and editor of *Fashion Studies: Research Methods, Sites and Practices* (Bloomsbury 2015). Her research focuses on fashion and consumption, including vintage and secondhand clothing and connections between the materiality of fashion, time, media, and cultural memory.

Christel Köhle-Hezinger, Professor Emeritus, was Chair of Cultural Anthropology/Empirical Cultural Studies at the Friedrich Schiller University in Jena, Germany, where she founded the cultural anthropology/cultural history program. Prior to this, she was Professor of European Ethnology and Cultural Studies at the Phillips University in Marburg, Germany (1994–1998); and at the Ludwig Uhland Institute of Empirical Cultural Studies at the University of Tübingen, Germany, where she was responsible for regional studies (1988–1994). She received her doctorate from the Ludwig Uhland Institute, Tübingen,

Germany. Her books include *Der neuen Welt ein neuer Rock: Studien zu Kleidung, Körper und Mode an Beispielen aus Württemberg* (K. Theiss 1993); *Europas Mitte—Mitte Europas. Europa als kulturelle Konstruktion* (Collegium Europaeum Jenense 2008); *Alltagskultur Sakral-Profan. Ausgewählte Aufsätze* (Waxmann 2011). Her research interests include material culture, fashion and dress in everyday life, manifestations of custom, tradition, and religion in the histories of material culture, regional and rural dress cultures, and relationships between urban and rural life.

Susan B. Kaiser is Professor of Gender, Sexuality and Women's Studies, and Textiles and Clothing at the University of California, Davis, United States. Her research and teaching span fashion studies and feminist cultural studies. Recent and current interests include shifting masculinities, issues of space/place (e.g., rural, urban, suburban), and possibilities for critical fashion studies through popular and political cultural discourses. She is author of *The Social Psychology of Clothing* (Fairchild 1997), *Fashion and Cultural Studies* (Bloomsbury 2013), and approximately 100 articles and book chapters in the fields of textile/fashion studies, sociology, gender studies, cultural studies, popular culture, and consumer behavior.

Christina H. Moon is Assistant Professor at the School of Art and Design History and Theory at Parsons School of Design, The New School, New York. She holds a PhD in Anthropology from Yale University, United States. Her research explores the social ties and cultural encounters between fashion design worlds and manufacturing landscapes across Asia and the Americas. Her research explores how modes of production and communities of making remake twenty-first-century workplaces, global cities, and material culture. Her work is published in *Vestoj, The Baffler, Pacific Standard Magazine,* and the journals *Design Issues* and *Critical Studies in Fashion and Beauty.* She is currently working on a book on the fast-fashion industry and the city of Los Angeles.

Daniel Purdy is Professor of German Studies at Pennsylvania State University, United States. He was born in Berlin and raised bilingually in New York City. He received his PhD from Cornell University, New York, in 1992. Before arriving at Penn State University, Pennsylvania, United States, he taught for nine years at Columbia University, New York. His research specializes on the connections between material culture and philosophical thought. Much of his writing concentrates on the *Goethezeit.* Having written about consumer culture and architectural theory, his current project focuses on the German reception of Chinese culture in the early modern period. His publications include *The*

Tyranny of Elegance: Consumer Cosmopolitanism in the Era of Goethe, a study on fashion culture and male identity (Johns Hopkins University Press 1998); *The Rise of Fashion*, a collection of historical writings about fashion and style (University of Minnesota Press 2005); *On the Ruins of Babel: Architectural Metaphor in German Thought* (Cornell University Press 2011). His most recent co-edited volume with Bettina Brandt is *China in the German Enlightenment* (University of Toronto Press 2016).

Lola Shamukhitdinova is a specialist in clothing, textile technology, and design. She received her doctorate from Moscow State University of Design and Technology, Russia. She is currently a research fellow at Technical University of Dortmund, Germany, and coordinator of the international research project "Modernity of Tradition: Uzbek textile heritage as cultural and economic resource," funded by the Volkswagen Foundation. She previously held positions as Associate Professor at Tashkent Institute for Textile and Apparel Industry, Uzbekistan, and served as Head of the Department of Technology and Design of Apparel Industry Products (2005–2006). Her research interests include contemporary Central Asian textile design, technology and consumption, and technology and design of traditional textiles. She has also participated in multidisciplinary team research on the creation of a textiles database for international use. She is co-editor (with Gabriele Mentges) of *Modernity of Tradition: Uzbek Textile Culture Today* (Waxmann 2013) and *Textiles as National Heritage: Identities, Politics and Material Culture* (Waxmann 2017).

Otto von Busch is Associate Professor of Integrated Design at Parsons School of Design, The New School, New York. He holds a PhD in design from the School of Design and Craft at the University of Gothenburg, Sweden, and was previously Professor of Textiles at Konstfack, Stockholm, Sweden. He has a background in arts, craft, design, and theory, and many of his projects explore how design, especially fashion, can mobilize community capabilities through collaborative craft and social activism. He has published articles in *The Design Journal, Critical Studies in Fashion and Beauty, Organizational Aesthetics, CoDesign Journal, The Journal of Modern Craft, Textile Cloth and Culture, Craft Research, Creative Industries Journal, Journal for Artistic Research* and *Fashion Practice*. His book chapters have appeared in *The Routledge Handbook of Sustainable Product Design* (2017), *The Routledge Companion to Design Research* (2015), as well as *The Routledge Handbook of Sustainability and Fashion* (2014).

Jutta Zander-Seidel received her PhD in art history from Friedrich Alexander University of Erlangen, Germany. She has taught at the Academy of Fine Arts in Nuremberg, Germany, and the Technical University of Cologne, Germany, and was a fellow at the German Research Foundation. Between 1995 and 2016, she was the director of the textiles and jewelry collection at the Germanisches Nationalmuseum, and, since 2008, associate director of the museum. She has extensive research and exhibition experience in the textile and clothing history, including the new conception of the museum's permanent exhibition on the history of women's, men's, and children's clothes in the eighteenth to twentieth centuries. Her publications include *Kleiderwechsel. Frauen-, Männer- und Kinderkleidung des 18. bis 20. Jahrhunderts* (2002), and the accompanying catalogue *In Mode: Kleider und Bilder aus Renaissance und Frühbarock* (2015) for the recent special exhibition on fashion in early modernity. Since July 2016, she has been an associate scholar at the Germanisches Nationalmuseum.

Index